Advance praise for **Your Money's Worth**

"Wise advice—custom-tailored for Canadians—all investors will appreciate."
Charles D. Ellis, MBA (Harvard), PhD, author of *Index Revolution: Why Investors Should Join It Now* and *Winning the Loser's Game: Timeless Strategies for Successful Investing*

"Baby boomers in Canada are retiring in droves and this demographic trend is only going to accelerate. Shamez Kassam's *Your Money's Worth* is an excellent book describing the entire financial life cycle for individuals, including investment concepts, insurance and estate planning in simple, easy to understand language. This book is particularly timely for boomers who are concerned about their and their family's financial wellbeing."
Jai Parihar, MBA, CFA, ICD.D, Former Chief Investment Officer, Alberta Investment Management Corporation, Former President and CEO, UBC Investment Management Trust

"Everyone who reads *Your Money's Worth* will be immediately struck by the passion of its author, Shamez Kassam. If you truly desire to understand how to master your personal finances, *Your Money's Worth* is an urgent must-read."
Tom Deans, PhD, author of the *New York Times* Top-Ten Book *Every Family's Business*, and *Willing Wisdom*

"This book is a must-have and must-read for every investor—young and old. It is comprehensive, with practical advice for every stage of life. It is especially important for millennials, who have received little education on managing their finances, planning for the future, and saving."
Tania Willumsen, corporate director, past Director of The Canadian Foundation for Advancement of Investor Rights (FAIR Canada) and the Association of Canadian Pension Fund Management, and a 40-year veteran of the investment industry

"As an institutional investor, I am intimately familiar with the complexities of the financial markets and the inherent burden it places on individuals in managing their personal wealth. Shamez's ability to simplify the roles and responsibilities of industry professionals, products and services is a strong step forward in providing clarity to an otherwise opaque industry."
Jagdeep Singh Bachher, Ph.D, Chief Investment Officer, University of California

"A wonderful guide for any Canadian considering investment or insurance products to protect their family's financial health. *Your Money's Worth* provides an easy read on what to look for in everything from seeking an advisor to different types of investments, insurance products, and estate planning. This book would be your first great investment."
Karim Manji, former Managing Director, Goldman Sachs

"As a single woman who has always had to manage my own financial affairs, I am always looking for the best possible advice. This book is such a resource. There is something in it for everyone, from the novice to the pro. Shamez has taken a complex subject and made it simple. Written in plain words with lots of resources, this is a 'must read.' In fact, buy a few copies for your friends and families—you, and they, will not be disappointed."
Irene E. Pfeiffer, CM (Order of Canada)

"More than ever, consumers need to be careful about who they get financial advice from. The industry is a patchwork of designations, licences, and specialties that are often clouded by misleading titles and potentially conflicted motives. *Your Money's Worth* is essential reading for those who seek financial empowerment."
John De Goey, portfolio manager and author of the *Professional Advisor IV*

"*Your Money's Worth* is a must-read for all Canadians. It provides a clear and comprehensive guide to understanding the financial landscape in Canada. Whether you're a DIY investor or use a financial advisor, this book teaches people to become more knowledgeable about their financial future and ensure that they have the tools to be prepared for retirement."
Anil Tahiliani, CFA, private investor and former Head of Research at McLean & Partners Wealth Management Ltd.

"Shamez Kassam has written a book that speaks to all of us. *Your Money's Worth* takes us on a journey of financial literacy. Kassam's style is clear and concise when dealing with the financial industry, investment vehicles, and insurance options. He points out that 'the hallmark of a great advisor is his or her ability to ask the right questions.' Well, in *Your Money's Worth*, Kassam gives the right answers."

Martin Parnell, professional speaker, author, and five-time Guinness World Record holder

"As a finance professor at the business schools of Harvard, Columbia, and MIT, my goal in teaching is always to distill complicated concepts into information that is both easy to understand and interesting to learn. My friend and former student, Shamez Kassam, has accomplished that goal in his new book on financial advisors, investing, insurance, and estate planning. The more people who take the time to read this book, the more people who will be on a better financial footing!"

Matthew Rhodes-Kropf, PhD, Associate Professor of Finance, MIT Sloan School of Management

"As both a student of, and a participant in, the Canadian financial markets, I find it refreshing to see such a comprehensive look at the choices and challenges Canadians are confronted with. *Your Money's Worth* provides truly valuable insights into why advice matters."

Barry H. Gordon, LLB, President and Chief Executive Officer, First Asset, a CI Financial company

"*Your Money's Worth* is a book that everyone can read to immediately improve their financial literacy. Shamez Kassam has provided a 'road map' that all Canadians can consult to learn their options when it comes to securing their financial future and determining what financial advice they need. Anyone looking for the road to prosperity for their personal and family's financial needs will want to find their place on the map and then consider the possible routes the author points to."

Hon. Kevin Sorenson, former Canadian Minister of State (Finance)

YOUR

MONEY'S

WORTH

THE ESSENTIAL GUIDE

TO FINANCIAL ADVICE

FOR CANADIANS

SHAMEZ KASSAM MBA, CFA

YOUR

MONEY'S

WORTH

Shazam! PRESS

Shazam! Press
Calgary, Alberta

Cataloguing data available from Library and Archives Canada
978-0-9952509-0-1 (paperback)
978-0-9952509-1-8 (ebook)

Editing by Donna L. Dawson, CPE
Copy Editing by Lindsay Humphreys
Cover and interior design by Peter Cocking

17 18 19 20 21   5 4 3 2 1

To my son, Izmir. It is a privilege to be your father.

I cherish every moment we spend together.

Disclaimer

THIS BOOK is written by Shamez Kassam in his individual capacity and not as a registered representation of Raymond James Ltd. (RJL) or any of its affiliates. It expresses the opinions of the author and not necessarily those of Raymond James Ltd. This book is provided as a general source of information and should not be considered personal investment advice or financial planning advice. It should not be construed as an offer or solicitation for the sale or purchase of any product and should not be considered tax advice. The author is not a tax advisor and recommends that clients seek independent advice from a professional advisor on tax-related matters. The author recommends that any individual seek independent advice from a financial advisor prior to making any investment decisions and from a professional accountant concerning tax-related matters. Statistics, factual data, and other information are from sources RJL believes to be reliable, but their accuracy cannot be guaranteed. This book is furnished on the basis and understanding that Raymond James Ltd. or any of its affiliates are to be under no liability whatsoever in respect therefore. This book may provide reference to third-party services. Raymond James Ltd. is not responsible for the availability of these external services, nor does Raymond James Ltd. endorse, warrant, or guarantee the products, services, or information described or offered. Commissions, trailing commissions, management fees, and expenses all may be associated with mutual funds. Please read the prospectus before investing. Mutual funds are not guaranteed, their values change frequently, and past performance may not be repeated. Securities-related products and services are offered through Raymond James Ltd., Member-Canadian Investor Protection Fund. Insurance products and services are offered through Raymond James Financial Planning Ltd., which is not a Member-Canadian Investor Protection Fund.

Contents

Abbreviations

ACB	adjusted cost base
CFA	Chartered Financial Analyst
CFP	Certified Financial Planner
CIPF	Canadian Investor Protection Fund
CIM	Chartered Investment Manager
CLU	Chartered Life Underwriter
COLA	cost-of-living adjustment
CRA	Canada Revenue Agency
CRM	Client Relationship Model
CSA	Canadian Securities Administrators
CSV	cash surrender value
DAF	donor-advised fund
ETF	exchange-traded fund
ETP	exchange-traded products
GIC	guaranteed investment certificate
IIROC	Investment Industry Regulatory Organization of Canada
IPO	initial public offering
IPS	investment policy statement
IRS	Internal Revenue Service (in the US)
IVIC	individual variable insurance contract
KYC	know your client
KYP	know your product

LIF   Life Income Fund
LIRA   Locked-In Retirement Account
MER   management expense ratio
MFDA   Mutual Fund Dealers Association
        of Canada
MLM   multi-level marketing
MTAR   Maximum Tax Actuarial Reserve
OSC   Ontario Securities Commission
PFIC   passive foreign investment company
PTF   platform-traded fund
REIT   real estate investment trust
RESP   Registered Education Savings Plan
RRIF   Registered Retirement Income Fund
RRSP   Registered Retirement Savings Plan
S&P   Standard & Poor's
S&P/TSX s&P/TSX Composite Index
TDF   target date fund
TER   trading expense ratio
TFSA   Tax-Free Savings Account
TIA   temporary insurance agreement
TSX   Toronto Stock Exchange
YRT   yearly renewable term

Introduction

WHEN I BEGAN my investing journey 20 years ago, I had no financial background. I believed that a financial advisor could help me, but I was unable to find any kind of simple resource that answered the questions I had. So, I struck out on my own. Since then, I have been fortunate and have come a long way on my journey toward becoming a successful investor.

I started out my professional career as an occupational therapist and worked in that field for several years, starting in the late 1990s. Once I'd accumulated some money, I became interested in investing and began to learn about it by reading countless books and through trial and error. I quickly made thousands of dollars in stocks like Nortel, Ballard Power, and some e-commerce companies (that no longer exist). However, I lost it just as fast—probably faster, actually. But the process of investing intrigued me, and I decided to go back to school and was fortunate to be accepted to the MBA program at Columbia University in New York.

Today, I am a financial advisor and have professionally managed money for large institutions with global reach as well as for individual investors in Canada. In fact, I am one of the few financial advisors in Canada who has seen the industry through the lens of both world-class institutional money managers and average individual investors.

But I still believe there is no simple resource that educates Canadians about the financial advice industry and answers basic questions that I feel are critically important to consider when selecting a financial advisor in Canada, such as the following:

- How is the financial advice industry structured?
- What types of financial advisors are there?
- What services can advisors provide?
- How are advisors compensated? What costs should I be aware of?
- What types of qualities and qualifications should I look for in a financial advisor?
- How will I know whether my advisor is doing what's right for me?
- What are some successful long-term investment strategies?
- What else do I need to know about my financial future?

It is my hope that this book will be the "how to" guide for Canadians who are seeking to manage their financial affairs either by working with an advisor or on their own. One of the biggest misconceptions today is that advisors only provide investment advice. This explains why the term "investment advisor" is so commonly used in Canada today. However, I much prefer the term "financial advisor" because, although advisors certainly do offer investment advice, they can provide so much more. If you want to utilize the services of an advisor solely for investment advice, there is nothing wrong with that. In my opinion, however, investing is only one part of making sure your financial house is in order—financial planning, insurance, and estate planning are critical areas you also need to address. Having an investment plan in isolation is not enough. I also want to emphasize that most advisors are not trained as accountants and lawyers, and so expecting precise tax and legal advice is not realistic. The best advisors, however, put themselves in the shoes of their client, offer big-picture concepts and solutions, and then coordinate with your accounting and legal professionals, so that you—the client— receive the optimal and most effective outcome.

This book represents everything I have learned over my career working with institutional investors, individual investors, financial advisors, and companies that create and distribute investment products. The book is organized into four parts. Part 1: Making Sense of It All: The Financial Advice Industry in Canada walks the reader through the structure of the financial advice industry in Canada, the different types of financial advisors and the areas in which they can help consumers, how to select and work with an advisor, and associated costs to be aware of. While I believe that a general understanding of the financial advice industry is important for all Canadians, I also acknowledge that some readers prefer to handle their financial affairs on their own. If this is the case for you, feel free to skim over Part 1, and focus on the remainder of the book. Part 2: Being an Informed Investor provides information on key investment principles. Part 3: Your Finances Beyond Investing: Insurance and Estate Planning covers important considerations about managing risk through obtaining adequate insurance and developing an estate plan. There are entire books about each of the subjects covered in Parts 2 and 3; this book serves as a reference of key principles for all the topics, in one package. At the end of Parts 1, 2, and 3, there is an Action Call of simple steps you should take to be on track for ensuring your financial house is in order. The final section, Part 4: Your Financial Future Is in Your Hands, provides practical worksheets designed to help you determine if you need advice, select and work with an advisor if you choose to do so, and make sure that all the vital areas of your financial life are being addressed.

If you are interested in growing your wealth in a responsible way, protecting your future, and taking care of your family, this book is for you. All Canadians can benefit from the information in this book, whether you hire an advisor or choose to manage your financial affairs yourself, and whether you are a new university graduate, a business owner, a wealthy professional athlete, a mid-career professional saving for retirement, or a senior getting ready to retire. Professionals such as lawyers and accountants can also benefit from the information in this book, as it will improve their understanding of how the financial advice industry in Canada works and better equip them to point their clients in the right direction when it comes to seeking financial advice. Undoubtedly, the financial industry will continue to evolve and the way Canadians access financial advice may change, but the core principles behind the successful management of our financial affairs will stand the test of time.

Good advice is more important today than ever before. The reason is simple—we are living in unprecedented economic times, largely due to the actions of central banks around the world over the last several years in response to the financial crisis of 2007–08. If you are not completely sure what is meant by the term "central bank," you're not alone. But it's important to understand the term because central banks have significant influence over capital markets and how your investments perform. Every country has a central bank, which is a public institution that manages the currency of the country and has as its goals growing, promoting maximum employment, and keeping the level of prices stable. One of the main powers a central bank has is the ability to change the level of interest rates. Because interest rates have such a major impact on investing, before delving into this book it's important to make sure you understand some fundamentals about interest rates. Let's start by looking at how central banks around the world have attempted to use interest rates to deal with financial crises in the past and more recently.

The financial crisis of 2007–08 was driven by several factors, including a bubble in the US housing market and proliferation of debt around the world. Central banks around the world responded to the crisis by dramatically lowering interest rates and by using unconventional policies known as "quantitative easing" (which is equivalent to printing money out of thin air) to purchase assets such as government bonds, which have the result of keeping interest rates artificially low. Some central banks, such as the Bank of Japan, have even been buying equities! While the initial response of central banks probably saved the world from entering another Great Depression (something for which they deserve a great deal of credit), they have kept using these unconventional policies for too long and, as of the end of 2016, interest rates continue to remain exceptionally low. In some countries, during 2016, government bonds had negative yields, meaning that investors were paying the government to take their money. In fact, at one point during 2016, one-third of all government bonds in the world had a negative yield! It is possible that we may be in a relatively low interest-rate environment for some time and Canadians will need to adapt their financial strategies to get through a "lower for longer" interest-rate environment while also being prepared for potential inflation down the road.

You may be asking, why have central banks engaged in unconventional policies in order to keep interest rates so low? It has to do with the fact that economic growth remains challenged for many reasons. The world remains awash in debt, particularly at the consumer and government levels. Whenever you have a debt situation such as this, there are only three potential remedies: austerity measures (reducing spending and dedicating more cash flow to debt repayment), default (declaring bankruptcy), or inflation. The first two options are considered too painful, so the preferred choice is inflation. Thus, central banks around the world have been desperately trying to create inflation. Why? Simply because inflation erodes the real value of debt over time. In an inflationary environment, debt can be paid back with future dollars that are worth less. Make no mistake: inflation is a form of taxation to you and your family.

The action by central banks has significantly benefitted prices of stocks, bonds, and real estate. This has benefitted the owners of these assets (baby boomers and their parents), while in many ways harming the younger generations. Today, there are several questions. What happens to asset prices when central banks stop using unconventional policies? Nobody knows for certain. When will interest rates rise? Although it is possible that we may have already seen generational lows in interest rates, nobody knows for sure. What we do know, however, is that the track record of central banks is to create bubbles (remember the technology stock bubble of 1999–2001 and the US housing bubble in the early 2000s), which then invariably deflate. Some economists have referred to central banks as "serial" bubble creators. At some point, the actions of central banks will cause more volatility and uncertainty.

If you are interested to learn more about how central bank policy is impacting our collective financial future, I highly recommend reading *Code Red: How to Protect Your Savings from the Coming Crisis* by US-based authors John Mauldin and Jonathan Tepper. I also recommend watching Consuelo Mack's weekly television program, WEALTHTRACK, which features a different highly regarded investment professional each week who explains in simple terms how they approach investing. In Canada, Michael Campbell's *Money Talks* is an extremely informative weekly radio program that is also available as a podcast.

Looking ahead, I strongly believe that the need for financial advice will only increase. The *2015 BlackRock Global Investor Pulse Survey* showed that only 42% of Canadians understand how much they have to save for retirement. Canadians have double the cash investments they feel they should, and knowledge is a barrier to investing. All of this points to a major opportunity for financial advisors to help. Additionally, today most Canadians don't have an employment pension plan they can count on. According to a 2016 study published by the Broadbent Institute titled *An Analysis of the Economic Circumstances of Canadian Seniors*, almost half of Canadians between the ages of 55 and 64 do not have access to an employer pension. Furthermore, as the study also stated, the "vast majority of these Canadians retiring without an employer pension plan have totally inadequate retirement savings." In my opinion, Canada is facing an impending retirement crisis that will have wide-ranging ramifications. As a country, if we are to avoid this crisis or at least manage it, Canadians need to have enhanced levels of financial literacy and know how and where to access the advice they need. Furthermore, younger generations are likely to have more difficulty finding suitable long-term employment—even the current federal Minister of Finance recently mentioned that Canadians should get used to "job churn." If this turns out to be the case, younger Canadians will have to improve their levels of financial literacy as well, to avoid making costly and preventable financial mistakes.

At the time of writing this book, despite record-low interest rates, economic growth in Canada is sluggish and incomes are stagnating. Governments are now considering massive investments in infrastructure to further stimulate the economy. The reality is that prosperity for many, especially those in the middle class, seems elusive. In my opinion, the Canadian economy is facing long-term structural challenges, increased tax burdens from all levels of government, and rising healthcare costs and an aging population. A recent commentary from the C.D. Howe Institute revealed that "the unfunded liability of federal employees' pension plans was $269 billion at the end of the 2015 fiscal year—$118 billion worse than reported." How will this gap be filled? All of these factors lead me to believe that over time, the level of tax burden on Canadians is only likely to increase. Also of concern is the fact that, at the time of writing this book, the rates of return on money in bank accounts, guaranteed investment certificates (GICs), and bonds are close to zero and, in some cases, negative after you factor in taxes and inflation. This makes it exceedingly difficult for pension plans to meet their return objectives, and in many cases this situation is forcing individual investors in need of income to take more risk and invest differently, even though they may not be familiar with such investments. Something else Canadians need to prepare for is that a massive wealth transfer is going to take place over the next decade. In their 2016 report, *The Looming Bequest Boom—What Should We Expect?*, CIBC Capital Markets estimated that Canadian baby boomers will inherit an estimated $750 billion in wealth over the next decade. Without the right knowledge and advice, those on the receiving end of the wealth transfer may not be prepared to manage their inheritance prudently.

Improving financial literacy is a global challenge. In Canada, there is a wide scope of activity in this area through the work of both private organizations and governments. Under the umbrella of the Financial Consumer Agency of Canada, there is an appointed Financial Literacy Leader who is responsible for developing and implementing the national strategy for financial literacy in Canada. The current Financial Literacy Leader, Jane Rooney, has said that financial literacy today is "as important as basic literacy and numeracy" and that "financial literacy is everyone's responsibility." I could not agree more.

Over the years, I have been frustrated and saddened to see so many of my fellow citizens make mistakes that significantly impacted their retirement plans negatively. Even more frustrating and saddening is that, in a large number of these cases, the mistakes were entirely preventable with more financial education and the right advice. It is my hope that this book will be a significant step forward in both reducing the knowledge gap of consumers of financial services in Canada and generally enhancing the level of financial literacy of Canadians. I also hope to make it clear how important good financial advice is and how to find it. I am particularly optimistic that my work will have a significant impact on young people by positively influencing their saving, investing, and financial-planning habits. Giving back has always been important to me. To this end, 25% of the sales of this book will be donated to the community, with the proceeds going to the Raymond James Canada Foundation (which manages the philanthropic work of Raymond James Ltd.), Calgary Food Bank, Accessible Housing in Calgary, and the Institute for Stuttering Treatment and Research, to help fund treatment for those who stutter and need treatment but cannot afford it.

It is an honour and a privilege for me to work in the financial advice industry. I particularly enjoy educating people, helping to "turn on lights" and show clients new and different ways of thinking about various financial issues. My focus has always been on helping clients simplify issues that are complex, being forthright and objective, and providing the client with the best integrated solution for their situation, rather than selling any particular investment product. I sincerely hope that this book will arm you with the necessary knowledge and perspective that will enable you to take charge of your financial future and, in the process, avoid the mistakes that I made and that tens of thousands of Canadians continue to make every day. I wish you much success in your journey and hope that in reading this book you do indeed receive "your money's worth."

SHAMEZ KASSAM
Canada's Candid Advisor
January 2017

1

MAKING SENSE OF IT ALL: THE FINANCIAL ADVICE INDUSTRY IN CANADA

Do You Need Advice?

HAVING THE KNOWLEDGE and ability to successfully manage our own personal finances is vital but, unfortunately, it is a subject that is largely missing from the curriculum in the Canadian education system. I have never understood why a topic so critical to a student's future is so ignored, and I urge provincial governments around the country that have jurisdiction over curriculum development to do more to rectify this. Because many Canadians aren't adequately informed, when they get to a point in their lives when they're able to invest, they go in "cold" and have to learn from the school of hard knocks (that's how I started). If you go this route without knowledge of core concepts, you will inevitably make mistakes—and sometimes those mistakes will be expensive. Enlisting the services of a professional financial advisor can help you avoid making costly errors.

In fact, regardless of financial status, just about everyone can benefit from the services of a competent financial advisor. I even know of many highly skilled financial advisors who have *their* own advisors! Having an objective third party provide you with guidance and direction is extremely valuable. What most people tend to forget is that the role of a financial advisor includes more than just selecting the right investments. Great advisors provide comprehensive services, ensuring that their clients have a financial plan and an estate plan, that they are adequately insured, that (when possible) they are taking advantage of government vehicles to minimize tax, and that

11

they have appropriate investments to meet their long-term goals and objectives. For their clients who are approaching retirement, advisors also can provide tremendous value in customizing a tax-efficient income stream.

According to a 2014 study by Advocis and Pricewaterhouse-Coopers, there are nearly 100,000 financial advisors in Canada. That same year, the *Globe and Mail* reported that roughly 10 million Canadians use the services of financial advisors, also noting that the percentage of Canadians using an advisor rises with age. As an increasing number of baby boomers retire and seek assistance to maximize their retirement income, it is very likely that the need for competent financial advisors in Canada will only increase. Thankfully, there is no shortage of advisors in Canada to meet an increased demand.

While I believe that everybody can benefit from good financial advice, you as an individual must decide for yourself if seeking the services of a financial advisor is appropriate, beginning with asking yourself whether you want to spend the time and energy required to manage your own money (by using self-directed accounts at discount brokerages, for example) and get your financial house in order. If you're certain you want to be a "do-it-yourselfer," keep reading—this book will still provide you with lots of valuable information. And if after reading this book you remain committed to handling your finances without professional guidance, make sure to also read Bruce Sellery's *Moolala: Why Smart People Do Dumb Things with Their Money (and What You Can Do About It)*.

If you're not sure if you need financial advice, ask yourself the following questions:

- Am I willing to spend the time required to learn about investing?
- Do I have the ability and discipline to create, execute, and stick with a long-term investment plan?
- Do I have an emotional tendency that will cause me to overreact to short-term market volatility and make poor financial decisions?
- Can I calculate my insurance needs so that my family is taken care of if I become disabled or die?

- Do I have the knowledge to put together an effective financial and estate plan?

In addition to answering these questions, consider the following. In all aspects of life, the actions you choose have consequences. These can be referred to as opportunity costs—they are the cost of what you choose to forgo as a result of your chosen action. For example, if you choose to go on a vacation, you will have less money to save and that would be the consequence, or cost, of your decision to go on a vacation. The opportunity cost of not having a financial advisor can be staggering. For example, if you have large amounts of cash sitting in your bank account because you are afraid of investing or you don't know how to invest, the opportunity cost of this would be not having your money working for you. Acknowledging that future returns may not match historical returns, equity markets have historically returned, on an inflation-adjusted basis, about 6%-7% annually compounded, before fees; it's clear that the consequence of not doing anything with your money can be significant. If you need advice and do not have an advisor, or if you are working with the wrong advisor, the opportunity cost of not having the right professional guidance is potentially not meeting your retirement objectives.

In life everything has an opportunity cost—don't forget this. Be serious when it comes to your finances. You cannot afford not to be. You are responsible for your future financial well-being and that of your family. Take the time to educate yourself—the road to financial success is manageable if you are a disciplined saver, you follow time-tested principles, and above all else, you keep it simple. It is also critical to understand the areas in which you may need advice. Part 4 contains several tools, including a Financial Advice Needs Assessment™. Completing this form will help you determine if you need advice.

....

➤ **TAKE NOTE:** A good financial advisor provides guidance on investing, financial planning, insurance, and estate planning, also acting as a sounding board to prevent you from making poor financial decisions.

....

Are You a US Person?

If you have citizenship or residency ties to the United States, you'll want to pay particular attention to this section. According to US law, if you are a citizen or a resident of the United States, you are considered to be a "United States person." Even if currently living in Canada, the following types of individuals are considered United States citizens: those born in the US, those born in Canada to two US citizens, and those born in Canada to one US citizen if the US parent resided in the US for five years (two of which were after the individual was 14 years old). If you are a Canadian and also hold US citizenship, you are considered a US citizen for tax purposes. If you have a "green card," you can also be considered to be a lawful permanent resident of the United States and be subject to US federal tax.

The rules for determining US citizenship can be complex. If you think you may be a US person, I strongly recommend you see a competent immigration attorney to make a definitive determination, then consult with a financial advisor who has experience in dealing with US persons, and also consult with an accountant who is licensed in both countries. If you are both a Canadian and a US person, you need to be aware of the many additional requirements that exist when it comes to investing and managing your finances. The United States is one of the few countries in the world that taxes people based on citizenship and not purely on residency. US persons living in Canada are therefore required to file both Canadian and US tax returns each year. Thankfully, because of tax treaties between Canada and the US, people in this situation are not generally double-taxed. In fact, for moderate income earners, it is likely that no additional US tax will be owed (depending on your specific situation, of course). Note that a US person living in Canada would be subject to only US federal tax and not state tax.

For US persons, there are numerous potential investment pitfalls to avoid. For example, Canadian mutual funds and exchange-traded funds (ETFs) are classified as passive foreign investment companies (PFICS) under US tax law (even though most Canadian mutual funds and ETFs are organized as trusts!). One of the goals of the Internal

Revenue Service (IRS) is to encourage US citizens to use US invest- ment vehicles. As a result, Canadian mutual funds and ETFs held in non-registered accounts (those outside of RRSPs, for example) are taxed very punitively in the United States. Additional tax reporting must be completed every year for each PFIC owned. If you do hold mutual funds and ETFs created by Canadian fund companies, make sure they are in registered accounts.

For US persons living in Canada, I strongly advise simplifying and structuring your investments in order to minimize not only the tax owing but also the filing and compliance requirements. There are a few things you can do to help "bulletproof" your portfolio against the IRS: consider minimizing the use of Tax-Free Savings Accounts (TFSAs) and ensure that Canadian mutual funds and ETFs are in registered accounts only (i.e., LIRAS, RRSPs, LIFs, or RRIFs). All non-registered accounts should be invested only in individual stocks and bonds. I cannot emphasize how important it is to have a competent cross-border accountant if you are a US person living in Canada.

➤ **TAKE NOTE:** US persons in Canada have additional tax and report- ing requirements. Choose an advisor who is aware of these issues and is capable of managing assets in an IRS-compliant manner in order to minimize US filing and tax requirements. Ensure that your advisor and accountant speak to each other so that you will obtain the best results.

Can the Value of Financial Advice Be Measured?

One challenge with the financial advisory business is that the value of the advice your advisor provides is difficult to measure. A traditional method of determining the value of financial advice given is to look at the return of your portfolio at the end of the year and compare it with what a reasonable market benchmark returned during the same time frame. If your advisor is providing a better return than the market, he or she must be adding value, right?

Not necessarily. If you are working with a financial advisor with the sole expectation that the advisor will do better than the market consistently, you definitely want to revisit that expectation. Even the best-educated and most experienced investors have difficulty beating the market over the long term—this has been proven time and again. This fact doesn't mean that nobody can beat the market consistently, but it does mean that very few can. While it is important for the investment strategy to be working effectively, the reality is that much of an advisor's value comes from making sure all the rooms in your financial house are in order. There is great value in knowing that your financial affairs are being well taken care of by a professional.

So, if it's not based solely on comparing market returns, how can you measure the value of financial advice? To answer this question, The Vanguard Group—one of the largest providers of exchange-traded funds (ETFs) in the world—published a paper in May 2015 entitled *Putting a Value on Your Value: Quantifying Vanguard Advisor's Alpha in Canada*, which looks at several areas whereby financial advisors add value, which are summarized below:

- **Asset allocation**: Your advisor will recommend an appropriate allocation of various asset classes (including stocks and bonds) based on your individual risk tolerance, goals, and financial circumstances, and help you ignore the day-to-day "noise" in the markets. Vanguard acknowledges that it is difficult to estimate the value of asset allocation, but it is important.

- **Cost-effective implementation**: Your advisor can add value by recommending cost-effective ways to implement your investment strategy. Vanguard estimated the added value of this to be up to 1.3% of investment assets annually.

- **Rebalancing**: Your advisor should recommend periodic rebalancing (usually annually) to make sure your portfolio is in line with your long-term asset allocation plan. Rebalancing is a means of controlling risk—it forces you to sell assets that are performing well and to use the proceeds to purchase assets that have performed poorly (that is, buy low and sell high). Vanguard estimates that regular rebalancing can be valued at up to 0.5% of investment assets annually.

- **Behavioural coaching**: The way in which an advisor adds the greatest value is by acting as a behavioural coach, helping you take emotion out of the investment process. The human mind is simply not optimally wired for successful investing. We have a tendency to succumb to fear and greed as a result of our natural "fight or flight" response. An advisor can play a critical role in making sure you avoid doing the wrong thing at the wrong time, whether that might be chasing investment fads or selling your investments when the media feature stories of economic doom and gloom. Vanguard estimated the value of behavioural coaching at 1.5% of investment assets annually.

- **Asset location**: A key role of the advisor is to place your investments in the best type of account with respect to tax efficiency. The value of asset location is difficult to quantify but important nonetheless.

- **Spending strategy/managing drawdown**: The way an advisor can add value in this area is by designing your retirement income plan and determining the best way to withdraw income from non-registered accounts, TFSAS, RRSPs, and so on, so that your income stream is as tax efficient as it can be. The value of tax efficiency is difficult to quantify, but keep in mind that every dollar of tax you save is an extra dollar in your pocket to save or spend.

- **Financial and estate planning**: Beyond dealing with your investments, an advisor should be able to add value by making sure you have an effective financial, retirement, and estate plan that meets your goals and objectives and is tax effective.

Vanguard concluded that the overall value of advice can be up to approximately 3% of investment assets annually. While it could be argued that Vanguard has an interest in promoting its investment products through advisors, I can tell you from experience that good advice is extremely valuable. It can mean the difference between achieving or not achieving your retirement goals, being adequately insured or not, and having or not having an estate plan that is tax efficient and maximizes the value of your estate for your heirs. Good advice can also prevent you from making potentially big financial mistakes.

This proved to be true for Heath, a client who was referred to me, initially for investment advice. An engineer, Heath was 44 years old and had two children in elementary school when we discussed his financial situation. Heath's wife, Donna, is a homemaker. Heath let me know that he did not own a home and had $150,000 of cash set aside for a down payment. As part of my effort to get to know his entire financial picture, I asked Heath about his existing insurance coverage and estate plan. He let me know that he had about $100,000 of life insurance coverage through his employer and that he had not yet completed his will and the related documents. I asked Heath what financial position he would want his wife to be in if he were to pass away suddenly, and he said he would prefer that she not have to work outside the home. As we discussed his priorities and ensured that his will was completed, adequate insurance coverage was of primary concern, while the investment advice was secondary. Although Heath wanted to discuss investments, his needs in other areas were far more immediate and urgent. Being inadequately insured could have been a mistake for Heath and his family.

Over the years, I have come across countless Canadians who are not receiving the advice they need. This typically happens to people for one of two reasons. First, they may not be with the right advisor. In my opinion, advisors should be paid to give advice in a range of areas, not only to manage investments. Consumers need to be aware of the areas in which their advisor can and should provide advice. If the relationship you have with your advisor focuses exclusively on investments and you want more, try being proactive and discussing your concerns with your advisor. If the situation does not change, find an advisor who better meets your needs and who provides the service and advice you require. The second reason many Canadians don't get the advice they need is that they don't seek advice in the first place. This is often because they have a negative view of the financial industry, perhaps as a result of bad experiences with advisors in the past or because of what they hear in the media.

Too frequently advisors are criticized by the media, usually in relation to the costs of using an advisor. The criticism often stems from the fact that the total annual cost (including the cost of advice and investment products) for those using an advisor could be up to 2.5% of their total portfolio value in cases where investments are made exclusively in mutual funds, compared with a cost of 0.5% or less if an individual doesn't use an advisor but instead uses a portfolio of ETFs in a self-directed account, through which they could possibly even obtain better long-term investment results. There is no doubt that costs do matter, but the value of professional advice is not limited to investment returns. This is the key point often missed by the media, and it bears repeating: **the value of professional advice is not limited to investment returns.** Good advisors provide advice in several areas—I refer to this as The Advice Wheel,™ shown in the illustration below. As in any area of professional service, good advice costs money. You get what you pay for.

The Advice Wheel™

A good financial advisor will be able to provide advice or direction in all of these areas.

As a client, you may not see consistent value—the value you derive from your financial advisor may be very different from year to year. For example, let's assume the following sequence of events. In Year 1, your portfolio returns 4%, while a market-based ETF returns 7%. From this perspective, as a new client you might conclude that your advisor is not only not providing value but also costing you money. In Year 2, during a market drop of 10%, you panic and want to sell your investments for cash; however, your advisor provides coaching and, as a result, you avoid fearfully selling at the bottom of the market. You then witness the inevitable market bounce-back. If you had sold at the bottom, you may have lost 10% of your portfolio value—but you didn't, so in effect your advisor has added 10% value. In Year 3, your advisor reviews your insurance, discovers you do not have adequate disability insurance, and works with you to enhance your coverage. Sometime after that, you become disabled and make a claim on your policy because it is in place. Having disability insurance provides financial flexibility so that you can focus on your recovery. In this example, it's almost impossible to quantify that value. Advisors will create value at different times, and that value cannot be judged solely on investment returns.

➤ **TAKE NOTE:** Advisor value cannot be judged on investment returns. Advisors add value in many areas, and that value will differ from year to year.

Advisor Alphabet Soup

Unlike other professions, such as medicine and law, there is no standard designation for professionals in the financial advice industry in Canada. Instead, there is an alphabet soup of credentials and certifications an advisor may have, including B. Com. (Bachelor of Commerce degree), MBA (Master of Business Administration degree), CFP (Certified Financial Planner), RFP (Registered Financial Planner), CIM (Chartered Investment Manager), CLU (Chartered Life Underwriter), and CFA (Chartered Financial Analyst). While some advisors may not have any of these formal designations, every advisor will have completed the regulatory licensing requirements and will be a "dealing representative." Depending on the path they take to get into the industry, advisors are regulated by one of several regulatory bodies (at the national or provincial level) and may be able to offer only certain products to their clients (more on this in the next section).

As a consumer, you need to know that it's not difficult to enter the financial services industry and become an advisor. During my career, I have come across financial advisors from a wide range of backgrounds, from used car salespeople to former professional athletes to people who, from a very early age, have wanted to help people manage money. At one end of the spectrum, anybody with a high school education who can pass three multiple-choice exams offered by the Canadian Securities Institute (CSI) with a minimum mark of 60% can be licensed as an advisor to deal in mutual funds and individual securities such as stocks and bonds. (A 90-day training program is also typically required when the advisor joins an investment dealer.) The majority of advisors, however, go far beyond this and complete further education to receive other designations, most of which require the advisor to meet annual continuing education requirements. But it is important for you to know that a certain level of formal education is not required for a person to operate in the financial advice industry.

The lack of a standard industry designation poses a major challenge for you as a consumer. I strongly believe that the minimum qualifications or standards to become an advisor need to be increased, and will increase over time. I hope that one day there are standard designations or credentials that apply across the industry. But for now, the financial advice industry is different from other professions. When you go to see a financial advisor, keep in mind that every advisor is different when it comes to their educational background and the types of investments and services they can provide.

Being that all financial advisors are not created equal and that there can be immense variation in the advice provided by different advisors, your challenge is to find one who can provide the advice, appropriate products, and services for your specific needs and, most importantly, one who puts your interests before his or her own. We will take a closer look later at how to choose the advisor who's right for you. Before you start your search, it's important that you have some background on the financial advice industry.

> **TAKE NOTE:** Advice is only as good as the person giving it.

How Advisors Are Regulated

Be it medicine, accounting, or law, in the vast majority of professions there is a regulatory body that serves to ensure certain standards are upheld and to protect the public. When it comes to the regulation of financial advisors, the picture can be somewhat confusing. As was touched upon above, different advisors are regulated by different bodies depending on the licences they hold and the products and services they are allowed to provide. In addition, the industry has both self-regulatory bodies and government regulatory bodies. The following chart provides a breakdown of the ways in which Canadian financial advisors are regulated according to the four main bodies.

Organization and status	Advisors regulated and geographic scope
Investment Industry Regulatory Organization of Canada (IIROC); self-regulatory	Advisors licensed to deal in individual securities such as stocks and bonds (these advisors are automatically licensed to sell mutual funds); national organization
Mutual Fund Dealers Association of Canada (MFDA); self-regulatory	Advisors licensed to deal in mutual funds; national organization

Provincial insurance councils; government regulatory	Advisors licensed to sell insurance products (e.g., life insurance, disability insurance, annuities, segregated funds); provincial organizations
Canadian Securities Administrators (CSA), comprising securities regulators from each province and territory; government regulatory	According to its website, the CSA brings provincial and territorial securities regulators together and is "primarily responsible for developing a harmonized approach to securties regulation across the country." CSA members regulate investment counselling firms, RESP scholarship plan dealers and private capital (exempt market) dealers, and oversee self-regulatory associations such as IIROC.

Note that in Quebec, the Autorité des marchés financiers (AMF) is the government organization that regulates the province's financial markets.

One of the challenges with the existing regulatory system is that sometimes different regulatory bodies have not effectively communicated with each other regarding disciplinary decisions. In the past, for example, there have been cases where advisors who have been disciplined by one regulatory body (such as IIROC) have maintained a license allowing them to continue operating in the insurance industry and sell insurance products. Regulators are now trying to work together more proactively to enhance investor protection. Although regulators are very much focused on enhancing investor protection, investors also need to help themselves, particularly by understanding how the financial advice industry in Canada is structured. While this may seem like a daunting task from a consumer's perspective, it does not have to be that way. Just understand that different advisors can be licensed to sell different products, and each advisor may ultimately be overseen by a different regulatory organization. If you have questions or require further information, refer to industry websites (such as the Investment Industry Regulatory Organization of Canada, Mutual Fund Dealers Association of Canada, and the Ontario Securities Commission Investor Office). These organizations have made available fantastic resources that could really help. Also be sure to ask your advisor, if you work with one.

In addition to the regulatory bodies listed in the chart above, there are voluntary professional membership associations such as Advocis, which refers to itself as The Financial Advisors Association of Canada. If your advisor is a member of Advocis, he or she may have different licences (e.g., insurance only; insurance and mutual funds; or insurance, mutual funds, and securities).

One of the major challenges Canadian investors have historically faced is limited transparency on costs for advice because, in many cases, the cost is embedded in the product or is deducted from the performance results of the product (such as a mutual fund). This issue has been longstanding and was identified and discussed at length by Glorianne Stromberg, former commissioner of the Ontario Securities Commission, in her 1998 report *Investment Funds in Canada and Consumer Protection: Strategies for the Millennium* that spanned 177 pages. Although it has taken time, the industry, led by the CSA, has taken bold steps to enhance disclosure through the Client Relationship Model (CRM), which was amended in 2013 with a Phase 2, known as CRM2, that includes new requirements. This new set of rules, developed to increase disclosure and transparency, will apply to the securities side of the financial advisory industry (insurance advisors are not subject to this—for now). In my opinion, Ms. Stromberg's work was visionary and far ahead of the curve when it comes to so many matters relating to investing and securities in Canada. Indeed, investors in Canada owe her a debt of gratitude.

One of the key parts of CRM2 is that, as of July 2016, regulations are now in effect requiring investors to be provided with annual reports on operating charges (account administration charges and transaction fees), compensation paid to investment dealers, and account performance. Due to the implementation period, investors can expect to receive these reports starting early in 2017. The new regulations mean that dealer compensation (how much you pay the firm your advisor works for, of which the advisor gets a certain percentage) will now be fully disclosed in dollar terms, allowing clients to clearly see what they pay for advice and thereby more easily determine whether the value they receive justifies the cost. Previously, dealer compensation was disclosed on various documents as a percentage and only in dollar terms for certain types of accounts. Be aware that these new statements will not show a breakdown of how much of the cost paid went to compensate the advisor and how much was kept by the company the advisor works through.

It is important to note that, unfortunately, these new disclosure requirements will not necessitate the disclosure of costs paid by clients to the investment manager (for example, you won't be told what amount is paid to mutual fund companies or other companies that manufacture and manage the investment products you purchase). In the future, disclosure requirements may become even more stringent and include a more thorough breakdown of costs so that the investor will see the total cost of investing and receiving advice.

In terms of performance reporting, investors will be provided with an annual performance report that will detail deposits and withdrawals from their account, the change in the value of the account, and the returns in percentages for the last year as well as for the prior three, five, and ten years. Returns will not be compared to any particular benchmark. Performance calculations will be based on a concept called the "money-weighted rate of return"—essentially all this means is that the calculation takes into consideration when the investor contributed to or withdrew money from their account. If the investor happens to make a contribution to their account right before a market downturn, the money-weighted return calculation would reflect this. The "time-weighted return" (historically used by the industry), on the other hand, ignores when contributions and withdrawals are made. This method is ideal for comparing managers or fund returns to benchmark indices. If you have questions on the return calculations on your statements, be sure to ask your advisor.

Investors must be aware that the new disclosure rules do not apply to insurance products such as segregated funds. This fact could lead to problems—for instance, advisors opting to sell segregated funds instead of regular mutual funds because the associated disclosure requirements are more lax. In industry lingo, this is called "regulatory arbitrage." In the future, I expect that this will change so that there is a level playing field between advisors who deal in securities and those who sell insurance products.

From a consumer perspective, you should know what the regulators are focusing on. For example, in June 2016, the Ontario Securities Commission (OSC) released its annual *Statement of Priorities*. In this report, the OSC noted that its first goal was to "deliver strong investor protection" and that it is proposing certain steps to improve that protection. The OSC stated that it is

> committed to achieving better alignment between the interests of investors and their advisors... Investors are placing increasing reliance on financial advisors and need to be confident that the advice they receive is appropriate and unbiased. We will continue to seek improvements to the culture of financial services businesses, including the incentive structures they use... The OSC is committed to achieving better alignment between the interests of investors and their advisors.

The OSC also noted that it will continue to consider the "impact that advisor titles and proficiency standards have on investor protection" and that it plans to "publish and conduct consultations on proposed regulatory provisions to create a best-interest standard." When it comes to titles, a December 2016 CSA notice stated that advisor titles may be based "on their ability to reach certain sales and revenue targets." It is interesting to observe that the Financial Consumer Agency of Canada's website even states: "The terms 'financial planner' and 'financial advisor' are used broadly; in fact, anyone outside the province of Quebec can call themselves a 'financial planner' or 'advisor.' What sets some apart are their education and training, and the qualifications that they hold."

The push to create a formal requirement for advisors to put their clients' interests first is gathering momentum globally. In April 2016, the U.S. Department of Labor put forward a fiduciary rule that will formally require financial advisors to put their clients' interests first when dealing with retirement accounts. At the time of writing, there are ongoing legal challenges to the rule as well as questions about whether the new US administration led by Donald Trump will repeal the rule. Barring any changes as a result of these factors, full implementation is expected by April 2017. It is important to understand that there are many legal nuances to how a fiduciary standard can actually be applied and enforced from a practical perspective. This is also something that Canadian regulators are thinking carefully about. It is my expectation that Canadian regulators will impose a higher standard on advisors, be it a fiduciary standard or a "best-interest" standard. This is a concept that I support, and I believe it is only a matter of time. If you are interested in learning more about the case for a fiduciary standard in Canada, one of the best papers I have come across on the topic is authored by Canadian financial advisor Nick Punko and titled *"Held to a Higher Standard"—Should Canada's Financial Advisors Be Held to a Fiduciary Standard?*

There has also been some discussion in Canada about banning the practice of having costs embedded in investment products, a measure that has recently been implemented in Australia and the United Kingdom. Embedded costs are commonly referred to as embedded or trailing commissions. As a result of the changes in Australia and the UK, many financial advisors in those countries have been forced to change to a fee-for-service business. In his April 2016 paper that was published by the University of Calgary's School of Public Policy, Pierre Lortie concluded that in countries where the cost of financial advice has been unbundled from investment products, an "advice gap" has been created, resulting in actually increasing the total cost of the services for some retail investors, while also denying access to others. In my opinion, generally speaking there is nothing inherently wrong with the embedded-fee structure, as long as proper disclosure is provided and costs are clearly understood. I believe that what is critical is that consumers should have a choice in how fees are paid.

From an advisor's perspective, one of the challenges of working in industry is that, in an effort to protect investors, Canadian regulators are continually increasing the compliance burden on advisors, to the point where it is common for advisors to spend one-third or more of their time dealing with these issues. Ironically, this takes more and more time away from advisors who could (and should) be spending the time working with clients to truly understand their goals and objectives, and helping clients to achieve them. From my perspective, while regulation is important and will always be needed to a certain extent, fundamental reform is required in three areas:

1. The Canadian education system absolutely, positively must include basic financial and investing concepts.

2. The advisory industry should move to a stronger and common educational standard that is required to be an advisor.

3. Guidelines for use of titles by advisors should be improved to ease consumer confusion.

Advisor Responsibilities

As part of the regulatory framework, financial advisors and the dealers through which they work have certain key responsibilities, categorized as follows:

- Know your client (KYC).
- Know your product (KYP).
- Recommend suitable investment products (suitability).

In addition to having to know their client, know their product, and make suitable investment recommendations, financial advisors are required to deal with each of their clients in good faith, fairly and honestly. The advisor also has an obligation to disclose all the risks of an investment to a client before proceeding with the investment. Let's look at how the three main responsibilities are satisfied.

Know Your Client

From a practical perspective, the requirement to know your client means that advisors should have an in-depth understanding of not only their client's financial situation but also of their goals and objectives. Let's assume you're deciding whether to hire a particular advisor. The advisor should start to get to know you from your first conversation. If you engage in a business relationship, the advisor will get to know you in more detail and will gather further information during the process of opening your new accounts. All of this information is gathered and put on what is known as the KYC (know your client) form. The information gathered typically includes personal information (your age, social insurance number, etc.), employment information, financial information (your income and net worth), risk tolerance, investment objectives, and time horizon (how long you plan to invest for and when you will need to start taking money out of your accounts). It is up to the advisor to *reasonably* assess your risk tolerance, investment objectives, and time horizon. Based on this assessment, your advisor must ensure that each type of account opened for you is appropriate. For example, if an elderly individual with a limited net worth and income wanted to open a margin account to trade stocks (borrowing to invest), this would likely not be appropriate. The requirement of knowing your client is an ongoing one, and it continues for the duration of the client–advisor relationship.

As part of the KYC responsibility, your advisor will either directly ask you what your risk tolerance and investment objectives are, make a determination based on the information you provide, or ask you to complete a risk tolerance questionnaire. At the individual investment level, risk tolerance is typically thought about in the terms low, medium, and high. As a rule of thumb, I would consider "low risk" to be assets such as cash, money market funds, and high-quality bonds. "Medium risk" would include blue-chip stocks (well-established companies that pay dividends such as TD Bank and Enbridge), while "high risk" might include assets such as stocks of smaller companies, especially those in highly volatile industries. Your advisor will need to make a determination of what percentage of your investments should be exposed to low-risk, medium-risk, and high-risk investments.

Investment objectives are most commonly described as income, growth (capital appreciation), or speculative. If you are in your retirement years and require your portfolio to generate cash flow to live on, the appropriate objective is likely income. If, on the other hand, you are in your peak earning years and trying to save for retirement, the appropriate objective may be capital appreciation. For example, a speculative investment objective is appropriate only if you are seeking investments that offer the possibility of large capital gains (but may involve a high probability of loss). A combination of objectives is also possible. The bottom line is that your investment objectives must accurately reflect your financial circumstances and goals.

When recommending individual securities, to help advisors assess risk some firms have developed their own risk-rating system. Within the system, each security—be it a bond, stock, or mutual fund—is given an objective and a risk rating. For the duration of the relationship between you and your advisor, the advisor must make sure that your investments comply with the agreed-upon percentages for the risks and objectives stated on the KYC form you completed and signed when you opened your accounts.

Throughout the client-advisor relationship, your advisor is required to ask whether there have been any material changes in your circumstances (e.g., retirement, a change in marital status or employment) and you, as the client, are obligated to inform your advisor of such changes. After all, if your advisor does not truly know you, how can he or she provide you with appropriate investments and advice? Good practice is for the advisor to review your situation annually, at minimum.

....

➤ **TAKE NOTE:** During the account-opening process, you should review the accuracy of the KYC information, ensure you understand it, sign the document, and keep a copy.

....

Know Your Product

It is critical that advisors understand in detail the features and associated risks of the investments and other products they recommend. Of particular importance is that they understand the anticipated return, risk, and costs involved in the investment, the time horizon of the investment, and its overall complexity. The advisor is also required to maintain documentation to support their recommendations.

Suitability

Simply put, all investment recommendations must be appropriate for the particular client. Your advisor is required to be able to justify that each recommendation he or she makes is appropriate in relation to everything they know about you. This includes your financial situation, risk tolerance, investment knowledge, investment objectives, and time horizon. All investment recommendations must also be suitable in the context of your account's current holdings and risk level. Your advisor should be able to clearly explain why a specific investment is appropriate and suitable for your needs and how it fits into the overall portfolio. Any investment that is not consistent with your personal situation (whether in relation to your time horizon, investment objectives, or risk tolerance) is considered an unsuitable investment.

Types of Advisors

Before you can choose the financial advisor who's right for you, you need to educate yourself about the different kinds of advisors available and how much their services cost. Historically, the financial industry in Canada has been organized with two arms—product manufacturers (fund companies that create and manage investments such as mutual funds) and product distributors (companies that sell or distribute the products created by the manufacturers). Today these industry lines are blurring and may continue blurring further in the future, as business models change; however, for now, it still makes sense to separate the industry into product manufacturers and product distributors.

For example, different mutual fund companies create different mutual funds, and financial advisors are the distributors of those mutual funds—that is, one of their primary roles is to sell the mutual funds to the public. Thus, financial advisors can be classified as product distributors (they sell the product to the end client—you!). There are a number of ways they can do this, depending on what type of advisor they are. Recognizing that, historically, the most common type of investment product in the financial industry has been the mutual fund, I will focus mainly on this type of investment in the descriptions that are provided below to help you understand the differences between the various kinds of advisors.

Bank Branch Advisors

Most bank branches have financial advisors on staff who are licensed to provide mutual fund investments. When you ask your bank for financial advice, expect to be referred to one of these in-house advisors. Banks are interested in obtaining a "greater share of wallet"— that is, if a bank holds your deposit accounts and your mortgage, it also wants to manage your investments. Ideally, every bank wants its advisors to offer bank-run mutual funds (known as "proprietary product") as these funds generate investment management fees for the bank. From a consumer perspective, this is referred to as "brand bias." The *Investment Executive*'s 2016 Report Card on Banks stated that in terms of asset allocation, almost 25% of client assets held at banks were invested in proprietary management products versus less than 3% for the average advisor. Although at the time of writing most do not, in the future bank branch-based advisors may also offer other bank-run investment products, such as exchange-traded funds. Over the years, there has been speculation in the advisor community that there is an "invisible hand" guiding bank-based financial advisors toward selling proprietary products, using tactics such as additional incentives, amongst others. A December 2016 CSA notice stated that there can be monetary and non-monetary incentives to favour proprietary products at firms that provide advice and have in-house investment products.

If you use a bank branch advisor, the fees you pay will likely be embedded in the returns of your mutual funds. For example, if the management expense ratio (MER) is 2.5% and your fund returns 8%, your statement will show a 5.5% return. Many investors believe that the financial advice they receive at the bank is free—it is not free.

Bank-based advisors are generally paid salaries with possible bonuses, and the bank also collects fees from managing the mutual funds.

If you are working with an advisor at a bank, it is important to understand that, legally, banks are not allowed to engage in what's called "coercive tied selling." This means that banks cannot unduly pressure you to buy a product or service you don't want before it will provide you with another product or service you do want. For example, if you qualify for a mortgage, a bank cannot approve your mortgage only if you agree to move your investments to that bank. Although coercive tied selling is not allowed, banks, like any business, can offer preferred pricing if you use additional products or services of theirs.

For new investors or those with low investable assets, using a bank-based advisor makes sense because of the convenience. But keep in mind that banks tend to move their personnel fairly frequently, so it may be difficult to develop a long-term relationship with one particular branch advisor who really gets to know you and your family.

Mutual Fund Representatives

Licensed to provide only mutual funds, mutual fund representatives can work for mutual fund companies, financial planning firms, or mutual fund dealerships. Examples of these types of companies include Investors Group, Assante Wealth Management, Investment Planning Counsel, and FundEX Investments. Mutual fund representatives are paid through sales commissions and ongoing fees from products sold; therefore, keep in mind the potential for conflict of interest. When you purchase a mutual fund or any other investment product (regardless of from whom), ask yourself whether the advisor is recommending an investment because it is really the best one for you or because it pays the highest commission to the advisor. The possibility of brand bias also exists with mutual fund representatives: some may offer only funds that are manufactured by their own companies or related entities. This is very important to be aware of, because your investment options may be limited. In general, a portion of the fees you pay to the mutual fund company for managing your assets goes to the advisor for ongoing service and advice. We will discuss these costs in more detail a little later, but for now take careful note: make sure you do indeed receive this ongoing service and advice! Mutual fund representatives may (or may not) provide other services, such as financial planning or retirement planning, depending on the advisor. In the future, mutual fund representatives may be permitted to also provide clients with access to exchange-traded funds. If you have smaller amounts to invest or prefer not to own individual securities, having a mutual fund advisor may be worth investigating further.

Planning-Focused Advisors

Advisors of this type typically have the CFP designation and they will focus primarily on examining your overall financial situation and goals, providing you with a detailed plan for achieving your retirement and financial objectives. As a client, you may be asked to fill out an extensive questionnaire. The information you provide to the advisor is entered into a specialized software program that will generate your detailed financial plan. Financial planners may charge a flat fee for this plan (possibly in the range of $1,500–$2,500) and they may or may not sell investment products and provide investment recommendations, depending on the advisor. Even if you plan to manage your finances yourself, seeing an advisor of this type annually or semi-annually is useful to make sure you are on track to reach your goals and objectives, and to make sure your financial house is in order.

Full-Service Advisors

These advisors generally work through well-recognized financial institutions, which could be bank owned or independent (meaning non–bank-owned firms such as Raymond James and Canaccord Genuity Group). Generally, full-service advisors are a better fit for higher-net-worth individuals because of their access to a wider range of products and services. It is important to note that full-service advisors are usually licensed to provide individual stocks and bonds as well as mutual funds. Some advisors at full-service investment firms may also be licensed to deal in insurance products. Compensation models (which will be discussed in detail later) can differ from advisor to advisor, even within the same firm. Each full-service advisor is licensed by a regulatory body and uses the platform of their company to serve their clients, doing so under a brand name (e.g., RBC Dominion Securities, TD Wealth, Raymond James). Beyond this, advisors will have their own unique investment approach and focus. The level of competence, service, and work quality of two advisors at the same company can be totally different.

An important note about full-service advisors at banks: one key advantage of these advisors is that they have access to many different specialists under the same roof—for example, if you are a high-net-worth individual, you would likely be able to access the services of an on-site lawyer specializing in estate planning. Essentially, banks can provide one-stop shopping for almost any financial need. While full-service advisors at independent firms also have access to other professionals, they may not all be available under the same roof. One other thing to keep in mind, particularly with regard to advisors at bank-owned firms, is: be aware of the potential conflicts that could arise from the usage of proprietary investment products, as noted earlier.

Portfolio Managers

Portfolio managers generally service high-net-worth individuals and institutions and they can be found at banks, independent firms, or investment counselling firms. By managing accounts on a discretionary basis, portfolio managers are able to make buy or sell decisions in your portfolio *without your consent* for each transaction. Typically, portfolio managers are more experienced and have higher-level certifications compared with other advisors in the industry. If you hire a portfolio manager, he or she should work with you to create a detailed, customized investment policy statement (IPS) that explains your personal situation, your risk tolerance, and how your assets will be managed for the long term. An IPS is like a GPS device for your investments. To see a sample IPS, refer to Part 4 of this book. Whether you hire a portfolio manager or not, it is a good idea for every family to have an IPS to guide their investments.

Before hiring a portfolio manager, make sure you have a clear idea of the manager's investment strategy and ask to see his or her track record. Be wary of a strategy that involves a "back-test" or simulated results based on a given strategy. For example, in theory, a portfolio manager could design an investment strategy in 2016 and then test it to see how it would have done from 2006–16. This is a "back-test" and the results are not based on real "live" money. There's a saying in the industry: "Nobody's ever seen a bad back-test!"

Portfolio managers should be able to converse knowledgeably about the investments in their clients' portfolios. Probe their ability to do this when speaking with them. Note, portfolio managers can use individual securities, mutual funds, exchange-traded funds, or other investment products in their clients' portfolios. Ideally, portfolio managers should also have at least part of their own portfolios invested in the same securities as their clients are invested in. Known as "eating your own cooking," this practice increases the alignment of interest between the advisor and his or her clients. According to the Portfolio Association of Canada, "portfolio managers have a fiduciary duty to act with care, honesty, and good faith, always in the best interest of their clients. Investment decisions therefore must be independent and free of bias. This results in a higher level of trust placed on portfolio managers." Some portfolio managers also provide financial advice in other areas, while others do not. Some portfolio managers may have a minimum asset requirement for clients to qualify for portfolio management services, often in the range of $250,000 to $500,000. Note: your investment management fees may be tax-deductible in non-registered investment accounts.

Insurance-Focused Advisors

These advisors are licensed to sell insurance (usually life and disability policies), segregated funds, and annuities. Annuities provide a steady stream of income over time in exchange for a lump-sum investment up front. Segregated funds are similar to mutual funds but have principal guarantee provisions. We'll discuss them in more detail later, but for now it's worth noting that segregated funds are also creditor- and bankruptcy-proof, and they bypass probate (the process of establishing the validity of a will) if the owner dies. These additional features result in fees that are typically higher than mutual fund fees. Segregated funds definitely have a place in some clients' portfolios, but I have seen instances where clients invested in segregated funds but didn't need the additional features the funds offer, meaning the clients paid higher fees than they really needed to. This may have been because the advisor was only licensed to deal with insurance products. Keep this in mind—insurance-focused advisors may or may not be licensed to deal with mutual funds and individual securities. Advisors can be licensed to handle insurance products only; insurance products and mutual funds; or insurance products, mutual funds, and individual securities.

Insurance advisors are generally paid upfront commissions on insurance policies or segregated funds, in addition to receiving ongoing fees for products sold.

Online Advisors

Several companies, commonly known as online, digital, or "robo" advisors, now offer investment and related services online at a reduced cost. Robo-advisors are attempting to, as Goshka Folda of Investor Economics puts it, "uberize" the investment industry. The business model of robo-advisors is essentially to automate as much of the investment process as possible by leveraging technology to commoditize what can be commoditized, including portfolio construction and the account-opening process. For example, accounts can be opened entirely online and well-diversified portfolios can be constructed (using low-cost exchange-traded funds) on the basis of completion of an online risk-assessment tool as well as a conversation with a human portfolio manager. Portfolios are rebalanced to target asset allocations on a yearly basis. Assets are typically held with a third-party custodian who is a member of the Canadian Investor Protection Fund, meaning client accounts receive the same standard of protection that traditional financial advisors provide.

Online advisor fees can vary among firms, but expect to pay approximately 0.5% of your assets per year plus the cost of the investment products used (ETFs), which could be up to another 0.5% of your assets. In total, the cost should come in at no more than about 1% of your assets annually. Be aware that there are some companies that charge a flat dollar amount on a monthly basis, so your costs may come in even lower than you think! In general though, don't forget to keep in mind that your total cost is the fee of the robo-advisor plus the cost of any investment product used.

Dollar for dollar, robo-advisors are cheaper than a traditional human advisor—there is no doubt about this. However, I caution you not to conclude that online advising is necessarily your best choice just because it is cheaper, despite what you might hear or read in the media (e.g., stories with headlines such as "It's time to hand your investments over to a robot"). As I stated earlier, in my opinion the media gets it wrong when it focuses only on investment costs and doesn't recognize the value of the advice traditional advisors can offer in all the other areas of The Advice Wheel.

Today, I would characterize robo-advisors as providing an online investing service for a lower cost than is possible with a human advisor. This is a relatively new part of the financial services industry, but it's one that represents a tectonic shift that will likely accelerate in the future. Going forward, expect to see continued innovation as machine learning and artificial intelligence gather steam! Currently, robo-advisors are trying to gather enough economies of scale with an objective of driving down costs by using ETFs rather than using traditional mutual funds. While online advisory companies are better established in the United States, where they have gathered billions of dollars of assets under management, these companies are definitely gaining traction in Canada.

The extent of advice offered by online advisors doesn't come close to what traditional advisors can provide, but I expect that over time online advisors will move toward a more complete service-offering that will appeal to an increasing number of Canadians. In addition, banks and other companies will continue offering more online advisory services to certain segments of their clients, such as millennials. That said, I believe traditional advisory channels will continue to be best equipped to serve clients who require thorough financial, insurance, and estate planning as well as those who have complex situations that necessitate coordination between their financial, accounting, and tax professionals.

Even executives at robo-advisor companies do acknowledge there can be immense value in the traditional human-advisor relationship.

Human advisors are essential in facilitating difficult conversations that many people don't want to have. For example, it takes a human to really engage a client to talk about insurance and estate planning. Furthermore, traditional advisors are better placed when it comes to behavioural coaching—preventing clients from getting emotional and doing the wrong thing at the exact wrong time. In investing, staying calm and not selling during a market fall can be critical to achieving long-term financial goals. Users of online advising services could potentially react to a market downturn with emotion and log in to their account to sell their investments at the wrong time. With a traditional advisor relationship, it is more likely that the advisor and client would have a detailed conversation that could lead to a different outcome.

Online advisors should appeal primarily to the following groups:

- **Investors with smaller amounts to invest.** Online advisors can provide services to investors with $5,000 (or even less) to invest. If you're in this category, the most common alternative to online service is to invest through an advisor at your bank branch. Full-service advisors generally do not work with clients having only small amounts to invest.

- **Cost-sensitive investors.** For investors who want to keep the cost of investing down, using an online advisor is a viable option. Remember, though, that often you get what you pay for. If you have a complex situation and want comprehensive advice, a full-service advisor may be a better solution.

There is no doubt that technology is transforming and disrupting the financial advisory industry. Industry participants on all sides acknowledge that we are in the midst of a paradigm shift. That said, in my opinion, any predictions of the impending demise of the financial advisor are greatly exaggerated. Canadians will always need advice and every person and their situation is unique. Advisors are critical in engaging clients to think and talk about issues that can be challenging, such as taking the right amount of risk in their portfolios, their risk appetite, the mechanics of delivering tax-efficient retirement income, and having adequate insurance for death and disability. Technology will never be a substitute for human judgment—sound judgment is indeed a very valuable commodity. Advisors will have to adapt, utilize technology to their benefit, ensure they are providing comprehensive services, and do a better job of articulating their value proposition. Needless to say, the next few years will be very interesting. I expect that online services will continue to evolve further. Some online advisors will make it in their current form, while others will be unable to gather the scale and assets necessary to survive. Banks and independent firms have also started to use their own or third-party online platforms. It looks like it will all result in the client experience being better: advice and planning will become more interactive, with clients able to access their investments, see their asset allocation, and also manipulate their financial plans for different life scenarios online whenever they want. It will be exciting!

. . . .

➤ **TAKE NOTE:** Online advisors are a practical option for people who have limited funds to invest or who are focused purely on keeping investment costs down. If you need comprehensive advice, you'll have to find an advisor who can provide it.

. . . .

Multi-level Marketing Advisors

As stated earlier, most companies operating in the Canadian financial advice industry fit into one of two categories: they are either bank-owned or an independent firm. Understanding how these types of firms and their advisors work is relatively straightforward, but you should also be aware that there are a handful of other advisory firms that operate under a different business model called multi-level marketing (MLM). To learn more about firms using this model, try googling "financial advisor MLM Canada." Companies using this business model tend to focus on Canadians who they believe are not well served by banks and independent companies.

Typically, MLM firms employ sales representatives who are usually licensed to sell mutual funds and insurance products. Similar to how many other advisors are paid, their compensation comes from sales charges (upfront fees), ongoing fees from selling mutual funds, and commissions on insurance policies. The key difference in compensation between MLM and other firms is that in MLM firms every sales representative receives incentives for recruiting other sales representatives.

For example, John, a sales rep, recruits Tim. As a reward, John will receive a portion of Tim's future earnings. Later, Tim recruits Isobel. Tim will receive part of Isobel's earnings. But John will also receive a small portion of Isobel's earnings. So John now receives his own income plus residual income from both Tim and Isobel. This cycle continues such that the more new recruits John brings in himself (or that his recruits bring in), the more income he will receive. The bottom line is that an advisor with an MLM firm is very much motivated to recruit as many new advisors as possible to build their business and increase their income.

While there is nothing wrong with MLM firms per se, in my experience advisors at such firms tend to be too heavily focused on making sales and recruiting new advisors. I have actually heard of instances where an individual has a full-time day job in a different industry and is working part-time as an advisor. Another interesting situation I came across was where an investor became the client of an MLM advisor and, shortly thereafter, the advisor tried to recruit the client as an advisor. As a potential client, you should think about how much time you would be comfortable with your advisor spending on recruiting new advisors. When evaluating advisors from MLM firms, it is also critical to consider their qualifications and experience.

....

➤ **TAKE NOTE:** Understand what type of business model your advisor operates in—that of a bank, an independent firm, or an MLM firm. MLM advisors may be more focused on sales and recruiting.

....

RESP Scholarship Advisors

Some companies and advisors focus exclusively on group Registered Education Savings Plans (RESPs), which are long-term savings instruments for education. Group RESPs (sometimes called pooled plans) are sold only by scholarship plan dealers (firms that specialize in selling this product). Participating investors pool their capital for investment purchases—every investor buys units in the plan. It is important to understand that the rules of each group plan are unique and every plan is different. In general, if you stop contributing to the plan and leave early, you will get your contributions back (less any applicable penalties), but the earnings on the investments will go to the other participants in the plan.

When it comes to using group RESPs, another option is opening RESP accounts through advisors at firms such as banks or independent investment dealers. If you are considering using a group RESP scholarship, be aware that, generally, group RESPs are less flexible and may have higher costs than if you open your own individual or family RESP. For example, if you miss a regular contribution to a group RESP, you may face penalties. If you set up your own individual or family RESP, you can make contributions when you are in a position to do so.

Additionally, some of the withdrawal rules for group RESPs may be more restrictive and the investments within a group RESP may be excessively conservative with little exposure to stocks that, while more volatile, can provide better longer-term growth. Being conservative with funds for your children's education is a good thing, but if your child has a 15-to-18-year time horizon before college or university, a reasonable amount of exposure to quality stocks may be warranted (this is especially true when interest rates are very low).

➤ **TAKE NOTE:** Group RESPs are generally less flexible and can be more costly than opening your own plan. If you are considering participating in a group RESP through an RESP dealer, make sure you understand the details.

Exempt-Market Advisors

In Canada, before a company is allowed to issue securities, it must file a prospectus with the applicable securities commission. The prospectus serves to provide investors with detailed information about the investment, including the risks involved, so that they can make informed decisions. The process of filing a prospectus is costly and time-consuming.

Exempt-market dealers can issue securities that are exempt from the prospectus requirement. Generally, these investments are called "private" investments because they are not traded publicly. Until recently, you needed to meet certain criteria to participate in these investments, such as having a minimum income level or net worth. Recently, though, investment rules have been relaxed so that Canadians with lower income and net worth levels can participate to a certain degree (see your advisor for further details).

In general, exempt-market dealers and their representatives are, however, still subject to the KYC, KYP, and suitability guidelines. While there are always exceptions (depending on the specific investment opportunity and your circumstances), in my experience exempt products may not be appropriate for all Canadians because of their reduced transparency, higher complexity, and potentially high sales commissions. For further information about exempt-market products and advisors, refer to the Private Capital Markets Association of Canada.

Advisor Authority

When you begin working with a financial advisor, be aware that there are two main types of investment accounts—non-discretionary and discretionary. The key difference is the decision-making authority you give your advisor.

Non-discretionary Accounts

With non-discretionary accounts, your advisor does not have the authority to make investment decisions without speaking to you, the client, to obtain specific verbal authorization. With this type of account, advisors call clients periodically (typically annually, at minimum) to review the account and to recommend specific transactions (buys or sells). One of the drawbacks of these accounts is that when you approve a trade, depending on the terms you agreed to, you may be charged a commission, which then leads to the question of alignment of interest: Is your advisor contacting you because you need to make changes to your account, or is the primary reason so that the advisor will earn a commission?

Non-discretionary accounts can also be operated on a fee basis—you are charged a specific percentage of your assets annually and allowed to make a certain number of trades at no additional cost. For example, you may pay a fee of 1% annually, with 20-40 trades included at no additional cost. With this type of fee structure, there is less concern about alignment of interests.

Discretionary Accounts

For a discretionary account, the client must hire an advisor who is also a licensed portfolio manager—only advisors who are registered portfolio managers are able to manage discretionary accounts. The advisor will develop an IPS for the client, based on the client's goals, objectives, and risk tolerance. The advisor will then manage the client's account according to the IPS, which states the guidelines for management of the account, making investment decisions on the client's behalf. The client typically receives a quarterly performance report, which is essentially the advisor's report card for the investments.

When you open a discretionary account, you essentially hand control of your account to your advisor. In my experience, I have found that many investors find discretionary accounts convenient and effective. This is especially the case for those who, in the past, had non-discretionary accounts and regularly followed the direction of their advisor. Their perspective is, if you are going to do what your advisor recommends, why not have it done on a discretionary basis? In such cases, discretionary accounts can be more efficient for both you and your advisor—your advisor can do what needs to be done without having to contact you every time and potentially not reaching you quickly.

For example, if an advisor has a hundred clients and wants to buy BCE stock, it won't be very efficient for her to do so if the clients have non-discretionary accounts and there is potential for unfairness: Who does she call first, who does she call last, and who can she not reach? If the advisor is a portfolio manager with discretionary accounts, however, she can make the change to every account affected by this trade at the same time. To do this, the advisor will go through all her client accounts (often using a software or trading platform) and decide how many shares of BCE are required to be purchased in total for all the accounts together. The advisor will then place one trade to buy BCE (for example, for 50,000 shares) and then distribute those shares across all of his or her clients' accounts in the appropriate proportions. This way, every client involved in the trade is treated fairly and the advisor is able to get the trade done in an efficient manner.

➤ **TAKE NOTE:** Understand whether your accounts are non-discretionary or discretionary. With a non-discretionary account, document every trade you authorize. Before opening a discretionary account, be comfortable with your advisor's investment philosophy, risk management ability, and track record.

How Is Your Advisor Paid?

One of the key questions to ask your advisor is how he or she is compensated. As a client, it is critical for you to understand not only the sources of the advisor's compensation but also the financial relationship between the dealer (the company through which the advisor works) and the advisor. For every dollar of revenue the advisor generates, the dealer firm will take a certain percentage—we will examine this later, in Understanding the Role of the Dealer. For now, be aware that each advisor is really running an individual business. Some advisors may work as part of a team, but this is more the exception than the norm. Advisors tend to use one of three business models—transactional, commission-based, and fee-for-service (fee only or fee-based)—and each has advantages and disadvantages, as you will read below.

Transactional Compensation

The transactional business model has been historically used by the traditional stock broker who gives only investment advice. Such an advisor is paid a commission whenever the client makes a trans-action such as buying or selling a stock or bond. For example, say your advisor recommends purchasing 100 shares of TD Bank for a total transaction value of $5,500. The advisor provides you with a rationale for why this is the right time to buy shares of TD Bank and how this purchase fits your investment goals, objectives, and risk tolerance. After considering the advice, you authorize the transaction. The advisor then charges you a commission—let's say it's 2.5% of the value of the trade ($137.50 in this case)—which then becomes revenue generated by the advisor for the dealer. Commission rates vary by advisor and by firm but usually range from 0.25% to 2.75% of the transaction value, depending on the size of the transaction. Typically, the higher the transaction dollar value, the lower the commission rate. Advisors who are compensated according to the transactional model may also provide ancillary services, such as financial planning, but in my experience this is not the norm.

In the 2010s, the transactional business model has become less common, for several reasons: investors are becoming more sophisticated and have increasing amounts of financial information at their fingertips, and the proliferation of low-cost alternatives such as online trading, online advisors, and ETFs has put pressure on fees, making this business model less attractive for advisors. Today, more consumers require a holistic level of service, beyond just investment and trading recommendations. Dealer firms are also encouraging their advisors to change their business model to a fee-based model, whereby a monthly or quarterly percentage fee is charged on client assets. Fee-based models generate consistent, predictable revenues, while the year-to-year revenue of a transactional advisor is inconsistent and less predictable.

ADVANTAGE:
- You pay only when you authorize a transaction.

DISADVANTAGES:
- Commissions can be significant and can add up quickly because you must pay a commission each time you buy or sell an investment.

- An advisor who does not have your best interests in mind may make unnecessary recommendations in order to generate additional commissions. This practice is known as "churning" and is widely frowned upon in the industry.

- While advisors using the transactional model can (and some do) offer ancillary services in areas such as financial planning, insurance, and wills and estate planning, in my experience this is less likely than it is with advisors using a fee-based model.

Commission-Based Compensation

Operating in the most common business model in the financial advice industry, commission-based advisors generally receive upfront and/or ongoing (trailing) commissions from the sale of mutual funds, segregated funds, and other insurance products.

Advisors who sell mutual funds or segregated funds can receive upfront commissions, which are referred to as the "load" or "sales charges." The upfront commission is meant to compensate the advisor for the initial work of meeting with the client; understanding their goals, objectives, and risk tolerance; making appropriate recommendations; and completing follow-up work. The load can be paid upfront by the investor ("front-end load") or by the mutual fund or insurance company whose product is being sold ("back-end load" or "deferred sales charge"). Front-end loads can range from 0% to 5% of the initial fund purchase, depending on what you negotiate with your advisor. Back-end loads pay the advisor 3% to 5% of the initial purchase and subject the investor to potential early-redemption penalties because the mutual fund company has paid the advisor a commission upfront and has to earn this back via the management fees from managing the client's assets. If the client withdraws the assets from the fund company, the fund company needs to recoup the commission. In recent years, back-end loads have dropped in usage within the advisor community. Recently, one major Canadian mutual fund company announced that, as of 2017, new purchases would no longer be allowed using a traditional back-end load structure. You should also be aware that there are some mutual funds available on a "no-load" basis, meaning that there are no sales charges or commissions to purchase the mutual fund.

Advisors selling life insurance will also receive an upfront commission from the insurance company. As a rule of thumb, this upfront commission is approximately the same as the first year of the insurance premium. For example, if you buy a $1-million life insurance policy and your payments are $200 per month (totalling $2,400 per year), your advisor will receive an upfront commission of about $2,400.

Ongoing or trailing commissions are meant to compensate the advisor for providing ongoing service to the client. The advisor may provide regular meetings and ongoing services in various areas, including financial planning, investments, behavioural coaching, and tax and estate planning. In the industry, trailing commissions are generally a percentage of the investment assets. The actual percentage depends on the type of funds the investor holds, as well as on the fund company. The trailing commission for equity funds is usually in the range of 1% to 1.25%, while fixed-income or bond-fund trailing commissions are usually about 0.5%. For example, if you work with an advisor and have a $100,000 portfolio invested in mutual funds, you will probably pay your advisor's firm about $1,000 per year for ongoing services (the advisor will receive a portion of the $1,000). If you have invested in a mutual fund and were not aware of this, it's because the annual trailing commissions are a form of embedded compensation—the cost is deducted from fund returns rather than billed directly to the client.

In Canada, the regulators of financial advisors have taken major steps to enhance transparency surrounding trailing commissions. As mentioned earlier, in July 2016 regulations went into effect that will require dollar amounts of trailing commissions—including those that are embedded—to be disclosed to investors on their statements. There is an implementation period, so from a practical perspective, 2017 will be the first year that many Canadian investors will see what financial advice costs them in dollar terms.

If your advisor uses a commission-based business model, you should be absolutely sure you receive the ongoing service you are paying for. If you're not, find another advisor. I know of many competent

MAKING SENSE OF IT ALL   49

advisors using a commission-based business model who do provide their clients with ongoing service and comprehensive advice, but I'm also aware of cases in which the ongoing service was not provided to a sufficient standard or was lacking altogether.

ADVANTAGES:

- For some investors, embedded commissions is psychologically an easier way of paying costs because they prefer not to see the dollar amount being paid.

- By the time this book is published, new regulations will have come into effect requiring transparent disclosure of embedded commissions.

DISADVANTAGES:

- There is a potential conflict of interest between the product that is best for the client and the product that pays the advisor the highest ongoing commission. Theoretically, an advisor who does not have your best interests in mind could choose products that may not be the best for you but generate high commissions or trailing fees for them.

- You may not receive the ongoing service you pay for through embedded commissions.

Fee-for-Service Compensation (fee only or fee-based)

Recently, the fee-for-service model has gained more traction in the financial advice industry. I have seen two main applications of this type of model.

First, some advisors who have been trained as financial planners may charge a flat fee or an hourly rate to provide advice and provide services such as creating a financial plan. I refer to this as a "fee only" compensation model. For example, an advisor might charge $1,500–$2,500 for a financial plan or bill you $250 per hour. The advisor may or may not make product recommendations. If you are knowledgeable and disciplined enough to invest on your own, but you want to make sure you are on the right long-term path, this type of fee-for-service option might be right for you.

Second, and more commonly, many advisors charge an annual fee that is a percentage of the assets they are managing for you. This is known as "fee-based" compensation. (Be aware that these advisors may require a minimum amount of investable assets—typically $250,000.) The annual fee pays not only for the investment management but also for other services such as client meetings, financial planning, and tax and estate planning. As is the case with fee-only (flat fee/hourly cost) compensation, a key advantage of this type is that the advisor does not receive any form of embedded or trailing commissions. The percentage fee varies significantly from advisor to advisor. In general, the more investible assets you have, the lower the percentage should be. I have seen fees ranging from 2.5% for smaller accounts to 0.5% for accounts in the millions of dollars. If you work with an advisor using an annual percentage fee, it is critical that you ask the following questions:

1. **Is the advisor a licensed portfolio manager permitted to make discretionary trades in your account?** Portfolio managers provide a higher level of service because they are permitted to make changes to a client's account without obtaining verbal authorization from the client, as long as the trades are within the parameters of the client's IPS. As discussed, discretionary portfolio managers can make a single "block" trade for all their clients at the same price and then allocate the shares to client accounts, resulting in greater efficiency.

   Some advisors using the fee-for-service model are licensed as discretionary portfolio managers and some are not. If your advisor is not, you will be required to authorize each trade in your account. Making a trade without explicit authorization from the client is strictly prohibited if the account is not set up for discretionary management.

2. **What types of securities will the advisor use in managing your accounts?** The answer to this question is critical in assessing the true cost of the advisor's services. In addition to the annual percentage fee you're paying to have your accounts managed, you need to know about any other costs you might be subject to, depending on which investment products your advisor has chosen for you. For example, assume you are paying 1.5% annually to your advisor to manage your assets. If the advisor has 50% of your investments in a mutual fund with an MER of 1.4%, your total

cost is really 1.5% + (50% × 1.4%), or 2.2%. In fee-based accounts, advisors can use a special class of mutual funds, known as the F-class. These funds have lower MERs than do regular mutual funds. Nonetheless, make sure you fully understand the total cost and that you are getting value for that cost. From an investment perspective, if having more foreign investments is the right thing to do, there is nothing wrong with the advisor using mutual funds or ETFs to accomplish this—a small incremental cost makes sense in this case. However, if an advisor is charging an annual fee of 2% and then using mutual funds for the entire portfolio, it may be a problem.

3. **Are there any additional costs for maintaining the account and/ or trading?** In fee-based accounts, most commonly there are no additional costs for having an account, and at least a certain number of "free" trades are allowed annually. For example, if you had a fee-based RRSP and TFSA, you would most likely not pay an annual administration fee to keep the accounts open (by contrast, an account that is not fee-based would have a potential cost of $125 and $25 annually for an RRSP and a TFSA respectively). Also, in a fee-based account you will likely be allowed at least 15-20 free trades each year. Accounts in which discretionary trading is permitted would have an unlimited number of trades at no additional cost.

ADVANTAGES:
- One all-in fee covers your advisor's services, as well as administration and trading costs.

- There's less potential for conflict of interest because the advisor does not receive trailing commissions.

DISADVANTAGES:
- Investors are also subject to the associated costs of the investment products chosen by their advisor.

- Investors should ensure that their portfolios are being actively monitored and that they are receiving the advice they require on a regular basis. Regulators are now becoming more focused on "lack of activity" in fee-based accounts, or what is also known as "reverse-churning."

> **TAKE NOTE:** Understand that each advisor is running a business and may use any one of a variety of business models. As a client, you must decide which one is right for you.

Costs Matter

In many areas of life, you can do the necessary work yourself for minimal cost or you can hire a professional at a higher cost. Just as you can either do your own repairs around the house or hire someone to do the work for you, you can either manage your own finances or you can hire a financial advisor.

As I commented on earlier, we often see articles in the media criticizing the financial advice industry for supposedly charging unjustifiably high fees to clients, but good advisors add value in numerous ways that those in the media often don't write about or consider. What is the value of an advisor preventing a client from doing the wrong thing at the wrong time, like selling at the bottom of the market? What is the value of an advisor who makes sure a client who works at WestJet doesn't have 30% of his retirement account in WestJet stock? (More on this later.) What is the value of an advisor who structures retirement income for a client in a way that minimizes taxes? Some in the media often overlook to what extent good advisors help families by encouraging retirement savings, assisting to make sure clients are on track to meet long-term financial goals, and making sure clients are adequately insured. In times of need, like when a family member passes away, the financial advisor often receives the first call. When you think about it, a good advisor can be invaluable.

The reality is that nothing is free and, like any other professional, advisors must be paid reasonable compensation for their time and expertise. As long as you are receiving the service and advice you are paying for, your costs should be examined relative to the value your advisor provides rather than in absolute terms. Keep in mind that the value you receive can be "lumpy"—more value may be added in some years than in others.

I expect that the debate about investor costs for advice will continue, but the good news is that the industry is becoming more transparent. Furthermore, investment product fees are likely to come down (especially for funds) over time due to an increasing number of low-cost investment alternatives, such as exchange-traded funds, and increased competition as investment companies continue to fight to maintain or increase market share. That said, it is every investor's responsibility to pay attention to the costs of investing and advice—after all, every dollar you pay in fees is one less dollar working for you in your portfolio, and excessively high fees can eat into your returns.

Let's look at a simple example. If an investor started with a $100,000 portfolio and earned an annual gross return (before costs) of 7% over 10 years, the closing portfolio value would vary as follows, depending on the annual costs the investor paid:

Annual Fee	Closing value
2.50%	$155,297
1.00%	$179,085
0.25%	$192,167

Clearly, costs do matter, especially in a low-return environment. The investor who paid costs of 1% annually has almost $24,000 more in their portfolio than the investor who paid 2.5% in annual costs. The investor who paid 0.25% annually in costs (likely a do-it-yourself investor without an advisor) has almost $37,000 more than the investor who paid 2.5%. (Of course, this assumes the do-it-yourself investor put in the time and effort to achieve the same return the advisor was able to provide while also keeping their financial house in order.)

....

➤ **TAKE NOTE:** Good financial advice costs money. Pay attention to the cost and make sure you are getting value for your dollar. According to some studies, financial advice can be worth up to 3% of assets per year.

....

Selecting and Working with an Advisor

If you have concluded that you would benefit from professional financial advice, the information in this next section will help you find the right advisor to meet your specific needs. Even if you feel confident in managing your own financial affairs, this section will provide more insight into the financial advice industry and the different areas in which you need to be competent to successfully manage your affairs.

Selecting a financial advisor should not be taken lightly. You should consider your advisor a business partner because he or she will have a lot to do with your financial success (or lack thereof) in the future. So, what attributes are important to look for in your advisor? A colleague of mine brought to my attention the qualities that Yale University desires in its partners who manage the institution's endowment funds, and these qualities apply equally well when selecting a financial advisor. In its search for fund managers, the qualities that Yale looks for include the following:

- **High integrity:** The advisor should have a philosophy of doing the right thing for the right reason, every time.

- **Sound investment philosophy:** The advisor should have a disciplined investment philosophy (and be committed to it!) that is proven to be successful in the long term. You want your advisor to be unaffected by the wealth-destroying emotions of fear and greed.

- **Strong track record:** The best advisors have a strong track record and have withstood different investment cycles and investment environments.

- **Superior organization:** In my experience, superior investment organizations have a well-defined and clearly articulated investment philosophy, and are process-driven, with a clear focus on controlling risk. Such organizations are driven to optimize long-term risk-adjusted results, rather than short-term investment performance. Having a culture focused on learning from mistakes is also critical.

In addition to the above, I highly recommend seeking an advisor who has these qualities:

- **Alignment of interest:** Advisors should have a vested interest in the financial success of their clients. This means if the client does well, the advisor does well. The ultimate demonstration of alignment of interests is when at least a portion of the advisor's own investment portfolio mirrors that of his or her clients.

- **Humility:** Egos exist in all industries; however, participants in the financial industry can be particularly subject to having egos and showing hubris largely because they deal with money on a day-to-day basis. In my experience, the best advisors are humble, level-headed, and they understand that financial markets have a way of bringing everyone down to earth at some point. Being able to admit and openly talk about mistakes is also important. For the best advisors, it is not about "me" but rather "the client" and helping the client achieve his or her goals and objectives. It is true that if you take care of the client, the rest will take care of itself.

- **A passion for helping clients achieve their financial goals and objectives:** Top advisors love what they do—they're not in it just for the paycheque. In my experience, advisors who love their work are more likely to have a commitment to excel.

- **Transparency regarding costs:** The best advisors are upfront about how they are paid. If your advisor does not bring this subject up and clearly explain his or her compensation, or if you have to ask about costs but do not get a clear explanation, it is likely best to move on.

- **Works within a team:** Even though your advisor may work in the same office as others, chances are that each advisor only works with his or her clients. Having your advisor work within a team can be very valuable because a team brings broadened perspective and unique skill sets that can be used to enhance client outcomes. It is important to also consider what your advisor's succession plan is. What would happen if your advisor was to suddenly become disabled or pass away? Would you have to go through the process of finding another advisor? The reality is that, today, most advisors don't have a succession plan, which, in my opinion, puts their clients at risk.

- **Macroeconomic knowledge:** Given the increasing influence of central banks, governments, and geopolitics on the investment markets, having an advisor who has a clear understanding of these issues and their influence is critical.

Focus on Key Areas of Service

I strongly advise that when evaluating financial advisors, you look for one who provides a lot of value *beyond* only the area of investments. Chasing investment performance is a classic error many people make when determining which advisor to work with. The fact is that, over very long periods of time, most professional fund managers and advisors will have difficulty obtaining better-than-market returns. What you should really be looking at is the advice and service an advisor offers in all areas of The Advice Wheel—these are the services you are also paying for! While definitely important, investments are only one component of your overall financial health. Your advisor should be able to provide value in the following areas: financial planning; insurance, wills, and estate planning; investments (include taxation); and communication with other professional advisors.

Financial Planning

A financial plan, sometimes also referred to as a cash flow or retirement plan, answers the question "If this is where I am financially today, where will I be financially in the future (for example, at retirement), given these particular assumptions?" Advisors can use software, your information (such as age, income, current investments, anticipated retirement date, and planned savings and contributions), and assumptions about rates of return and inflation to forecast what your financial situation may look like in the future. One thing to remember is that a plan is only as good as its assumptions—after all: garbage in = garbage out. The assumptions must be realistic, especially for projected investment returns. For example, a financial plan can look spectacular with an annualized return assumption of 10% for years into the future, but is it realistic?

As of June 30, 2016, recommended assumptions from the Financial Planning Standards Council for net rates of return ranged from 3.3% for a conservative portfolio (25% equity/70% fixed income/5% cash), 3.9% for a balanced portfolio (40% equity/45% fixed income/5% cash), and 4.8% for an aggressive portfolio (75% equity/20% fixed income/5% cash). Note: this return assumed 1.25% for investment fees annually. If you would like more detailed information, google "projection assumption guidelines Financial Planning Standards Council."

In general, it is usually better to be conservative when building a financial plan. And because markets change, as do your own circumstances, your advisor should update your plan yearly. Your advisor's assistance with your financial plan should include the following:

- Educating you about risks that could affect your plan
- Helping you to set and achieve realistic financial goals and keeping you on track with saving
- Suggesting different methods to achieve your objectives
- Providing debt-reduction strategies
- Presenting strategies for minimizing taxation during retirement
- Making sure you are using tax-effective accounts such as RRSPs, TFSAs, and RESPs
- Educating you about employer pension plans (if applicable)
- Communicating with your accountant and other advisors as necessary
- Being aware of special requirements if you are a US person

Insurance, Wills, and Estate Planning

The areas of insurance, wills, and estate planning are often the most neglected part of The Advice Wheel, largely because death and disability are not topics most people want to deal with. I can understand this, but life is uncertain so it is important to address these areas of your financial life. I can't tell you how many people (many with young children) I have come across who are either inadequately insured or do not have a current will. This topic is covered in further detail in Part 3, but for now take note that your advisor should do the following for you:

- Review your existing insurance policies and recommend changes as necessary to protect you and your family

- Confirm that you have an up-to-date will package that consists of a will, a power of attorney, and a medical directive

- Refer you to other professionals such as lawyers and accountants to complete your estate-planning documents as necessary

- Educate you about the ways you can maximize your estate using insurance strategies

- Discuss the option of using charitable giving (sometimes referred to as "planned giving") as part of your estate plan

Investments (including Taxation)

In general, financial advisors are most well-known for providing investment advice. Investing is discussed in detail in Part 2, but for the purposes of this section you should be very much aware that studies have shown that your advisor's individual risk tolerance can have an impact on the construction of your investment portfolio. A 2014 working paper by Foerster et al. examined the investment portfolios of clients at three large Canadian financial institutions and found that the strongest predictor of risk taken by clients was the composition of their advisor's portfolio, even after controlling for the client's own risk tolerance. Tomas Dvorak's 2013 study of 401(k) plans in the United States arrived at a similar conclusion.

In the area of investments, at minimum your advisor should do the following for you:

- Determine your objectives and risk tolerance through discussion with you and by using an investment questionnaire

- Provide an investment policy statement based on your goals, objectives, and risk tolerance

- Recommend an appropriate allocation of assets in a tax-effective manner

- Conduct due diligence before recommending or selecting investments

- Rebalance your portfolio annually

- Stay on top of the macroeconomic and investment climate and know how to best position your assets accordingly. This is especially important today because of the unprecedented times we are living in given all of the central bank intervention in global markets

- Provide you with access to investment research if you request it

- Review your portfolio regularly and send you reports on how your investments are performing

Communication with Other Professional Advisors

At different points in their life, it's common for people to require the services of several professionals (that is, lawyers, accountants, and financial advisors) during the same period of time, but what's unfortunate—and a significant failing on the part of the professionals—is that a client's various advisors rarely speak to each other! Because the efforts of these professionals are not coordinated, their mutual client often does not achieve an optimal outcome.

As you gather more assets, it becomes more important for your professional advisors to speak with each other. As the client, it is your responsibility to make sure this happens when necessary so that everyone is on the same page. Tax planning, investment strategy, insurance, and estate planning can be interconnected. (For example, if you own securities with large capital gains, one way to minimize taxes owing at death is donating the securities in kind to a registered Canadian charity.) Therefore, it is critical to make sure efforts on your behalf are coordinated. One of the best ways to make sure your professionals talk to each other is to appoint the financial advisor you work with to be the coordinator, or quarterback, if you will. Most advisors would welcome this role. Be clear that you expect this person to connect with and get to know your other advisors, ensuring their efforts are coordinated on your behalf.

Understanding the Role of the Dealer

In this section, I will focus on advisors working in the securities industry. The vast majority of advisors dealing in securities are regulated by the Investment Industry Regulatory Organization of Canada (IIROC) or the Mutual Fund Dealers Association of Canada (MFDA). The exceptions are investment counselling firms, which are regulated by provincial securities commissions. Advisors registered to sell individual securities will work through an IIROC platform, while those licensed only to sell mutual funds will work through the MFDA platform. If you want to be able to hold individual securities in your portfolio rather than solely mutual funds, an IIROC advisor is more suitable. Also keep in mind that some MFDA dealers will sell only their own in-house products. In certain cases, the MFDA dealer could be owned by a mutual fund company, for example.

IIROC advisors can work with clients through a bank-owned or an independent (non-bank-owned) platform, or firm—that firm is known as the dealer. For example, if your advisor works through ABC Bank, the dealer may be called ABC Bank Securities. The majority of advisors are employees of their dealer. Like all businesses, dealers expect to be profitable; they provide advisors and their clients with various services in exchange for a portion of the revenue the advisor collects. Within an independent platform, such as Raymond James or Canaccord Genuity Group, advisors often have a choice of two structures—be an employee of the firm (in which case office space and overhead is provided by the firm) or be responsible for their own overhead expenses. The amount of revenue the advisor keeps from each dollar they generate would be dependent on whether they pay or the firm pays the overhead expenses.

There are two major differences between the bank and independent platforms. First, at independent firms, advisors "own" their relationships with their clients. Should an advisor decide to change dealers for any reason, his or her old firm will appoint a temporary advisor to serve the departing advisor's clients but will usually not actively seek to retain those clients for at least 90 days. By contrast, if an advisor at a bank (non-independent) firm moves to another dealer, the original firm will immediately assign a new advisor and also contact the departing advisor's clients to attempt to retain them.

The second major difference, which was discussed earlier, is that advisors at independent firms have more flexibility to use whatever investments and products they feel are in the best interests of their clients. Bank-owned firms provide their advisors with a certain level of independence, but they also want to make sure the bank products are well-represented in their client accounts (the bank collects management fees on those products). Bank-owned firms can have some advantages, due to the scale and resources they possess—this includes in-house access to other professionals such as insurance specialists and tax and estate lawyers, as discussed earlier. As a client, it is critical to understand whether or not the advisor is completely free to recommend what he or she believes to be in your best interest.

One of the roles of the investment dealer is to collect fees on behalf of the advisor—for example, portfolio management fees, trailing commissions from mutual funds, and stock commissions. These fees are then shared with the advisor based on the total revenue (known in the industry as "production") the advisor generates. The dealer firm keeps a percentage of the advisor's revenue as payment for the service it provides. Every firm has what is called a "grid" that lists the different payout levels (as a percentage of revenue generated) for different production levels. The more revenue an advisor generates, the higher his or her payout percentage.

Payout levels vary by firm and depend on whether the advisor runs an independent branch and is responsible for office overhead costs or whether these costs are covered by the dealer. Advisors who run their own offices can receive payouts of up to approximately 80% of their production, while advisors whose overhead expenses are borne by their dealer usually have maximum payouts closer to 50%. Grids can also vary by the type of product sold. For example, the payout for insurance products might be 85% for a top-producing advisor, while fees from managing investments may top out at 80%.

This system benefits advisors who generate more revenue for the dealer firm, while at the same time it encourages lower-producing advisors to grow their businesses or leave the industry.

In exchange for a share of the revenue that advisors generate, dealers provide the following valuable services to advisors and their clients:

- **Compliance:** Dealers monitor client accounts to ensure that the securities they contain fall within the objective and risk guidelines the client agreed to when opening the account. For example, if you set up your account to be invested as 100% medium risk and the investments in your account are 50% medium risk and 50% high risk, the dealer's automated reviews will pick this up. The individual assigned to supervise the accounts at the branch will contact your advisor to understand why the account is "off-side." Dealers also keep their advisors informed of any changes in regulatory requirements.

- **Opening and closing accounts:** The dealer facilitates all procedures for opening and closing client accounts. For example, when you open an account, the dealer processes and approves all the paperwork you sign before you begin to invest.

- **Custody of securities:** The dealer holds securities on behalf of clients. The CSA has recently stated that "ensuring safety of client assets" is fundamental to its mandate of protecting investors.

- **Reporting and tax information:** The dealer makes account statements available periodically (by mail or online) so clients can see how their investments are performing. After year-end the dealer sends clients their relevant tax slips.

- **Trading:** The advisor has access to the dealer's trade desk to facilitate the purchase and sale of securities.

- **Research and access to products:** Most dealers provide economic and investment research to advisors so that advisors can make better investment decisions for their clients. Dealers within the IIROC platform also participate in underwriting new stock issues and initial public offerings (IPOs) and provide advisors with the opportunity to enable their clients to participate too. The dealer may also have a research department that creates and monitors model portfolios, which advisors can use for their clients.

- **Practice management and marketing:** Dealers provide resources to help advisors serve clients better and attract new clients to grow their business. The dealer organizes periodic business conferences, which bring advisors together to share best practices and ideas and to hear the latest research on how clients can be best served.

- **Access to specialists:** When clients have complex needs in areas such as estate planning and insurance, advisors can refer their clients to specialists employed by the dealer. For example, a business owner may want to develop a succession plan and maximize his or her estate. This client would be referred to an estate-planning specialist, who would meet with the advisor and client and make recommendations for effectively meeting the client's objectives.

- **Top-advisor recognition:** One of the key roles dealers play is that of motivator. One way they do this is by recognizing top performers. Some firms have special conferences and gatherings of top advisors that serve as both networking opportunities and continuing education sessions. These are exclusive events—it is not uncommon for only 2% to 3% of advisors at a given dealer to qualify.

When it comes to selecting an advisor to work with, in my experience a common mistake investors make is basing their decision on the dealer. The thinking seems to be that if the advisor works with a dealer owned by CIBC, Bank of Montreal, TD Bank, or the Bank of Nova Scotia, for example, he or she must be good. After all, the big Canadian banks are very large and stable. Undoubtedly there are great advisors working through the major Canadian banks, but assuming an advisor is the right fit for you just because they work at one of those banks could be a mistake. Dealers (in this case, banks) do not have investment philosophies—those come from the advisor. Some advisors are value investors; others are growth or momentum investors. Two advisors in the same office can provide very different investment strategies and service.

When selecting an advisor, keep in mind that the name of the dealer the advisor works through is important, but it should not be the decision-maker. The dealer serves as the advisor's back office—as long as your advisor works through a large, stable, and well-known firm, such as any Canadian bank or a leading independent firm, you can be satisfied that the dealer's role will be fulfilled. There are differences between dealers, but if you are dealing with a well-known brand, those differences are not material. **The capability and competency of the advisor is paramount.**

Be sure that the investment dealer your advisor works with is a member of the Canadian Investor Protection Fund (CIPF), which provides protection within prescribed limits in the case of a dealer bankruptcy. See www.cipf.ca for further details.

....

➤ **TAKE NOTE:** Do not choose an advisor based on his or her dealer firm but, rather, based on the individual advisor. The difference between the major dealer platforms is not material.

....

Finding Your Ideal Advisor

So what is the best way to go about finding a great advisor? It can feel at first like a daunting task—there are advisors seemingly on every block. To complicate matters further, two advisors from the same company may be completely different in their approach and in the services they provide, as noted above. And depending on the amount of assets you have to invest, you may have access to only certain types of advisors. So where do you start? Generally, the best way to start seeking a great advisor is through word of mouth, keeping in mind that, similar to most professions, there are great advisors, good advisors, and advisors who may not be the best fit for you. Your goal should be to hire the right advisor for your particular needs.

I have found that people in search of an advisor often call an "expert" they heard on a local radio program. What most people don't realize is that sometimes such experts pay for their own airtime. Don't make the mistake of assuming that just because an advisor has a radio show, he or she must be extremely skilled. While some highly competent advisors do appear in the media, there are other advisors who are focused primarily on increasing their client base and they use media advertising to do so.

And so, rather than relying solely on names heard in the media, I strongly recommend you ask friends, family, acquaintances, and other professionals (such as your accountant or lawyer) about their advisors and whether their experience has been positive. Set up introductory meetings with the advisors who those in your network recommend, and expect to spend at least an hour with each advisor. Take along your investment statements, copies of your insurance policies, and a copy of your most recent notice of assessment from the Canada Revenue Agency (CRA). Be willing to provide any other information the advisor requests.

The hallmark of a great advisor is his or her ability to ask the right questions. When the meeting begins, pay attention to the questions the advisor asks and whether they truly strive to understand your situation. You should be doing most of the talking in the introductory meeting, because they should be asking you ample questions to get all of the information they need. Once the advisor has asked their questions, they should give you the opportunity to ask questions. To help you with this part of the process, I've developed the Advisor Interview Questionnaire™, which you will find among the forms provided in Part 4. Take careful notes of the prospective advisor's answers. At the end of the meeting, let the advisor know you are interviewing several potential advisors and that you will get back to him or her in the near future.

A 2016 article published in the *New York Times* titled "Deciding if a Financial Adviser is Right for the Job" referenced an exercise conducted by the Certified Financial Planner Board of Standards in the United States. The goal of the exercise was to see if investors would succumb to a smooth-talking, good-looking salesperson and hire him as a financial advisor. To do the test, the Board hired a professional DJ and asked him to change his appearance from a "rocker" with long braided hair and body piercings to a clean-cut business professional with short hair and a quality suit. The DJ was taught basic investment lingo and then met with investors who were looking for an advisor.

After spending 15 minutes with each person, all but one of the investors were ready to hire the DJ as their financial advisor. I must say, I am not surprised!

Choosing an advisor is a very important decision that should not be taken lightly. In the end, it comes down to selecting someone who you believe is competent (based on your interview and references), someone who will provide the services you require, someone who has their interests aligned with yours, and someone who you would enjoy working with. To help you find the advisor who will meet your requirements, follow the steps below, using the forms provided in Part 4 where noted:

- **Step 1: Determine what you need.** Completing the Financial Advice Needs Assessment™ will help you to establish a clear idea of what type(s) of advice, if any, you are looking for. Recall that the services offered by advisors range from investment advice only to comprehensive wealth management, including investments, insurance, and estate planning. Ideally, your advisor should be able to protect and grow your assets and provide you with comprehensive wealth management solutions—including a financial and estate plan as well as insurance, if required.

- **Step 2: Interview potential advisors.** Ask your friends for recommendations, keeping in mind that the best advisors don't advertise—they accept new clients by referral only. Once you have some suggestions, prepare to meet and interview three to five advisors. The Financial Advisor Interview Questionnaire™ will help you ask the right questions of each advisor you interview. Although the financial advice industry is built on a sales culture, the best advisors won't give you a sales pitch. Rather, they will ask lots of questions and pay careful attention to your responses. These advisors will also be determining whether you are a fit for what they look for in a client. If you are on the receiving end of a sales pitch, consider it a red flag and move on.

As part of your due diligence, make sure that prospective advisors have the registrations they claim to have and ensure that they haven't had any disciplinary action brought against them. You can do this through the self-regulatory bodies. To help you, the Canadian

Securities Administrators website has some valuable investor tools, including a National Registration Search through which you can verify that an advisor is registered. If the advisor you are researching is IIROC-licensed, be sure to go to the "Know Your Advisor" page on IIROC's website, for a more thorough report detailing the IIROC-regulated advisor's background, qualifications, and discipline history.

- **Step 3: Rank advisors.** I have created the Financial Advisor Ranking System™ to give you a systematic way of ranking each potential advisor you interview. I would like to emphasize, however, that the Financial Advisor Ranking System is only a tool. It will give you some idea of which advisor may be the best fit for you, but don't make your decision based exclusively on the tool. You should also give serious thought to which advisor is the best fit in terms of a long-term working relationship.

- **Step 4: Check references.** Once you have identified an advisor you would like to work with, conduct reference checks by speaking with two or three of the advisor's existing clients. The Financial Advisor Reference-Check Form™ lists important questions you should ask those clients (see Part 4).

➤ **TAKE NOTE:** Many of the best advisors don't advertise their services—new clients are constantly referred to them by existing clients. Seek recommendations from within your own network and interview potential advisors to find the one that is right for you.

Monitoring Your Advisor

One of the key regulatory requirements for advisors is to accurately document their discussions with clients, especially discussions regarding investment decisions and the purchase of other products such as insurance. The reasons a particular financial solution is appropriate given the client's goals, objectives, and risk tolerances should be clearly noted. Good advisors take detailed notes during each client meeting and keep them on record in the client's file. That way, if there is ever any question from the client, the advisor can refer to the notes. As you'll read a little further on, in rare cases a complaint may be launched against an advisor. In those situations, the notes—or lack thereof—form a crucial part of investigating the complaint.

I suggest that you, as the client, take notes during your meetings as well. Doing so will help not only to make sure you and your advisor are on the same page, but it can also help you keep track of tasks to follow up on. For example, if your advisor tasked you with seeing a lawyer to complete your will and the related documents, you'll have this on your list to remind you to do it. Furthermore, if there is ever any misunderstanding with your advisor, you can refer to your notes to clarify the situation and review what exactly was discussed and agreed to. I have created the Advisor Meeting Summary Form™ to help you with taking useful notes from the meetings with your advisor (see Part 4).

I encourage you to evaluate on an annual basis whether your advisor is still meeting your needs. I've provided the Annual Advisor Review Form™ in Part 4 to help you do this. You will also find it helpful to answer three simple questions to determine what I refer to as "net advisor value":

1. **Needs assessment**: Do you still need advice? If so, what kind of advice are you seeking?

2. **Advisor service**: During the time you have been with your current advisor, has he or she provided you with advice beyond recommending investments?

3. **Value proposition**: Are you getting good value for what you pay your advisor?

After answering these questions and completing the Annual Advisor Review Form, you should have a clear idea of whether the net advisor value you're receiving meets your needs. If you feel the value does not meet your needs or justify the cost, set up a meeting with your advisor to review your work together.

Over time, personal and financial situations can change, and a client's needs may become more complex. If your situation has changed, discuss this with your advisor to determine whether he or she is still a good fit for you—it's not unusual for clients to outgrow their advisors and vice versa. If your review identifies any concerns, be sure to share those with your advisor so that corrective action can be taken. Most advisors welcome feedback that enables them to improve the service they provide to clients.

Using Multiple Advisors

If you have significant investable assets, you may want to consider having more than one financial advisor. This is a personal decision, and people have different thoughts and opinions about the idea. Some people feel that having multiple advisors is like trying to build a house with multiple architects in the sense that different advisors could do different things in different ways, resulting in suboptimal outcomes for the client. There are advantages to consolidating all of your assets with a single advisor whom you trust, as long as you are confident that they provide advice in all the areas of The Advice Wheel. That way, you have one advisor who understands your big-picture financial situation and goals, manages your complete portfolio, puts the required insurance in place, and creates and implements an effective financial plan. This is ideal.

Other people believe that using multiple advisors is like not having all your eggs in one basket—it helps to diversify you away from what I call "advisor risk." For example, say your entire net worth is $5 million and your financial advisor (who manages the whole amount) makes some poor investment decisions, resulting in your portfolio dropping 20%. If you'd had two advisors, each managing $2.5 million, and one advisor's choices led to a 20% decline in the assets they managed while the other's returns were flat, your overall loss would be 10%, not 20%—that's a big difference in a $5-million portfolio.

One way to mitigate advisor risk is to have a primary advisor who manages a portion of your investments and serves as the financial quarterback who assists with insurance and financial and estate planning, and then have a secondary advisor (or more) who specifically manages the remaining investments. If you choose this route, be sure that your primary advisor has full access to any information about your finances so they can facilitate the planning process. Another alternative is to have a primary advisor but also have some assets invested in simple ETFs, which are low-cost investments that provide a return similar to the overall market or asset class they are tracking. Discipline is the key to success in this scenario. You know yourself best—if you are not disciplined when it comes to investing, keep it simple and just use an advisor.

If you are highly confident in your advisor, there is nothing wrong with having that advisor manage all of your assets. Just be sure you understand the potential consequences, both good and bad.

Changing Advisors

If you have an advisor but are moving to a new one, you'll need to have a conversation with your existing advisor to let them know about the change. For some people this can be a difficult conversation, but it doesn't have to be. A simple comment such as this would be sufficient: "I have enjoyed working with you and I appreciate all the advice you've given me. However, I have decided that another advisor would be a better fit for me at this point. I would appreciate if you would make sure the transition to my new advisor is as smooth as possible. Thank you."

Once you have told your advisor about the change, you'll want to ensure the smooth transfer of your assets to your new advisor. The main steps you should expect to go through are as follows:

- **Meet with your new advisor to sign account-opening documents.** These documents will list your personal and financial information, risk tolerance, and types of accounts being opened. You will also need to sign transfer forms to move the accounts to your new advisor. Be clear on whether you are opening discretionary accounts (in which case your advisor does not need your authorization for each transaction) or non-discretionary accounts (in which case your advisor must obtain authorization for each transaction). You should also clarify what costs to expect and how your advisor will get paid.

During this meeting, your new advisor should recommend whether you should transfer your assets in cash or in kind. The cash option means all of your existing investments would be sold and the proceeds would be transferred to your new advisor to be reinvested. If your assets are sold during a down market, this may not be the best option. In addition, selling all your assets can have tax consequences for non-registered accounts. In general, I recommend transferring your assets in kind (transferring all the investments as they are, not liquidating them and transferring cash instead) so that your new advisor can review the portfolio and then recommend changes as appropriate.

- **Clarify your new advisor's licensing.** Make sure you understand what assets you own in your accounts with your old advisor and what types of assets your new advisor can hold. The vast majority of traditional assets (stocks, bonds, and mutual funds) are highly liquid (meaning they can be easily sold) and can be held by most companies, as long as the advisor has the appropriate licensing. If, however, you have a stock portfolio and are moving to an advisor licensed only to sell mutual funds, your new advisor will be able to invest only in mutual funds on your behalf; you will therefore have to sell your individual stocks. One of the main areas in which I have seen problems with transfers is alternative investments such as real estate limited partnerships. If you hold any of these assets and are changing advisors, check with your new advisor to make sure the investments can be held in your new accounts. If your new advisor doesn't fill out the transfer form correctly, there can be lengthy delays and extra work for both your new and your old advisor.

- **Ask about administrative fees.** It is typical for firms to charge clients an administrative fee ($125 or thereabouts) per account to transfer accounts out of the firm. Ask your new advisor whether they or their firm can cover this fee, as you are bringing your business to them. They want your business, so don't be afraid to ask.

- **Check progress after one month.** Generally, the transfer of assets takes three to four weeks—sometimes longer for registered plans such as RRSPs and RESPs. Check with your new advisor after a few weeks to ensure the transfer is going smoothly. Once the transfer is complete, reconcile all the assets (including cash) in the new and old accounts to make sure everything was moved properly. Your advisor should do this as well, but it is a good idea to be proactive.

- **Follow up with your new advisor.** After the transfer is completed, follow up with your new advisor regarding next steps so you can start receiving the advice you need. Many investors don't understand how to read their investment statements. If you are in this camp, meet with your advisor to learn how.

....

➤ **TAKE NOTE:** Put your former and new advisors in contact with each other to ensure that the transfer process goes smoothly.

....

How to Make a Complaint

As detailed earlier, several national self-regulatory organizations oversee investment dealers and their advisors. Each of these organizations sets rules for dealers and their employees, and two of their primary goals are to ensure that rules are not broken and that investors are treated fairly. In addition, these organizations have the power to levy fines on dealers and advisors. The most common types of complaints relate to suitability of investments, unauthorized transactions, and misrepresentation of the risk characteristics associated with certain investments.

As an investor, if you feel you have been treated unfairly, you have the right to complain. In fact, when you open your accounts, the dealer will send you information about how to complain. But remember: simply losing money in the markets is *not* legitimate grounds for complaint if the investments were suitable for you based on your situation at the time the investments were made. If the investments were not suitable, that is another issue and one that *is* complaint-worthy.

All dealer firms take client complaints extremely seriously. If a complaint is successful, damages can be awarded and regulatory bodies can also levy fines against the advisor. In extreme cases, the advisor can have his or her licence revoked on a temporary or even permanent basis. The last thing an advisor wants is a complaint: not only does the resulting investigation take a lot of time for the advisor, but having a complaint on their record can damage the advisor's reputation and standing in the industry. For this reason, before you make a formal complaint, do your best to resolve the situation with your advisor.

It is important to keep a file of all relevant correspondence from your advisor, along with your meeting notes. If something goes wrong between you and your advisor, take action as soon as possible while the details of the situation are fresh in your mind. If you are unsure whether you have a legitimate complaint, contact the regulatory body to which the advisor belongs.

When you think making a formal complaint might be necessary, follow these steps:

1. Attempt to resolve the situation directly with your financial advisor.

2. If Step 1 is unsuccessful, ask to speak to the advisor's branch manager or other supervisor.

3. If Step 2 doesn't resolve the issue, send a complaint letter to the advisor's firm and send copies to the advisor and the regulatory body to which the advisor belongs. In the letter, explain your situation, specifically describe your complaint, and state the resolution you expect. Include any supporting documents. The firm is required to acknowledge the complaint quickly (usually within five business days). Within 90 days, expect to receive notification of the results of the firm's investigation, as well as a rationale for its decision, and any compensation awarded.

4. If you are not satisfied with the result of the investigation, consider contacting the Ombudsman for Financial Services and Investments for a free independent review of the case. You can also consider arbitration proceedings.

➤ **TAKE NOTE:** Launching a complaint against an advisor is serious and has a significant impact on the advisor's career; therefore, do not resort to this measure hastily. Always try to resolve the situation with your advisor first.

Client Responsibility

Like all relationships, the relationship between you and your advisor should be a two-way street. To maximize the benefits of the relationship as well as the probability of achieving your financial goals, plan to be an active participant in the relationship. Rather than just handing your money over to your advisor to invest (and hoping they make you rich), you can play an active role in shaping your financial future by doing the following:

- Take the time to really think about your financial goals and objectives. If you have a spouse, do this together. While this sounds simple, few people actually do it. The more clearly you can articulate your goals and objectives, the easier it will be for your advisor to help you achieve them.

- Live within your means and save a portion of your income. If you consistently spend too much and save too little or regularly withdraw money from your investment accounts, it will be difficult for your advisor to help you achieve your financial goals. The more you save (and the sooner you save it), the better the power of compounding will be able to work for you.

- Learn the basics of investing. Having at least a basic understanding of investment principles will make it easier for you to understand and follow your advisor's recommendations. If you have a solid grip on the material in this book, you will be more knowledgeable than much of the general public. Ask questions of your advisor during meetings in order to enhance your knowledge of the investment process. Showing an interest will motivate your advisor to go the extra mile for you; it's human nature for people to want to be of more help to those who try to help themselves, and professionals are no different in this respect.

- If your advisor makes recommendations that make sense to you, implement them! Advice is useless if you don't act on it.

- Look at your investment statements at least quarterly. If you don't know how to read them, ask your advisor for help.

- Focus on the big picture—don't get bogged down by short-term investment returns, good or bad.

- When your advisor asks for information, provide it as soon as you can.

- Keep your advisor informed of material changes in your life that affect your financial situation, such as changes in marital status, the birth of a child, or employment.

....

➤ **TAKE NOTE:** The relationship with your advisor is a two-way street. Be an active participant in shaping your financial future. Help your advisor help you.

....

For married or common-law couples, it is critical that both spouses have at least a basic understanding of their financial affairs, including investments, retirement planning, insurance, wills, and estate planning. Both should also understand general investment principles, such as how wealth is created over the long term. In my experience as an advisor, I regularly encounter situations where one spouse takes a more active role in dealing with the household finances while the other has little, if any, interest or knowledge in this area because they are busy working or raising the kids. But both spouses need to be involved—the important of this cannot be overstated. I can't tell you how many times I've seen situations where the spouse handling the financial affairs suddenly became disabled or passed away, leaving the other spouse with no clue about the family's financial status.

If you and your spouse are not both well-informed, don't worry. Here is a three-step process to quickly get you on the right track:

1. **Get educated**. Read books on personal finance and investing and you will be well on your way. For another perspective about the financial advice industry, refer to John De Goey's *The Professional Advisor IV*. Be sure to ask your advisor for additional materials on specific topics for further reading.

2. **Be an active participant**. Make sure both you and your spouse attend every advisor meeting. Yes, it'll take extra time, but it will be a great investment over the long term. If one of you absolutely cannot make it during the workday, ask your advisor whether he or she can accommodate an evening appointment. Be reasonable with your requests and your advisor should accommodate you if they can. If not, find an advisor you can work with more easily.

3. **Spend the time**. Allocate at least two hours each month to review your financial affairs—make a regular schedule. Call it "family finance time"; be creative and try involving your kids so that they can learn about finance from an early age. Believe me, it will pay dividends down the road with respect to your financial position!

Studies have shown that Canadian women tend to lag behind Canadian men when it comes to knowledge about investing and knowing how much money will be needed in retirement as well as how to save to meet retirement goals. For example, BlackRock's 2014 Global Investor Pulse Survey found that 41% of Canadian women are knowledgeable about how much money they will need in retirement, compared with 51% of men, and 39% of Canadian women knew how much they will need to save to meet their retirement goals, compared with 46% of men. The study also found that fewer women felt comfortable investing in the stock market, resulting in women holding more cash than men. (For women who want to increase their financial knowledge, I suggest reading any of the books written by Patricia Lovett-Reid.)

The most important benefit of having both partners involved in the financial decision-making is that, as noted, they will both be informed about the family's financial situation. But, for traditional couples, there is an added benefit. Because men and women have different emotional characteristics, having both parties involved in decision-making can lead to more balanced decisions. Studies have shown that women investors on average have lower risk tolerances and are more cautious than men (Barclays Wealth, 2011). This caution drives investment behaviour that is disciplined and focused on controlling risk and obtaining better longer-term returns. Men, by contrast, are more prone to being overconfident and may try to time the market; they may have a short-term focus and trade more frequently. Therefore, having the perspectives of both a man and a woman when making financial decisions is likely to bring more balance to the investment decisions that are made.

Action Call

1. Review the Advice Wheel and evaluate how you are doing in each area.

2. Note any areas in which you need help.

3. If you need help, be committed to finding the right advisor to meet your unique needs.

4. Evaluate the costs of advice and make sure you are getting value for what you pay.

2

BEING
AN INFORMED
INVESTOR

HAVE READ COUNTLESS investing books over my career, and one of the most interesting is *Winning the Loser's Game: Timeless Strategies for Successful Investing* by Charles Ellis. In it, Ellis compares investing to tennis, which he characterizes as a game in which many amateur players beat themselves by making too many mistakes. He makes the point that the best players are talented, no question, but that they also let their opponent (other investors) make the errors. I could not agree more.

While the book you're reading now is not meant to be another investing book, Part 2 will cover key investment principles because they are essential to your financial success—whether you hire an advisor or not. If you choose to manage your investments on your own, having knowledge of these principles will help prevent you from making mistakes and also will increase the probability of your long-term investment success. If you use a financial advisor, having a solid understanding of these principles will make it easier for you to communicate with your advisor and ask the right questions. The information covered in the pages that follow is the essential knowledge that I believe all Canadian investors should have.

As a supplement to the material in this part of the book, you may also want to refer to the Fact Cards prepared by the Investor Office of the Ontario Securities Commission. The Fact Cards cover a wide range of important investment topics.

What Is Risk?

For most people, when it comes to making an investment, the first thing that usually comes to mind is the potential return. I would strongly suggest, however, that you think about risk first, and return second. As such, let's look at risk first.

Risk is simply the possibility that something bad will happen. Risk is a part of life. Usually without realizing it, you take risks every day, from the moment you get up until the moment you go to bed. When it comes to investing, risk can be defined as making an investment and possibly losing money. From day to day, the value of any investment can be expected to change. You should think about risk in terms of permanent loss of your money—in the industry, this is referred to as "permanent capital loss." There is risk in any investment. Even if you keep all your money in a bank savings account that pays little or no interest, your decision to invest in cash means taking the risk of losing purchasing power to inflation.

The organizations that regulate financial advisors have certain ways of viewing risk. Commonly, every security is classified as low, medium, or high risk. Low-risk investments include very safe products such as GICs, Canada Savings Bonds, and some individual bonds and bond mutual funds. These investments are also expected to have lower returns. Medium-risk investments include most dividend-paying stocks of larger, well-established companies and other investment products holding such investments. For example, a mutual fund that holds mostly medium-risk investments would be rated medium risk overall. Anything that does not fit into the low-risk or medium-risk categories is considered high risk. Stocks of small junior oil and gas companies and mining companies, as well as some types of mutual funds holding assets in more volatile asset classes (such as those focusing on emerging markets), generally fall into the high-risk category.

As an investor, you should expect to be paid an appropriate return for the risk you are taking. The greater the risk in the investment, the greater the potential return should be. If you expect larger returns, expect to take more risk. If you are satisfied with lower returns, investments that come with lower risk may be fine for you. As an investor, you must understand that the concepts of risk and reward go hand in hand. In the investing world, risk cannot be avoided, but it can be managed.

....

➤ **TAKE NOTE:** When investing, focus on risk first, and return second.

....

Types of Risk

Below are the most important types of risks you should be aware of as an investor.

- **Longevity risk.** Simply put, longevity risk is the risk of outliving your money—a risk that is increasing with advancements in medical science and technology and, therefore, our increased life expectancy. While living longer is wonderful, investors who don't plan properly for their retirement will find themselves outliving their money. As lifespans continue to lengthen, it will become increasingly important for investors to be disciplined and start saving for retirement earlier.

- **Purchasing power risk.** Also known as inflation risk, purchasing power risk describes the situation whereby increases in the cost of living reduce the real value of the income stream your investments provide. For example, if you are a retiree with a portfolio of bonds that provides income of $40,000 per year and inflation rises from 1% to 3%, thereby making the goods and services you need more expensive, the income from your portfolio will no longer go as far.

- **Loss of capital risk.** This is the risk of permanently losing money in an investment. Permanent loss of capital is very different from a temporary loss due to market fluctuations. Market prices of investments change daily—that is normal. However, if you invested $10,000 in shares of a company and the company went bankrupt, your investment would be lost forever. This is permanent loss of capital. You can manage this type of risk by investing wisely in quality companies, diversifying your investments, focusing on the long term, and avoiding common mistakes. Doing these things can minimize (but not eliminate) the probability of permanent loss of capital.

- **Liquidity risk.** The ease with which a given investment can be sold and converted to cash is liquidity. For example, the liquidity of a large-capitalization, blue-chip stock such as Telus or Bank of Nova Scotia is likely very good because the stock is widely held by individuals and institutions such as pension funds. As a result, blue-chip stocks generally trade actively, and they have a ready market. By contrast, investments in real estate are generally less liquid—typically they cannot be sold at a moment's notice. If you make an investment with a short time horizon because you may need your money back quickly, taking into consideration its liquidity is very important. If you have a longer time horizon, liquidity is less critical. For most investors, having the majority of your portfolio in liquid investments is prudent.

- **Valuation risk:** When you invest, you are exchanging money today for the right to a certain amount of income (bonds) or portion of the future profit of the business (stocks). John Burr Williams is a noted 20th-century economist and the author of *The Theory of Investment Value*, in which he wrote, "The value of any stock, bond, or business is determined by the cash inflows and outflows—discounted at an appropriate interest rate—which can be expected to occur during the remaining life of the asset." It is very important to keep in mind the price you are paying for an investment. Even if you purchase shares of a solid company such as Visa, if you substantially overpay, you are facing an uphill battle. However, if you buy the shares on a day when the market is depressed and offering the shares at a low price (and at a better value), you're ahead of the game. You can think of valuation in terms of an elastic band: when value is stretched too far in either direction (too low or too high), like an elastic band snapping, value tends to return to more of a middle ground.

  With my clients, I often use shopping (not that I like to shop!) as an analogy when discussing valuation and investing. Usually when shopping, people tend to "stock up" and buy more of certain items when they're on sale. Think, for example, about when you purchase groceries, clothes, electronics, or shoes. Typically, when items are on sale, you are happy to buy, or to buy more. However, when buying or selling investments, people tend to behave in a totally different way. When the stock price of a company is down, the emotion of fear *prevents* investors from buying when there is a sale. In general, most average investors don't have the inclination or the skill set to judge the value of the investments they're buying. The solution to this? Have your investments managed by a professional!

▶ **TAKE NOTE:** Some degree of risk is present in every investment you purchase. Risk cannot be eliminated, but it can be managed and minimized.

Investing in "Buckets"

As an investor, you have many choices for where to put your money. You can invest in different types of assets, and in the financial industry each broad type of asset is referred to as an asset class. Think of each asset class as a unique "bucket." All the buckets, when taken together, form your portfolio. The process of deciding how much of your money to put into each bucket is called asset allocation, which we will discuss later.

When you make an investment, you are providing money (capital) to a company or, in the case of some bonds, a government. The lifeblood of any company is its access to capital for operating and growing its business, and companies obtain this capital from investors. In general, companies can borrow (issue debt in the form of bonds) or they can raise equity, which means selling an ownership stake (shares) in the company in exchange for capital. Typically, companies use both debt and equity financing. It is generally healthy for companies to use some debt because the interest on the debt is tax-deductible. The mix of financing that a company uses is referred to as its "capital structure."

From an investment perspective, you should understand that investing in different parts of a company's capital structure will have different risk and reward characteristics. Capital structures are often viewed from top to bottom, with the top being safer for investors and the bottom being riskier. The reason the capital structure is safer at the top has to do with what happens if a company fails and has to declare bankruptcy. If this should happen, any value remaining in the company has to be divided among the investors (debt holders and shareholders). Generally, investors at the top of the capital structure are paid back first and then, if there is any remaining value, lower parts of the capital structure will recover some or all of their investment. This is called the "order of priority." The lower in the capital structure you invest, the higher your expected return should be because your risk is greater.

In general, you can think of capital structure in relation to risk, order of priority, and expected returns as shown in the table below.

Type of financing	Risk	Priority	Expected returns
Senior debt (secured loans from banks)	Lowest	Highest	Lowest
Secured bonds			
Unsecured bonds (debentures)			
Convertible bonds (debt with some equity features)			
Equity (preferred shares)			
Equity (common shares)	Highest	Lowest	Highest

As you invest in different parts of the capital structure, your risk-and-return profile changes. For example, secured bonds are near the top of the capital structure and are generally safer, but they provide lower returns. This is because the company is only obligated to pay interest on the bonds, and so the investor does not benefit from any upside (growth) of the company. In the event of a bankruptcy, secured bond holders have a strong claim on the company's assets because the bond investment was secured by assets owned by the company. Contrast them with holders of common shares, who have all of the upside (benefit) in the company if it does well but who also have all the downside, because in the event of a bankruptcy, common equity owners are the last in line to collect any residual value.

As such, the risk of investing in common shares is higher than if you are a bond holder (lender to the company).

It is critical to understand that when you invest in *any part* of a company's capital structure, there is always risk. Just because secured bonds, for example, are safer, doesn't mean that you cannot lose money. If a business performs really badly and has minimal residual value, an investor in any part of the capital structure would take a loss on his or her investment.

> **TAKE NOTE:** A company's capital structure is the way by which the company obtains financing to operate and grow its business.

To simplify our discussion, think of all investments as falling into these asset classes, or buckets:

- **Cash**

- **Bonds** (also known as fixed income)—As a bond investor, you are a lender to a company.

- **Stocks** (also known as equities)—As a stock investor, you are an owner of a company.

- **Other**—This includes everything else, including commodities, real estate, hedge funds, private equity, and venture capital.

Each bucket has a different risk-and-return profile, just as different parts of the capital structure do. And the concept is the same: the lower the risk you take, the lower the return you should expect.

Now let's take a closer look at each of the four buckets, and the information investors need to know about each.

Cash

The cash bucket is relatively straightforward—cash is any money you have sitting in bank accounts or investments such as GICs. Cash is a very low-risk investment that provides low returns but offers safety of principal. Keep in mind, however, that with very low interest rates (such as we've seen in the mid-2010s), once you factor in taxes on interest income and inflation, what your cash investment buys tomorrow may be less than what you can buy with the same amount of money today. This means that with the cash bucket comes purchasing power risk, as described above.

Having your entire portfolio in cash is generally not suitable as a long-term investment strategy to meet your retirement goals; however, I believe that cash is a legitimate asset class and should be part of your overall investment strategy. The roles that cash plays in an investment portfolio include the following:

- **Acting as a buffer.** It reduces overall volatility in a portfolio. The low-risk, low-return characteristics of cash reduce the swings (both up and down) in the portfolio. Having cash in a portfolio can give you a smoother ride toward your investment goals.

- **Providing the opportunity to buy when prices are low.** A cash reserve built into a portfolio gives you (or your advisor) an opportunity to purchase investments at lower prices and at better valuations.

- **Offering flexibility.** If you need money from your investments, having a certain amount of cash available will prevent you from having to sell investments at low prices if the markets are down when you need the money.

When it comes to the correct amount of cash to hold in your portfolio, there is no right or wrong answer—it's something you should discuss with your advisor. That said, having a cash weighting of about 4%-5% as a goal, and then increasing or decreasing that allocation based on changes in the market or your goals and objectives, is a reasonable place to start.

➤ **TAKE NOTE:** Cash offers very low risk and low returns. Having some cash in your portfolio provides a smoother ride, opportunities to buy when markets are down, and fast access to funds.

Bonds (Fixed Income)
The bond market is the largest market in the world—three times larger than the equity (stock) market according to a 2011 study by management consultancy firm McKinsey & Company. A bond is

essentially an IOU from a government or company to you as the investor. Let's say you purchase a new five-year bond issued by Suncor. You are effectively lending Suncor a certain amount of money, and the company is agreeing to pay you a certain rate of interest per year with a promise to give you back your money in five years. Bonds are simple in principle but can be quite complex in practice—there are many different types of bonds as well as underlying features.

For example, some bonds are secured by certain (or all) assets of the company, meaning that if the issue of the bond fails to pay interest or principal, the investors can force liquidation of the assets that secured the bond to recover their monies owed by the company. This is similar to the bank repossessing and selling your home if you fail to make mortgage payments. Other bonds do not have any specific security (these bonds are unsecured; investors don't have any specific collateral). If something goes wrong and the company can't make payments, bond holders are still higher up in the capital structure relative to equity holders and therefore have a higher probability of seeing at least a partial recovery on their investment. In addition to secured and unsecured bonds, some companies issue convertible bonds, whereby holders can choose to convert their bond investment into shares, or issuers can elect to repay their debt obligation by issuing more shares in the company (usually this is a last resort if something goes wrong and the company cannot come up with cash), which they then use to pay the convertible debtholders. In general, when examining a bond investment, be aware that, while interest rates are generally fixed, some bond issues may incorporate features wherein the interest rate can change (these are known as "floating rate" issues).

For our purposes, consider bond investments to be a form of fixed income. All this means is that the income received from a bond is typically pre-set—the investor receives a set amount of interest for a set period of time, after which the initial amount invested (the principal) is returned. The date by which the investor is scheduled to get his or her money back is called the maturity date. By definition, when you purchase a bond, you are choosing to sacrifice upside potential or growth (equity holders have this) for more safety and an income stream. That does not mean that you cannot have capital gains in bonds; however, the main reason behind purchasing bonds for most investors is safety and income.

Risk in Bonds

Investing in bonds carries two main risks: credit risk and interest-rate risk.

Credit risk is the risk of the bond's issuer being unable to make interest or principal payments. For example, if you bought a bond from a corporation and the corporation's business then took a turn for the worse, the corporation would have less cash flow, which may negatively affect its ability to make interest payments or to repay the principal when the bond matures. Credit risk is the biggest risk of investing in bonds. When purchasing a bond, always consider what the probability is that you will receive ongoing interest payments and your principal when the bond matures.

Interest-rate risk comes into play because bonds are very sensitive to changes in interest rates. The relationship between the price of bonds and interest rates is an inverse relationship—that is, when interest rates decrease the price of bonds increases, and when interest rates rise the price of bonds falls. Think of it as a teeter-totter.

Bonds and Interest Rates: The Teeter-Totter

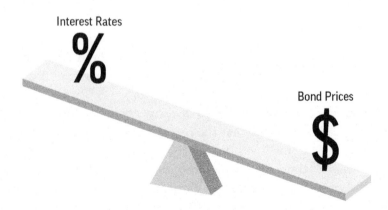

Higher interest rates mean lower fixed-rate bond prices, and lower rates mean lower bond prices.

One measure of a bond's sensitivity to interest rates is its "duration." A bond's duration tells you the approximate change in price you can expect for any 1% change in interest rates. For example, if a bond has a duration of five years and interest rates drop by 1%, the price of the bond will rise about 5%; if interest rates increase by 1%, the price of the bond will drop by about 5%. It is important to note that in the short term, market prices of bonds do change, although bond prices are generally less volatile than stock prices. If you invest in bonds and have to sell before the maturity date, it's possible you could lose money.

In general, short-term bonds are less sensitive to interest rate changes than are long-term bonds. The reason is simple—the investor is committing their money for a shorter period and will get their money back relatively quickly, which will give the investor the opportunity to reinvest in other bonds at the then-prevailing interest rate. Note: it is important to keep an eye on government bond yields because they can directly impact the cost of fixed-rate mortgages.

Anytime there's a low-interest-rate environment like we are experiencing now (at the time of writing), investors need to be especially careful about their bond investments and be aware that money can be lost in bonds. Today, bonds, especially long-duration government bonds, are expensive. The paradox of the low-interest-rate environment is that assets that have been traditionally safe (e.g., long-term government bonds) and generate little income, are now very expensive and carry significant price risk. In fact, many well-known investors are warning of a bubble in bonds, especially in longer-dated government bonds. The bursting of bubbles is notoriously difficult to predict; however, one day in the future, interest rates will rise, and it may happen suddenly. As an example, in the two days following the 2016 election of Donald Trump, $1 trillion of value vanished from bond markets worldwide. When interest rates do rise on a sustained basis, many investors will be presented with a rude awakening.

The previous paragraph is not meant to deter you from having bonds in your portfolio—quite the contrary. Bonds do play an important role as a shock absorber for the portfolio. You just have to be careful what you own—and this is where professional advice can be so valuable. I always tell my clients to think about their investment portfolio as an airplane ride and, as such, how much turbulence they want (and can withstand). Bonds can limit the overall fluctuations in your portfolio. In a low-interest-rate environment like we have today, focusing on shorter-duration, high-quality corporate bonds is prudent.

Assessing Risk in Bonds

When it comes to bonds, the most important thing an investor needs to know is whether the company or government issuing the bond has (and will continue to have) the financial capacity to repay the investor. For example, if you buy a 10-year bond, you must be sufficiently confident that the company or government will have enough cash flow to pay you interest each year, as well as the principal payment in Year 10. But making this assessment requires detailed analysis and financial modelling. Can the average individual investor really assess risk in bonds? For most investors, it's better to have bond exposure through an investment product such as a bond mutual fund or an exchange-traded fund.

If you do venture into the world of selecting your own bonds, be aware that most bonds have a rating, which describes the bond issuer's capacity to repay investors. The agencies that provide these ratings, such as Standard & Poor's (S&P), employ credit analysts who conduct detailed financial analysis on specific bonds and the companies or governments that issue them to determine the riskiness of the bond and how likely it is that investors will get their money back. Investors can use these ratings when making investment decisions. S&P uses a ratings scale that ranges from AAA for the highest-quality (and least risky) bonds to D for the lowest-quality (and most risky) bonds.

Rated bonds are divided into two major categories: investment grade and non-investment grade. These categories reflect the reality that some bonds are safer than others with respect to the probability of investors getting their money back. Investment-grade bonds are safer but pay lower interest, while non-investment-grade bonds (also known as high-yield bonds) pay a higher interest rate but are riskier. For example, bonds issued by provincial or federal governments in Canada are generally investment grade, while bonds issued by a small company with a high debt load that does business in a volatile industry would likely be considered non-investment grade. In the end, it always comes down to risk. Investment-grade bonds carry less risk (but not *no* risk), while non-investment-grade bonds carry more risk.

Keep in mind that ratings agencies are paid by bond issuers. If you're thinking this creates the potential for conflict of interest, you are correct. Analysts at rating agencies could feel conflicted because on one hand their job is to provide objective ratings, but on the other hand the bond issuer is paying the rating agency (and thus the analyst's wages). The issuer of the bond wants higher ratings so that its cost of raising capital will be lower. (Everything else being equal, investors will accept being paid lower interest rates from issuers with higher bond ratings.) The issue of objectivity and the potential for conflict of interest within ratings agencies was depicted very well in the 2015 movie *The Big Short*.

> **TAKE NOTE:** When investing in bonds, the key risks to consider are credit risk and interest-rate risk.

Stocks

A stock, or common share, in a company is simply an ownership interest in that business. For example, if you own 100 shares of Canadian Tire, as an owner you have the right to a share in the profits that Canadian Tire generates, based on the percentage of the company you own. A portion of the stockholder's share of the profits can be paid out by the company on a periodic basis (e.g., quarterly), and these payments are called "dividends." Many, but not all, companies pay dividends to their common shareholders. Remember, dividends are not guaranteed and they depend on the company's profitability. However, when the dividend level of a company is originally set, it will be based on a level that is sustainable based on cash flows normally generated by the company. That way, shareholders know what amount of income they can expect from their investment. Unless the business environment and profitability drastically deteriorate, a company will generally not reduce its dividend. Companies are very reluctant to reduce their dividends because it sends a negative message to shareholders and the broader market, which typically results in hurting the company's stock price because many investors react by selling their shares.

There are daily media reports on the major stock markets, such as the s&p/tsx Composite Index (s&p/tsx), the Dow Jones Industrial Average, and the Standard & Poor's 500 Index (s&p 500). Each country or region has its own stock index, which represents a certain group of companies that comprise the index. For example, the s&p/tsx is made up of the largest and most valuable companies in Canada.

Stock exchanges serve a great function for investors. They make it possible for people with excess cash to exchange that cash for an interest in a publicly traded business by purchasing shares. Conversely, people who own shares in publicly traded businesses but who need cash can convert their shares into cash by selling them. In this way, the core role of a stock exchange is twofold: to facilitate using cash to buy shares, and to facilitate raising cash by selling shares. A stock exchange is really a medium of exchange.

To help investors understand how stock markets work, one of the greatest investors of all time, Benjamin Graham, created a metaphor that he described in his book *The Intelligent Investor*. Graham suggested that investors view themselves as one of two owners of a business and to think about it this way: each day, as an investor, you have to deal with your business partner, "Mr. Market," who offers to buy your share of the business. Every day, the price Mr. Market offers changes, and in fact Mr. Market often offers prices that are either way too high or way too low, depending on whether his mood is pessimistic or optimistic. As an investor, you can accept the price of the day and transact with Mr. Market, or not. Graham's point was that investors should focus on the actual business performance of the companies they invest in (and whether business conditions are relatively better or worse) rather than worry about the day-to-day fluctuations caused by the short-term popularity of a company's shares. Unfortunately, however, many investors think of shares as pieces of paper to be bought and sold almost randomly. A prime example of this is day trading—buying and selling shares the same day to make a small profit.

You have likely noticed that the financial press reports on the stock market's movements constantly. One day the market may be up 2%, but down 1% the next day, and the financial media will always have a reason for the movement in the market. For example, in the fall of 2014 the S&P/TSX dropped by 10% in just over a month. The financial press attributed the dip to a slowing global economy, a drop in oil prices, and fears related to the Ebola virus. Could the real, long-term value of the largest businesses in Canada really decline 10% in one month? No. But investors were nervous and emotional and therefore willingly sold shares at lower prices. In general, investors do not like uncertainty, and as a result, stock markets can be very sensitive to geopolitics and headline news. Stock markets are also forward-looking, meaning that the market cares less about whether economic or company conditions are good or bad in an absolute sense, but more about whether things are getting relatively better or worse.

➤ **TAKE NOTE:** A share represents ownership in a real, live, operating business. If you keep this in mind, you will dramatically increase your probability of being a successful investor. Stay focused on long-term results, not everyday fluctuations. From time to time, investors will become emotional and stock prices will decline and be on sale—these are buying opportunities. As Warren Buffett says, "Be fearful when others are greedy, and be greedy when others are fearful."

Preferred Shares

Having characteristics of both equities and fixed income, preferred shares are oftentimes referred to as "hybrid" securities and can be a component of a well-diversified portfolio. From a priority perspective, preferred shares rank above common shares and below bonds. Holders of a preferred share have an ownership interest in the company but generally do not have any voting rights. Preferred shares generally pay a fixed dividend (similar in concept to interest income from bonds) that is often safer than common share dividends. If there is a cash crunch, companies will usually cut dividends to common shareholders before cutting dividends to preferred shareholders. But the term "preferred" does not mean guaranteed. Other key things to know about preferred shares include the following:

- Preferred shares represent an ownership interest but have less upside potential than common shares.

- Preferred shares are similar to bonds because of the fixed dividend they offer. As a result, preferred shares are interest-rate sensitive. As interest rates increase, investors can compare different fixed-income investments to meet their income needs; therefore, preferred shares may be relatively less attractive in that scenario.

- There are several different types of preferred shares, and some may include features where dividend rates vary or can be reset at certain periods. See your advisor for further details.

- Like common shares, preferred shares are eligible for Canadian dividend tax credits and are taxed preferentially compared to interest income from bonds.

Styles of Stock Investing

There are many different styles of investing in the stock "bucket." Entire books have been written about equity-style investing, and so the following discussion will take a very high-level focus. The two main types of investing styles are known as fundamental and technical. Fundamental investing focuses on "what to buy", while technical investing focuses on "when to buy." Some investors will also use a combination of the approaches.

Fundamental investors look at a potential investment from the viewpoint of how "fundamentally" sound it is. To do this, investors analyze various metrics of a company, including its balance sheet, whether the business is growing, and whether earnings are increasing. The goal of fundamental analysis is to identify undervalued companies, invest in them when they are trading at less than they are worth, and sell as the stock price of the company becomes fairly valued. This is what's referred to as "buying low and selling high."

There are also sub-styles of fundamental analysis. Some investors consider themselves to be *value investors* and focus only on stocks that are very cheap relative to their true worth, known as their "intrinsic value." (One of the all-time classic books about value investing, which I mentioned earlier, is Benjamin Graham's *The Intelligent Investor*.) Other investors are *growth investors* and are willing to pay higher prices for companies that are growing their revenues and earnings faster. (A classic book about investing in growth stocks is Philip Fisher's *Common Stocks and Uncommon Profits*.) Another sub-style of investing is referred to as "growth at a reasonable price," which combines the value and growth styles. Some investors focus on companies of a certain size—small, mid-size, or large.

Different styles tend to do better at different times. Work by Richard Bernstein has shown that growth investing tends to perform better than value investing during periods of lower economic growth, and value investing tends to perform better during periods of higher economic growth. This makes sense because in periods of slower growth, more money gravitates toward the stocks of companies that are growing, which bids those stocks up. When economic growth is more robust, value stocks tend to do better as there is less of a premium on growth stocks.

Rather than focusing on company fundamentals, investors who follow technical analysis (known as "chartists" or "technicians") study price and volume movements in securities to forecast likely future price action. Think of chartists as the weather forecasters of the financial markets. They study the "weather" of the markets and individual securities and forecast what the future is likely to hold. You may hear technical analysts say things like, "xyz stock closed above its two-hundred-day moving average, so it is a buy," or "abc stock closed below its two-hundred-day moving average, so sell." Sometimes they are right, but they are sometimes wrong as well. Technical analysts consider basic economic forces of supply and demand. When there is more buying interest in a stock (demand for shares) than selling interest (supply of shares), the price of the stock will increase, and vice versa. Be cautious about relying purely on a "price momentum" strategy (buying what is going up). While price trends can persist for periods of time, it's like walking on a high wire without a net underneath—trends can change fast (and when you least expect it!). In general, technical analysis is a valuable tool that even many fundamental analysts use in their decision-making process. If you would like to learn more about technical analysis, a great book I recommend you read is John Murphy's *The Visual Investor: How to Spot Market Trends.*

Analyst Ratings

The investment industry is divided into two main sides—the sell side and the buy side. Sell-side firms include brokerages and banks that sell investment services to institutional investors such as mutual funds and pension funds (the buy side). The buy side comprises money managers (e.g., managers of mutual funds) who invest on behalf of their clients. All firms on the sell side have research departments that employ stock analysts, who are known as sell-side analysts.

Sell-side analysts provide their clients with ongoing research on a list of companies in a specific industry group. Sell-side firms usually have one analyst for each market sector, which typically include

- energy,
- materials (e.g., mining companies),
- industrials (e.g., railways and transportation companies),
- consumer discretionary (e.g., department stores and movie companies),
- consumer staples (e.g., grocery stores and food companies),
- healthcare,
- financials,
- information technology,
- telecommunications services (e.g., cable and telephone companies), and
- utilities.

Sell-side analysts are expected to be experts in the industry they cover and to know each company they cover in great detail. To do this, they study company financial statements and talk to the company's management, customers, and suppliers. The analyst will build detailed financial models to project the company's quarterly earnings. Many investors track the trajectory of a company's earnings estimates and whether the company surprised the analysts by beating or missing earnings expectations. Earnings surprises on the upside can have a strong positive impact on a company's stock price, while a downside miss can significantly lower a company's stock price. While the investing community is fixated on quarter-to-quarter results, the average investor should consider this as "noise" and ignore it.

Analysts will also write detailed research reports that include a recommendation to buy, sell, or hold a stock, along with a price target. For example, a financial sector analyst may issue a report on a bank, giving the stock a "buy" rating with a one-year target price of $88 per share (meaning the analyst expects the stock price to reach $88 within a year).

Ratings change periodically—the stocks of some companies will be upgraded from "hold" to "buy" or downgraded from "buy" to "hold." These research reports are disseminated to the average investor ("retail" investors) and to larger institutional investors (the buy side). One of the main goals of sell-side firms is to generate trading activity (and commissions) from individual and institutional investors through the research. Analysts want to be valuable to the buy-side portfolio managers so that these firms will direct their trading to the analyst's firm, which is a revenue-generating activity.

The vast majority of analyst recommendations are "holds" or "buys"—it is quite rare to see a sell rating. Why is this? From time to time, companies will use sell-side firms to raise capital by issuing shares to the public. Although there is a strict division between the research and capital-raising arms of sell-side firms, when companies want to raise capital, they tend to use sell-side firms that have a favourable opinion of their stocks. The result is that there is a natural tendency for research departments to issue more favourable ratings.

A 2012 study, *Analyst Target Price Optimism around the World* by Bradshaw et al., examined the accuracy of analyst target prices, using data from 11,436 analysts from 41 countries. The study concluded that, based on a one-year time horizon, the accuracy of analyst price targets was approximately 30%. The study also found evidence that target prices can be optimistic and suggested that some analysts may have incentives to generate revenues from trading and investment banking activities. In a 2013 study of sell-side analysts entitled *Inside the "Black Box" of Sell-Side Financial Analysts,* conducted by Lawrence Brown, Andrew Call, Michael Clement, and Nathan Sharp, sell-side analysts were asked to rate the importance of several factors in their compensation. Interestingly, only 35% of respondents stated that the profitability of stock recommendations was very important, while 44% rated success at generating revenues from capital-raising activities and trading commissions as very important. This reiterates that analysts can be indirectly influenced or incentivized by factors other than solely the accuracy of their recommendations. The point here is not to say that research from sell-side analysts is not valuable—often, it provides significant insight into companies and their businesses. But it's critical for the average investor to have an idea of what other factors may influence analyst recommendations.

As with advisors, there are a lot of great sell-side analysts, but there are also a few who are not so great. Analysts are only human and, as such, they are subject to the emotions of greed and fear. Even they can be (and are) wrong. The bottom line for the average investor is this: use research from sell-side analysts as what it is—just research. Do not rely exclusively on analysts' buy, sell, or hold recommendations. Just because an analyst writes a report suggesting that they believe a stock will reach a certain price within a year, doesn't mean it will happen. Analysts also change their recommendations and revise their price targets in response to changes in the company's stock performance. Sometimes, however, the revisions are too late to benefit the average investor.

> **TAKE NOTE:** Do not make investment decisions based solely on the buy, sell, or hold recommendations of stock analysts. Use research from stock analysts as just that—research.

Alternative Investments

In investing, there is a bucket known as alternative investments. One challenge with the word "alternative" is that it means different things to different people. To keep things simple, I refer to alternatives as "other" investments—anything that does not fit in traditional asset classes like cash, bonds, or stocks. The investments I'll discuss here that fall into the "other" bucket are hedge funds, managed futures, gold, real estate, mortgages, infrastructure assets, private equity, and venture capital.

One of the main advantages of having some alternative investments in your portfolio is that they can be less correlated to traditional investments such as bonds and stocks and, therefore, can reduce volatility in your portfolio by increasing diversification and reducing total risk. You can look at it from the perspective that when some assets "zig," others "zag."

Alternative investments can be public or private market investments—the distinction is very important. Generally, private market alternative investments are more complex and can carry higher risk. In Canada, these investments are often sold through what is known as the exempt or private capital market. It is important to realize that, in some cases, the alignment of interests between the promoters and the investors is poor for these products, with large upfront commissions paid to sell these investments. As its name suggests, the exempt market offers certain exemptions from the full disclosure and sales requirements imposed by regulators of the public markets. As mentioned, until recently, this market was geared toward "sophisticated" investors who needed to exceed minimum requirements for income and net worth to participate (although, in my experience, investors who exceed these thresholds are not necessarily sophisticated investors). Recent rule changes now allow investors who do not exceed minimum financial requirements to participate in private investments on a limited basis.

The main thing for you to be aware of as an investor is that the exempt or private capital market is generally more loosely regulated. By contrast, alternative investments listed on the public markets generally have better disclosure and transparency. Examples of public market alternative investments are mutual funds that specialize in certain sectors such as real estate and infrastructure.

Hedge Funds
Hedge funds are private investment partnerships that were initially designed to capture upside in markets and limit downside by taking offsetting positions. For example, let's assume a hedge fund owned

20 stocks that the hedge fund manager felt were undervalued. The hedge fund manager was also worried that the broader market may decline, however, so she "shorted" the market by positioning part of the portfolio to be profitable if the market declined. When it comes to investing, you can either be "long" (meaning you own a security) or "short" (meaning you are positioned to profit if a security falls in price). In this example, assume that the hedge fund manager was correct and the market declined 10%, so the hedge fund made 10% because of its short position. The stocks owned by the hedge fund declined by 5%, so the hedge fund made a total of 10% minus 5%, or 5%. If the hedge fund manager was wrong and the market continued to rise, the fund would lose money on the short position. However, as long as the stocks in the portfolio went up in value more than the amount that was lost on the short position, the hedge fund would be profitable overall.

Today, however, the term "hedge fund" does not necessarily mean the investments really have limited downside. The way hedge funds are now managed is highly variable and depends on the manager of the particular fund. Funds can focus on a wide range of asset classes and sectors, use significant amounts of borrowed money ("leverage," which can magnify gains and losses), and choose to protect the downside (or not). Every hedge fund is different, and understanding the objective of the fund and the manager's style is very important. To keep it simple, when it comes to hedge funds, assume the manager has the flexibility to do anything.

Hedge fund clients are mostly large institutional investors. While some hedge funds are available to individual investors, often the best hedge funds in the industry are not open to individuals, unless you are very wealthy and can make a substantial investment. Historically, hedge funds have typically charged an annual management fee of 2% and also 20% of any profits generated (the "performance" fee). Sometimes investors must earn a minimum return (called the "hurdle rate") before any performance fee is generated, but this is not always the case. A hedge fund may also require investors to commit their money for a certain number of years, so keep in mind that you may not be able to sell the investment if you need cash unexpectedly.

In recent years, hedge fund fees have come under pressure due to lower performance and increasing investor focus on fees. Some large institutional investors such as CalPERS (California Public Employees' Retirement System) have exited hedge funds entirely, partly to reduce costs. That said, as of the second quarter of 2016, according to BarclayHedge, hedge funds as an asset class still manage $2.9 trillion. I expect hedge funds to remain an attractive option for investors looking for exposure to an asset class that can have a different risk-and-return profile compared with more traditional asset classes. Canadian regulators are also considering measures to enhance access to hedge funds for retail investors. If approved, in the future purchasing a hedge fund may be as simple as buying a mutual fund, and investors will also benefit from having a similar level of disclosure and protection.

Managed Futures
Managed futures are specialized funds run by commodity-trading advisors. These funds aim to produce profits by following trends in a wide range of markets, including equities, commodities of all types, and currencies.

Gold
In the investment community, there have historically been mixed opinions on whether investors should hold gold. Some argue that gold is an asset that doesn't generate cash flow (and has a cost to store it), and so it cannot be valued and therefore is not a worthwhile asset in a portfolio. Others point to the historic role of gold as a hard asset that has been used as a form of payment as an alternative to paper (or fiat) money, and as a form of portfolio insurance because gold can be an investment that benefits in times of market uncertainty and panic.

In recent times, more and more well-known investors are recommending that investors hold 5%-10% of their portfolio in gold because central banks around the world are engaging in so much quantitative easing, which, as was discussed earlier, equates to printing money. Central banks can print as much money as they want, but you simply cannot print more gold. Given where we are today from a macroeconomic standpoint, having some exposure to gold is likely prudent. Gold exposure can be in physical gold or stocks in gold companies. Gold companies can have more leverage and upside to the price of gold; however, you could also have situations where the price of gold goes up but a gold company has operational issues and its stock declines. See your advisor for further information.

Real Estate

An asset class most people are familiar with, real estate investments can range from owning raw (undeveloped) land to owning lower-risk properties that are generating income (such as apartment buildings, hotels, and strip malls). Real estate prices are very sensitive to migration and employment trends, as well as interest rates because a substantial portion of real estate is financed by debt (think about your mortgage!). When interest rates increase along with financing costs, real estate prices can decline due to the affordability factor.

For most people, their biggest investment and real estate exposure is in their own home, although some also own rental properties. If you are considering making investments in rental property, make sure you really want to spend the time and sweat equity managing the property and rental process (you could engage a property manager, but this of course comes at a financial cost). It is also important to be diversified. For example, some people I know have several rental properties (in addition to their day job), but all the properties are in Calgary, where, since the oil market turned down in 2014, vacancy rates have risen substantially while rents have declined, which, at the time of writing, is posing a major challenge.

Commonly, financial advisors can access real estate investments through limited partnership structures. Simply put, this means you invest money to buy a unit of the limited partnership and then the investment manager will purchase physical real estate. Limited partnership investments can be subject to limited transparency. Recent regulatory changes have also meant that these types of investments must be valued each year by a third-party accounting firm, so the values are accurate on client statements. Oftentimes, if the investment manager does not engage an independent accounting firm to provide a valuation, your statement may simply show "zero" value.

Be aware that you can also own physical real estate within your portfolio by purchasing publicly traded vehicles such as individual real estate investment trusts (REITs) or an ETF that owns REITs. REITs are a type of security that owns and usually operates income-producing real estate such as apartments and commercial buildings. These securities generally pay shareholders higher-than-average dividends and trade on stock exchanges as any other stock. The same level of due diligence applies when purchasing a REIT as it does with any stock or equity investment.

Mortgages

Mortgage investments are related to real estate; however, they differ in that the investor does not own the physical real estate but rather is a lender to the owner of the real estate. Mortgage investments can be in residential or commercial property. They provide investors with income and also offer security because the investment is backed by the underlying real estate—that is, if something goes wrong, the investor can always take control of the real estate.

For most average investors, it may be best to refrain from investing in single mortgages, unless you have the knowledge to be highly confident in this type of investment. A better bet is to have exposure to various mortgages (directly or through a fund) and to diversify geographically. While the concept of mortgages is simple to understand, these investments can get complicated, depending on how they are structured. For example, mortgage-backed securities have hundreds or even thousands of underlying mortgages and the cash flows are sliced and diced in such a way that certain investors receive particular cash flows, resulting in different investors having different levels of risk. When investing in mortgages, be mindful of liquidity provisions. If you need to liquidate the investment on short notice, this may be a challenge.

Infrastructure Assets

In recent years, infrastructure has emerged as an asset class. It can be broadly defined as those assets that represent essential facilities and services to society, ranging from transportation assets (airports, toll roads, railways, and bridges) to satellite towers and utilities such as pipelines. These assets are attractive to investors because of the steady performance and cash flow they generate. For example, even in a recession people will continue to drive and the owners of a toll road will continue to collect fees. The number of people driving may drop slightly, but if people have to drive, they will drive. Infrastructure assets are widely available on the public markets through mutual funds and ETFs. The popularity of infrastructure assets have increased since the financial crisis of 2007-08, when investors began in earnest to look to invest in stable assets with long-term cash flows.

Private Equity

Private equity investments are pools of capital traditionally used to directly invest in private companies or purchase publicly traded companies and turn them into privately owned businesses in leveraged buyout transactions (buyouts that are heavily funded by debt). A leveraged buyout is the acquisition of a company, mostly through debt. Private equity funds usually set their acquisition sights on mature businesses that generate significant cash flow. Because the acquisition is financed with large amounts of debt (sometimes up to 80% of the total purchase price), stable cash flows in the target business are very important so that the interest and principal can be repaid.

The result is that the investors have a good possibility of making large returns (20% or more annually is a common target). Private equity investors also often aim to make operational improvements to the businesses they buy in an effort to improve profitability. As the business becomes more profitable and the debt is paid down, the equity or ownership stake in the business becomes more valuable. Often, the private equity investors will eventually take the private company public again (by offering shares for sale to the public) as a way of exiting their investment. One example of a leveraged buyout transaction is the The Blackstone Group buying the Hilton Hotels Corporation in 2007.

Private equity funds also actively invest in companies that are struggling financially—these investments are generally referred to "distressed" investing. Typically, private equity investments buy such companies, bring in their own experienced management teams, and restructure the business and eventually restore profitability. These are often known as "special situations" or "turnarounds." If the turn-around is successful, the business will likely be sold, reaping large returns for the private equity investors.

Venture Capital

If you are familiar with the television program *Dragon's Den*, then you have already had some exposure to venture capital. Venture capital-ists are best known for making early investments in companies that have the potential to grow at exceedingly high rates by transforming an industry with a new product or service. Google, for example, was originally funded largely by venture capitalists. Typically, in a port-folio of 10 venture capital investments, one will do exceedingly well, two will fail completely, and the remainder will provide a modest return. The big winner, however, can provide returns large enough to compensate for the modest or negative returns on the others. Ven-ture capitalists may also invest in more established businesses that are growing and need capital to accelerate their growth.

In the 2010s, the boundaries between venture capitalists and private equity investors has blurred, with private equity investors sometimes becoming involved in investments that have tradition-ally been in the domain of venture capitalists and vice versa. It is not uncommon for hedge funds to have some private equity and venture capital investments in their portfolios.

➤ **TAKE NOTE:** The best private equity, venture capital, and hedge funds are very difficult (if not impossible) to access for the average investor. Top managers are able to attract more than enough capital from large institutional investors such as pension funds.

Cautions about the "Other" Bucket

In an ideal world, investments in the "other" bucket would bring additional diversification to an investment portfolio. Major pension plans around the world, including the Canada Pension Plan, have substantial exposure to these assets. Seeing this, some companies that cater to individual investors are recommending that the portfo-lio of the average investor should look like that of the Canada Pension

Plan in terms of the allocation to alternative investments, especially investments in private companies. The difference, however, is
that the staff of pension funds are highly competent, professionally
trained, sophisticated investors who have an in-depth understanding
of the investments, the skill set to monitor them closely and create
value, and the scale to drive down costs. For the average investor, a
good deal of caution is suggested when it comes to alternative investments for the following reasons:

- **Complexity.** Because of the complexity of some alternative investments,
  it is difficult for most investors to have a clear, detailed understanding of the risks involved. Some of these investments can also
  increase the complexity of ongoing tax filings when the investment
  concludes, especially if investments were made in the United States.

- **Lack of liquidity.** Alternative investments can be difficult to sell if you
  suddenly need cash. Because many alternative investments are not
  readily saleable, the time frame of the investment can be long. If a real
  estate asset has no buyer, for example, the investor will be forced to
  hold the investment for a longer period. In general, expected returns
  of less liquid investments should reflect a premium for illiquidity.

- **Leverage.** Many alternative investments use leverage, or borrowed
  money. Even though you personally may not be borrowing money
  to make the investment, the investment manager may borrow. Borrowing money will magnify the returns, whether they are positive or
  negative. If everything works out well, you will be very happy; but if
  the investment does not perform as expected, you could lose a lot of
  money.

- **Lack of transparency.** Because most alternative investments are
  not publicly traded, they have a relative lack of transparency that
  makes it difficult to get a sense of how the investment is really performing. Traditionally, the value of some alternative investments
  has stayed static on account statements until the investment concludes, which could take five to seven years or even longer. During
  this time, the value shown on the statement may or may not reflect
  how the underlying investment is truly performing. If, for example, you invest in a real estate limited partnership and some of the

properties purchased were unoccupied for a lengthy period, the value of the overall investment may in fact have dropped, but your account statement may not reflect that. Because there is no daily price on most alternative investments that are not publically listed, investors have a harder time knowing how the investment is performing. This situation creates the potential for a nasty surprise when the investment concludes. The good news is that recent regulatory changes now require most private investments to be valued annually by an independent source (such as a recognized accounting firm) to give investors a more accurate picture.

- **High commissions.** Upfront sales commissions can be quite high for those selling some alternative investments. I have seen sales commissions on private investments of up to 10%! If the person selling the investment is receiving 10% right off the bat, how are the investors going to make money?

To illustrate some of the complications of alternative investments, allow me to share the personal experiences of some investors I have met.

Ten years ago Jerome and his wife, Claudette, purchased a private real estate investment consisting of a mortgage loan and preferred shares in Seniors' Lodge, a company that develops, operates, and manages seniors' residence properties in Western Canada. Through an advisor, they invested $75,000, and the person who sold Jerome and Claudette the investment received an upfront commission of 10% or $7,500. The majority of the investment was in the couple's RRSP accounts. The mortgage had a maturity date of 2030. By making this investment, the clients were locking up their money for almost 25 years!

The company began a project once enough capital had been raised for two to three months of construction; capital-raising efforts continued. But because of poor economic conditions, not enough capital was raised, construction was stalled, and interest payments were suspended on the clients' investments. After many years, the project was finally completed; however, Seniors' Lodge was not fully occupied and was operating at a loss. The company did not have enough capital to continue operating at a loss until occupancy improved. The property was sold, and the clients received 30¢ for each dollar they had invested—a substantial loss. This loss was the result of investing a substantial amount in a single high-risk, illiquid investment.

Although this case demonstrates what can go wrong, not all alternative investments are bad. Let's look at an example of an alternative investment that worked out very well.

In 2010, Mike and Vanda were in their early 50s and had some excess capital to invest. Their advisor, Dave, recommended they invest in a real estate limited partnership that focused on buying income-producing real estate, such as hotels and multi-family units, in geographic regions that were having temporary economic issues (which made the real estate assets cheap to acquire). Dave knew that the principals making the investments were disciplined and would not overpay for assets. The principals also invested their own money alongside clients and the investment was structured with a modest upfront commission (3%), with most of the manager's compensation contingent on the long-term success of the investment. The principals were planning to buy at least five different properties within the same limited partnership. At the time, the principals were focused on buying US real estate, given the compelling value combined with a Canadian dollar that was at par with the US dollar. Mike and Vanda invested $75,000. The upfront commission their advisor received was $2,250. Five years later, they received a compounded return of 15% in US dollar terms, but 20% in Canadian dollar terms (because the US dollar had strengthened).

If you truly understand and accept the risks and you want some exposure to alternative investments, take the following measures:

- Know what you own and understand what you are getting involved in.

- Check the background of the people involved with the investment.

- Make sure the investment is properly structured and check alignment of interest. Is the deal too rich for the people putting it together? Ideally, the promoters and investment managers should get paid a small amount for coordinating and marketing the deal, but most of their reward should be based on the success of the investment.

- Ensure that you are not just investing in an alternative single investment but, rather, at least a handful of different investments.

- Be aware of whether there is a match between the structure of the type of investment you make and the ease with which the underlying investment can be converted to cash (liquidity). What I mean by this is, if you are buying a mutual fund that can be bought or sold at any time and the underlying investment is in physical real estate (an asset that cannot be converted to cash easily), if confidence suddenly collapses and many investors want to redeem simultaneously, the fund may freeze redemptions, leaving the investor stuck holding the fund. For example, shortly after Britain voted to leave the European Union in 2016 (i.e., Brexit), several UK property funds suspended redemptions because there was panic selling and not enough cash to satisfy redemptions requests.

For most investors, focusing on publicly traded, alternative investments such as mutual funds or ETFs in the areas of real estate and infrastructure is best. You could also consider the stocks of private equity funds or companies that own and manage real estate (e.g., REITs).

➤ **TAKE NOTE:** Alternative investments can reduce the overall risk of your portfolio because of the different risk-and-return profile compared to traditional stocks and bonds. However, it is critical to understand the risks before participating in these investments.

The Future of Investment Returns

Before concluding this section, I want to touch on what the future investing climate may look like. While predicting future returns is impossible to do accurately on a consistent basis, some assessment can be made about probabilities based on longer-term trends. In its 2016 *Thriving in the New Abnormal* report, McKinsey & Company states the following:

> [The] return environment of the past 30 years was an historical anomaly. It was a golden age characterized by declining inflation

and interest rates, strong global economic growth fuelled by demo-graphics, productivity, and rapid growth in China, and robust corporate profits boosted by access to new markets, low tax rates, and the rise of automation and sophisticated supply chains. These trends are all winding down in highly predictable ways and an unprecedented rise in productivity would be required to close the resulting gap. While productivity gains related to digitization and other disruptive technologies will certainly help, they are unlikely to counter a substantial long-term decline in the rate of global economic growth and the corresponding "mean reversion" of long-term returns for both equities and bonds.

McKinsey believes that the era of exceptional returns is over, and they expect that "over the next 20 years, average returns are expected to decline by a significant amount" as shown in the graph below.

Historical Asset Returns and Potential Scenarios for the Next 20 Years

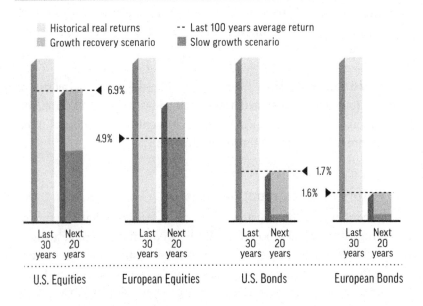

Over the next 20 years, average returns are expected to decline by a significant amount. *McKinsey & Company. "Thriving in the New Abnormal: North American Asset Management" (2016).*

So, what does this mean for investors? In my opinion, investors would do well to prepare for a lower-return environment in the future over the long term. Get great advice, be diversified, and have the right asset allocation for your risk tolerance. (More to come about all these things later.)

Types of Investment Products

Once you have an idea of which buckets you want to use, the next step is deciding what exactly you are putting in each bucket—you need to select investment products. The most common investment products are mutual funds, exchange-traded funds, and individual securities. Another set of products is sold through insurance licensed advisors, but we will focus on those later.

Thousands of investment products are available, with more created almost daily it seems. Different investment products have different objectives. At a very basic level, a product can have one of two objectives: to beat the market return or to match the return of the market. The two types relate to two particular ways of thinking in the investing world—one that believes that over time very few people, if any, can achieve higher-than-market returns in the long run, and another that believes investors with superior skills do exist and that they can indeed beat the market.

Products intended to provide a better return (after fees) than a certain market or index, such as the S&P/TSX or S&P 500 are known as "active" investments. The goal of active managers is to provide excess return over and beyond the market—in the industry, this is known as "alpha." (Interestingly, I once met a fund manager whose first name was Alpha! That's a lot of pressure!) In general, active investments usually come with a higher price tag than passive investments because of the cost of obtaining the services of qualified investment professionals to actively manage the money. Active management simply means that the investor or fund manager chooses securities within a portfolio he or she feels will do better than the relevant market benchmark, net of fees.

Products that aim to provide about the same return as a certain market or index are known as "passive" investments. In industry lingo, these investments provide market exposure known as "beta." Passive investments are generally available to investors at a lower cost than active investments. Passive investors believe that in the long run it is not possible for investors to do better than the market and that all investors are better off investing, at a lower cost, in products that provide market returns (slightly less after fees).

You will recall that earlier I referenced a paper by The Vanguard Group called *Putting a Value on Your Value: Quantifying Vanguard Advisor's Alpha in Canada.* In it, Vanguard classifies the additional value that advisors can add in various areas the "Advisor's Alpha." Morningstar's Paul Kaplan and David Blanchett use the term "Gamma" to explain how advisors can add value through enhancing client income levels in retirement using financial-planning strategies. So, there is alpha (for active products), beta (for passive products), and advisor alpha or gamma (for advisor value). Enough of the Greek letters! Let's go on to a question that you may be itching to ask: Can mutual fund managers beat the market in the long run? Standard & Poor's Indices Versus Active (SPIVA) methodology was designed to answer that question. It compares the performance of mutual funds (after fees) run by highly trained professional investors versus market benchmarks, producing quarterly scorecards. The Canadian 2015 scorecard looked at funds with different mandates, such as Canadian equity, US equity, and global equity, and reported the following percentages of funds that outperformed the market over 1-, 3-, and 5-year periods:

Funds Beating the Market

	1 year	3 year	5 year
Canadian Equity	57%	52%	34%
International	21%	17%	7%
US Equity	15%	4%	1%

The above results are for funds managed by highly trained investors who do it for a living, and you can see that even they have difficulty beating the market over a longer period. You may be wondering why a higher percentage of fund managers with Canadian mandates seems to outperform. The reason is that the Canadian market is highly concentrated in three sectors: energy, materials, and financials. In the years preceding 2015, the energy and materials sectors have performed poorly and managers could have outperformed by just having less exposure to those sectors. When these sectors eventually outperform, these same managers may have a hard time keeping up with the Canadian market. It is also important to note that over the measurement period for the 2015 scorecard, the Canadian dollar has weakened, which has made it even more difficult for Canadian managers with international and US equity mandates to keep up with their respective benchmarks.

The reason that it is so difficult to beat the market is that, as mentioned earlier, investing is a zero-sum game. For somebody to win, somebody else must lose. Competition is intense, and the best and brightest are playing the game: it is you against them. The players across the net could be institutional fund managers or hedge fund managers with Ivy League pedigrees, financial advisors, a computerized high-frequency trading system, or your neighbour. It is not for the faint of heart.

In my humble opinion, there is a role for both the active and passive investment approach in a portfolio. When markets are roaring higher (a "bull" market), it may be difficult for active managers to keep up; however, when the markets are dropping significantly (a "bear" market), active managers can protect the downside and outperform by having more cash in a portfolio or by being in more defensive sectors of the market. Additionally, certain parts of the market and regions of the world are very well-followed and more efficient, while others are not very well-followed and less efficient. In general, it makes more sense to have an active management approach in parts of the market and regions of the world that have less coverage from research analysts and are less efficient. For example, large capitalization companies in the United States are an example of a market that is relatively efficient—it would be hard for an active manager to outperform the market in this area. Small capitalization companies or stocks in emerging markets are generally not as well covered by analysts, therefore making an active approach more viable, with a higher probability of outperformance. Rather than focus on passive or active investing, I subscribe to the mantra of having the "right investment product in the right place."

....

➤ **TAKE NOTE:** Don't expect your advisor to consistently beat the market—this is an unrealistic objective. Individuals will often compare their returns to that of their friends, family members, or neighbours, asking them, "How did your advisor do?" If you do ask this question, then be sure to also ask, "What risk did your advisor take to get that return?" It is risk-adjusted return, rather than return, which is important. I strongly suggest that instead of focusing solely on performance, you focus on good investment results and advice in all aspects of The Advice Wheel.

....

Now that we've covered the difference between active and passive products, let's take a look at product choices in more detail.

Active Products (Mutual Funds)

At a basic level, mutual funds pool investors' money. The funds are then managed by a professional fund manager for a fee. Different mutual funds have different mandates—there are equity mutual funds, bond funds, and balanced funds (a combination of stocks and bonds). The mandates can also specify a geographic focus (e.g., Canada, Europe, India), a sub-asset class (small or large companies), and an investment style (value, growth, or growth at a reasonable price—GARP). Minimum initial investments are often $500 or less. The fund manager will manage a diversified portfolio (the average equity mutual fund usually holds stock in at least 50–75 companies).

Mutual funds are extremely popular: according to the Investment Funds Institute of Canada, as of September 2016, Canadians had $1.32 trillion invested in mutual funds. In Canada, 4.9 million households (33%) held mutual funds in their investment portfolios at the end of 2015 and mutual funds accounted for 31% of Canadi-ans' financial wealth. Mutual funds provide average investors with an opportunity to participate in the markets in a diversified way, using professional management, which may not be possible if they invested on their own.

Mutual funds are broadly classified by asset class, as follows:

- **Money market funds** invest in high-quality cash-like instruments such as treasury bills. These funds are appropriate if you want to "park" your money for a shorter time and earn more than you might in a regular bank account.

- **Fixed-income funds** have a mandate to invest in bonds and other secu-rities such as mortgages to provide the investor with interest income. Traditionally, fixed-income funds have also been used to diversify portfolios and limit volatility. Don't forget that the investments inside fixed-income funds can still fluctuate, so capital gains and losses are possible. These investments are also interest-rate sensitive. As interest rates decrease, fixed-income funds will tend to increase in value, and vice versa. Remember the teeter-totter analogy!

- **Equity funds** generally invest in the stocks of publicly listed com-panies. Investment objectives can vary substantially among funds. Some funds may invest in large, well-established companies that pay dividends, while others may invest in smaller companies in cer-tain sectors of the market or certain countries. Some funds can be allowed to invest a small portion of the total assets of the fund into private companies. The return from equity funds is composed pri-marily of dividends and capital gains (or losses).

- **Balanced funds** are typically a hybrid of fixed-income and equity funds. Typically, the investments within balanced funds are a mix of bonds and stocks. The word "balanced" is relative—the mix of stocks and fixed income in any particular balanced fund can vary. A common mix is 60% stocks and 40% fixed income. The return on balance funds comprises a mixture of interest income, dividends, and capital gains (or losses).

Even within the same type of mutual funds, all funds are not created equal. Before buying a mutual fund, dig in and make sure you understand what the underlying investments are and how the fund is managed. This is where an advisor can provide tremendous value.

Mutual funds offer several benefits to investors:

- **Trained investment managers:** Most fund managers, who make the buy and sell decisions, hold the Chartered Financial Analyst (CFA) designation. When you invest in a mutual fund, you can be confident that a trained professional will make investment decisions on your behalf. All you have to do is make sure your overall portfolio is allocated properly, be disciplined, and invest regularly.

- **Diversification:** Mutual funds are a great vehicle to create a diversified portfolio even with a smaller amount of money. For example, an investor just starting out with $10,000 to invest would have a hard time creating a diversified portfolio by investing in individual securities. So instead of trying to select 25–40 different stocks, you can own a fund that owns many different securities.

- **Access to specialty markets and managers:** Mutual funds give investors access both to markets where it may be difficult to invest on their own and to managers who are highly skilled in certain areas of the market. For example, it is much simpler for the average investor to purchase a mutual fund to invest in India's growing economy than it is to try to choose individual securities in this region. Funds are also a good way to obtain exposure to certain sectors of the market. If you want exposure to energy stocks, but don't know which ones to choose, pick a good energy fund. Investing in mutual funds also gives the average investor the chance of investing with certain managers who have demonstrated skill investing in a certain sector or part of the market, such as smaller companies.

- **Liquidity:** Mutual funds can be bought and sold daily. Generally, the price of the fund is determined at the end of each business day, and all orders are executed at the daily ending price, known as the net asset value. Be aware that many mutual funds have minimum holding periods, typically 30–90 days. If you sell a fund before the minimum holding period, additional charges may apply. This provision is meant to discourage short-term trading, which is detrimental to longer-term fund investors, as discussed below.

What are the drawbacks of investing in mutual funds?

- **Cost:** Mutual funds tend to have higher costs because you are paying for active management. These costs are currently embedded in the returns of the fund. Overall, the trend for mutual fund costs is down, largely as a result of the popularity of passive products such as ETFs, which can provide the market return for a very low cost. To maintain market share, mutual fund companies have had no choice but to gradually reduce costs. Mutual fund costs are discussed in more detail later.

- **Bigger is not necessarily better:** As a given mutual fund increases in size, it can become more difficult for the manager to select investments that will contribute significantly to make a difference to the fund returns. Large multi-billion-dollar funds, for example, are often indirectly restricted to investing only in the largest, most liquid companies because taking a large enough position in a smaller company is not feasible.

- **Impact of other investors:** One of the main benefits of investing in a mutual fund is the ability to pool your money with that of other investors. Ironically, that is also one of the drawbacks of mutual funds. As an investor in a mutual fund, your investments are influenced by the actions of other investors over whom you have no control. Most investors have a very difficult time avoiding the emotions of fear and greed. When the markets are doing well, they are happy to invest more even if the market is expensive from a valuation perspective. When the markets are declining, the same investors are fearful and scared of losing capital, so they sell, even if the market is actually attractive at those prices. In short, many investors end up buying high and selling low, even though this is the exact opposite of what they should do!

Here's how this affects you: Assume you are an investor in XYZ Canadian Equity Fund, and you are disciplined and invest regularly and have a 20-year time horizon. Because you are well-informed about the fund, its holdings, and the manager's investment process, you are not too concerned about short-term market fluctuations. However, some other investors in XYZ Canadian Equity Fund are less informed, undisciplined, or have shorter-term time horizons. These investors could end up buying high and selling low. The manager is mandated to keep the fund invested and will not hold a lot of excess cash in the fund. Therefore, when the markets are doing well and money is flowing into the fund because some investors want to buy, the manager is forced to buy even if the valuations are less attractive. And when the markets are down and investors are redeeming funds, the manager may be forced to sell when the holdings are actually attractive to buy because of their lower valuation. These activities have the potential to decrease the investment performance of the fund; to some extent, the manager is also being forced to buy high and sell low. This phenomenon can be offset to some extent by the manager's ability to determine what to buy and sell, but it is possible that your investment's performance could be negatively affected by the actions of other investors.

Mutual Fund Costs Explained

If you invest in mutual funds, you need to be aware of the costs. Mutual funds carry three main costs: the management expense ratio (MER), the trading expense ratio (TER), and sales commissions paid to advisors (commonly known as loads).

Many investors are familiar with the management expense ratio. The MER represents the combined total of the management fee, operating expenses, and taxes charged to a fund during a given year expressed as a percentage of a fund's average net assets for that year. All mutual funds have an MER, which also includes the cost of ongoing advice and service offered by your advisor.

The returns you earn as an investor—whether reported on your statement, in the media, or in promotional materials—reflect performance data that is reported *after* the fund's MER is deducted. For example, if your fund's investments gained 9% last year and its MER is 2%, the reported return will be 7% for that time period. Remember, as of July 2016, additional transparency requirements were implemented by regulators so that investors can see the amounts paid to dealers. However, the actual fees charged by the mutual fund companies to manage the investments are still not fully transparent. The move to enhance transparency by regulators is a welcome step in the right direction, but it's only a half measure. Investors therefore should still pay attention to the costs of investment products.

MERs have two components:

- The fee paid to the manager covers professional investment management, supervision of the fund, administration of fund operations, and service support. Operating expenses include costs for regulatory filings, legal advice, record-keeping, accounting and fund valuation costs, custody fees, audit and legal fees, costs of preparing and distributing reports and prospectuses, and taxes. Note: most mutual fund companies will also invest substantial resources in providing advisors with ancillary services such as access to mutual fund portfolio managers, speakers at client events, and other tools and resources to help the advisor grow their (and, therefore, indirectly the mutual fund company's business). When it comes to pricing, be aware that many mutual funds have lower pricing available if you (or your family in total) have a certain dollar amount invested with the fund company. This concept is known as preferred pricing—ask your advisor for details. Some companies are now automatically applying discounted pricing when investment thresholds are met, rather than the advisor having to complete paperwork or request the discounted pricing for their clients.

- Trailing commission is an ongoing fee paid to the advisor you work with and the advisor's firm. This fee is paid for the advisor's investment recommendations; portfolio construction; ongoing monitoring and portfolio rebalancing; retirement, tax, or goal-specific planning; and administration, which covers account openings and closings, reporting and issuance of quarterly account statements and client communications, and regulatory compliance activities. The payment goes from the fund company to the advisor's firm, which then pays the advisor according to the applicable grid.

In addition to the MER, mutual funds have other costs you should be aware of. The TER is a measure of a fund's trading costs. Generally, the higher a fund's TER, the more actively the fund manager has traded in a given year. The TER is typically expressed as a percentage. For example, if a $100-million fund incurs $1 million in trading commissions (expenses) for the year, the TER is 1%. If a portfolio manager buys and sells securities more often or invests in less-liquid securities, the fund tends to have a higher TER. This is because there is a wider spread between what buyers will pay and what sellers will accept to transact in less-liquid securities (this is known as a wider "bid-ask" spread). Funds with low turnover rates that invest in more-liquid securities tend to have lower TERS. The TER is independent of a fund's MER, and it typically does not apply to fixed-income transactions because commissions for fixed-income funds are already embedded in the price of the bond.

Initial sales charge, or sales commission, practices are highly variable among advisors. There are several types of initial sales charges they can use:

- **Front-load** charges, paid upfront by the investor, are one of the most common types of initial sales charges. With this method, the investor pays up to 5% of the initial investment to compensate their advisor. For example, if you invest $100,000 in a mutual fund and pay a front load of 5%, your initial investment is really $95,000 and you pay $5,000 to the investment dealer, of which your advisor receives a portion. Because you paid that cost upfront, the minimum time you must hold the funds is short, usually 30-90 days, depending on the fund company. This form of commission gives the investor the most flexibility because there are no fees to sell or redeem the funds.

- With the **back-end load** method, the investment dealer receives a sales commission of up to 5% from the mutual fund company, which flows to the advisor through the grid. The back-end load is commonly referred to as a deferred sales charge (DSC). For example, if you invest $100,000 in a mutual fund, the fund company will pay the investment dealer 5% of the investment ($5,000); your investment would still be $100,000. With this type of commission, you would face substantial penalties if you sold the fund within the first seven years. Here's why: if you sell the fund too soon, the mutual fund company would be in a loss position because it has not had a chance to earn back the sales commission it paid to the dealer, by earning management fees on the assets. Therefore, a penalty will apply to the investor so that the fund company can at least break even. The advantage of this type of initial sales charge is that you have more money working for you because there is no upfront cost. The downside is you are required to pay penalties if you redeem early. If your investment needs change or you need money, the downside can be substantial. The penalties usually decline from 6% or 7% of the investment if you sell in Year 1 to 1% in Year 6 and 0% in Year 7.

It is important to understand that the back-end load generally allows you to switch your investment within the same fund family. For example, if you invested in the Fidelity Canadian Large Cap Fund on a back-end-load basis and wanted to switch to the Fidelity U.S. All Cap Fund after six months, you could do this without penalty because you are leaving your investment with the same fund company (Fidelity Investments) and so it will continue to collect management fees. If you do this, however, check to make sure that your new investment will not be subject to a new six- or seven-year redemption schedule. You should also find out whether your advisor will charge a fee to switch your funds.

One of the challenges with the back-end load method is that the investor is not always aware that while they are committed to the fund company for several years, they do have flexibility to move to another fund within the same company. As a result, investors are often reluctant to redeem a fund with a deferred sales charge due to the penalty, even if redeeming is the best thing to do from an investment perspective.

For example, in the late 1990s before I had any financial training, my first advisor was a fellow at Merrill Lynch in Edmonton. I had $2,500 of savings to invest from my first job. He recommended a science and technology fund, which did well for a couple of years, until the technology market crashed. As the fund began to drop in value, I was concerned and spoke to my advisor, who told me I could sell but would be charged a penalty of 5%. I did not want to pay the penalty, so I held on, thinking the fund would come back. By the time the penalty period for selling ended, the fund was down another 50%. Had I known a switch into another fund within the same fund family was possible, it would have been a viable option for me.

Another feature of back-end load funds to be aware of is that each year, investors are allowed to redeem 10% of their mutual fund investment without penalty. How the free redemption is applied may vary slightly among companies. For example, the 10% may apply to the original cost of your investment or it may apply to the number of units of the fund you own. The 10% free redemption cannot be carried forward.

In the industry, the use of back-end load funds has declined substantially in recent years and will likely continue to do so. In my experience, back-end load funds can work for certain investors, but it is usually best for longer-term investments. Make sure the fund company has a good lineup of funds you can switch into if needed.

- **Low-load** funds are a variation of the back-end load or deferred sales charge approach. The low-load option works in a similar way, but the fund company pays the investment dealer approximately 3% of the initial investment upfront (of which the advisor receives a portion); penalties apply if the investor sells the fund within three years.

- **No-load** funds do not have any sales charge attached to them. Advisors who use these funds will not charge anything on the sale because they believe the compensation from the ongoing (trailer) commissions is adequate.

Remember, sales charges are negotiable, so don't be afraid to talk to your advisor about them.

It is important for you to be aware that there can be many different series of a given mutual fund. Each different series has its own fund code. For example, ABC Canadian Equity Growth Fund may be available as Series A, D, and F with the fund codes hypothetically being ABC265, ABC266, and ABC267 respectively. Different classes are meant for different types of accounts or different sales structures. If you have a regular-commission account, you would purchase a Series A, while somebody with a self-directed account (through a discount brokerage, for example) would purchase Series D, and somebody with a fee-based account would purchase Series F. Note: if you own mutual fund through a discount brokerage account, make sure you own Series D funds, as these funds have lower costs because they exclude costs of advice (why pay for advice you are not receiving?).

How to Select Mutual Funds

With literally hundreds, if not thousands, of mutual funds to choose from, how do you pick the best funds? In deciding to purchase a mutual fund, you are choosing active management over passive management. If you are choosing active management (and paying the manager a fee), make sure the fund does not look exactly like the market index (otherwise you are paying a fee for market performance).

In my experience, investors often make two big mistakes when choosing mutual funds. The first is buying last year's best performer. Mark Yusko, CEO and CIO of Morgan Creek Capital Management, has summarized the phenomenon of investors chasing top-performing funds in this way: "Investors buy what they wish they would have bought." For example, technology funds did very well in the late 1990s, and many investors began investing in them because prior returns had been so good. Ultimately, most of these funds declined significantly or collapsed. **Past performance does not indicate future returns.** The second mistake is that sometimes investors pay for active management but don't receive it. That is, investors purchase actively traded mutual funds, but the funds are really passive investments (basically representing an index).

One reason many fund managers essentially replicate an index is that manager performance is usually measured against a market index. Deviating too far from the index (i.e., actively managing) could result in career risk (being fired!). A manager who is consistently underperforming the index to which he or she is compared could earn lower compensation, and money could flow out of the fund because many investors mistakenly tend to chase performance. In the industry today, very substantial sums of money remain invested in active management strategies that are really closet index-type investments. In its 2016 *Thriving in the New Abnormal* report about the North American asset management industry, McKinsey & Company stated it "expects that a large pool of benchmark-hugging active assets—up to $8 trillion—will be up for grabs over the next several years as clients re-examine their core investment beliefs and manager relationships." To give you some Canadian context, a 2015 study entitled *Indexing and Active Fund Management: International Evidence* (conducted by Martijn Cremers, Miguel A. Ferreira, Pedro P. Matos, and Laura T. Starks) estimated that about 37% of all assets in Canadian equity mutual funds are in closet index funds. That likely equates to over a billion dollars of costs being paid *annually* by investors for active investment management that is not really active.

To explain the typical behaviour of institutional fund managers, in his book *A Zebra in Lion Country,* Ralph Wanger (a well-known and respected portfolio manager in the United States) used a clever analogy that outlined the similarities between zebras and portfolio managers. Wanger wrote that both zebras and portfolio managers have difficult goals—zebras seek fresh grass, whereas portfolio managers seek above-average returns. Both zebras and portfolio managers do not like risk. As Wanger put it, "portfolio managers can get fired; zebras can get eaten by lions." Furthermore, Wanger explained that both zebras and portfolio managers move in herds: "They look alike, think alike, and stick close together." Every zebra living in a herd has to make an important decision—where to stand relative to the rest of the herd. If conditions are safe and there are no lions in sight, the outer edge of herd is the best place to be because grass is fresh (in the middle of the herd, the grass has already been picked at or is trampled down). However, the zebra positioned at the outer edge of the herd when predators, such as lions, arrive could be targeted and may die. The zebras in the middle of the herd may eat stale grass, but it is easier for them to stay alive. Wanger went on to state that most portfolio managers cannot afford to behave like the zebra at the outer part of the herd. For portfolio managers, the optimal strategy is simply to stay in the centre of the herd at all times. If the manager is invested like most of their peers, they are less likely to be criticized. If the portfolio manager is too different from their peers and fails, they would be subject to criticism and even potentially losing their job.

The main point here is that if the manager invests like a zebra in the middle of the herd, performance is likely to be no better than the market, and the investor would be better off in an index fund. There is no doubt that mutual funds that closet index will usually under-perform after fees. In the industry there is a saying that "the return of an index fund with a high fee will always be lower than an index fund with a low fee." For example, if the index returns 10%, a closet index fund will provide a pre-fee return of very close to 10%—let's say 9.5%–10.5%. With a typical fee of 2.5%, the investor's return would be between 7% and 8%, less than the index return of 10%. As John Bogle, the legendary founder of The Vanguard Group, puts it, "The math is the math."

If you do invest in mutual funds, make sure you are really getting active management. One of the key metrics to ask about is "active share," which describes how different the fund is from its passive index benchmark. In this context, active means different. The higher the active share number, the better. Mutual funds that have a very low active share (they look pretty much like the passive benchmark index) are known as "closet indexers"—that is, the fund presents itself as being actively managed, but it is essentially replicating an index such as the s&p/tsx, which the investor could access for a much lower fee using an ETF. Another consideration is how patient the fund manager is. A 2015 study titled *Patient Capital Outperformance* by Martijn Cremers and Ankur Pareek introduces the concept of having a patient investment strategy. According to the study, funds with high active share portfolios and whose managers are patient (with less portfolio turnover) do better than the applicable index on average by 2% per year. Funds that trade frequently tend to underperform, even with high active share numbers.

Morningstar is a company that provides independent research on mutual funds and, more recently, also ETFs. In his book *Fund Spy: Morningstar's Inside Secrets to Selecting Mutual Funds that Outperform*, Russel Kinnel makes the following key points about selecting mutual funds:

- Expense ratios are the most powerful predictor of fund performance. In general, there is an inverse relationship between fund performance and cost. Look for low-cost funds with sound investment strategies—choosing them will double or triple your chances of success.

- Look at the long-term performance history of the fund, which will reveal how the fund performed in different market cycles. Look at the best years and the worst years. Short-term performance data is not useful—funds that have performed best in the past couple of years may do well over the short term but are likely to then fall back to earth.

- Manager discipline is critical because every strategy is going to have periods of stronger performance and weaker performance.

- On average, funds managed by managers who themselves have a significant investment in the fund perform better because of the enhanced alignment of interest. In Canada, it is difficult for the average investor to obtain this information, and this is something that regulators should consider mandating and that fund companies should provide. But if you ask your advisor, he or she may be able to find out from the mutual fund company.

Be Patient
Many individual investors who invest in mutual funds achieve returns that pale in comparison to the funds themselves. Consuelo Mack has referred to this as the "underperformance trap." The root cause is that investors as a group lack the patience to deal with periods of underperformance. (By the way, this problem is not unique to

individual investors—sophisticated institutional investors can also experience difficulty being patient!)

Davis Advisors studied the top-performing US large cap investment managers from January 1, 2004, to December 31, 2013, to see how many of them suffered a three-year period of underperformance. The results are as follows:

> 95% of these top managers' rankings fell to the bottom half of their peers for at least one three-year period. A full 73% ranked among the bottom quarter of their peers for at least one three-year period. Though each of the managers in the study delivered excellent long-term returns, almost all suffered through a difficult period. Investors who recognize and prepare for the fact that short-term underperformance is inevitable—even from the best managers— may be less likely to make unnecessary and often destructive changes to their investment plans.

Furthering this point, in his book *The Success Equation: Untangling Skill and Luck in Business, Sports, and Investing,* famed investor and author Michael Mauboussin talks about how short-term investment results are mostly dictated by luck.

In summary, no active approach will outperform the market all the time. If the manager is a good one, his or her skill will be evident in the long run. In the short term, results are often related to, in large part, luck! If you find a disciplined, truly active manager, stick with that manager until there is a reason not to. Joel Greenblatt put it best in an interview with *WEALTHTRACK* when he said, "The strategy for you is not only one that makes sense, but one you can stick with." In my opinion, patience is a powerful factor in long-term investment success.

Some investors believe that mutual funds are all "bad." I want to make it clear that, in my opinion, this is not the case. There are some very high-quality active mutual funds that do add value over time, especially in certain areas of the market where passive exposure makes less sense. There is definitely room for mutual funds in certain areas of a diversified portfolio.

> **TAKE NOTE:** Choosing a mutual fund with high active share will by no means ensure that your investment will do better than the market, but combining active share with assessment of other qualitative or subjective factors will stack the odds in your favour. Be patient and focus on high active share, relatively low cost, and manager patience.

Passive Products (Exchange-Traded Products)

In the 2010s, exchange-traded products (ETPs) have risen in popularity. ETPs are a type of security that trades on an exchange similar to a stock. ETPs can be referenced to different assets including stocks, market indices, commodities, or bonds and are priced according to price movements of the assets to which they are referenced.

The most popular form of ETP is called the exchange-traded fund (ETF), which usually tracks equity or fixed-income indices. In the last few years, ETFs have grown at a phenomenal pace, especially since 2009, and even with this phenomenal growth, there is lots of runway left for ETFs to continue to grow in assets, as shown in the graphs that follow.

Active vs. Passive Funds Assets Breakdown

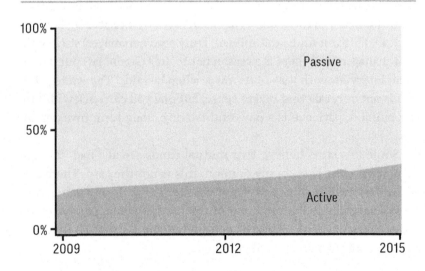

Cumulative Flows into Passive vs. Active Funds

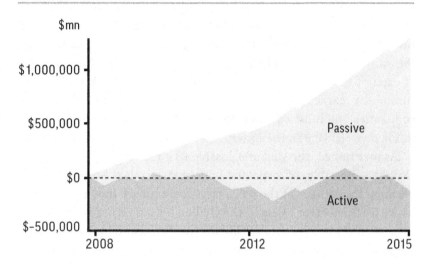

Source: PwC analysis, BofAML, US Equity and US Quantitative Strategy, Valuewalk.com.

Much of the increased assets in ETFs have come at the expense of traditional mutual funds. As regulatory changes increase the care of duty by advisors to a best-interest standard or fiduciary duty, ETF growth may accelerate further because there may be more pressure on advisors to use lower-cost products rather than go through the process of justifying why a higher-cost active product is appropriate. Ironically, if the assets in actively managed funds decrease substantially, this may make it easier for the remaining active managers to outperform because there will be less competition.

In Canada, actively managed equity mutual funds, which try to outperform the market, have historically cost approximately 2.5% of the funds invested annually (recently, mutual fund fees have started to decline). By contrast, most ETFs are passive, meaning the goal is not to outperform the market but rather to provide a return very similar to that of a specific benchmark index. The goal of a traditional ETF is to mirror the return of a benchmark.

If the goal is to closely match the return of an index, it makes sense that the best way to accomplish that is to own the securities that are in the index. Like a mutual fund, an ETF pools the assets of multiple investors and invests according to its mandate. Each share of an ETF represents an undivided interest in the assets owned by the ETF. For example, if you want exposure to the companies in the S&P/TSX Index, you can invest in a single ETF that owns some of each of the companies in the S&P/TSX Index. Stock indices are commonly market-capitalization weighted, meaning that the largest companies and most valuable companies have the largest representation or weighting in the index.

As mentioned, the goal of a passive ETF is to track the return, as closely as possible, of a specific benchmark index. Any difference between the returns of the ETF and its benchmark index is referred to as "tracking error." One of the challenges with ETFs is that investors can never be sure they are buying the ETF near its net asset value; instead, the investor relies on market participants that provide liquidity, such as market makers, to keep the price very close to the net asset value. In periods of volatility, this can be especially challenging.

ETFs can have substantially lower management fees than mutual funds—in some cases as low as 0.1% of assets per year. This makes sense because the investor is not paying for (or receiving) active management and financial advice. Keep in mind, though, that there are costs associated with buying and selling ETFs. But given the proliferation of discount brokerages, trading costs can generally be kept reasonable. Many companies in Canada make ETFs available, including Vanguard, BlackRock (iShares), Bank of Montreal (BMO), and Invesco. Some mutual fund companies have also started to bring ETF products to market. Be aware that costs for ETFs can vary widely depending on the issuer and the specific mandate of the ETF. Like mutual funds, ETFs also have a trading expense ratio that should be considered by investors.

When you purchase an ETF, "look under the hood" to see what underlying assets it holds. Let's say you are looking for a Canadian bond ETF. The most common ETF for the Canadian bond market has an average duration (or sensitivity to interest rates) of seven. This means that for every 1% rise in interest rates, the price of the ETF will decline by about 7%. If you are concerned that interest rates may rise, you may be better off considering a short-term bond ETF or investing with an active mutual fund manager who can manage the duration risk for you. It is also important to remember that the liquidity of an ETF is only as good as the liquidity of its underlying investments. Lastly, make sure you review the costs of the ETF— some have higher relative costs.

Given the popularity of ETFs, there has been a proliferation of new kinds of ETFs, and the innovation of products will continue in the future. Although ETFs are most well-known for being passive investments, today you can find actively managed funds in an ETF structure. Some of the types of ETFs you should be aware of include the following:

- **Leveraged ETFs** aim to provide increased exposure to a certain asset class and deliver double (2×) or triple (3×) the performance of the index they track. There is, for example, an ETF that aims to provide twice the daily return of the price of oil. In theory, it sounds simple—if you think the price of oil will increase, buy an ETF that gives you double the exposure to the movement in oil. If the price of oil rises 5%, the ETF you own should rise 10%. In practice, however, the returns will not closely track double or triple the price of oil if your holding period is more than a day (which it should be—otherwise you are speculating as a day trader). The reason has to do with the way 2× and 3× ETFs are structured and the daily rebalancing required. In my experience, novice investors who try leveraged ETFs are often disappointed with the results.

- **Inverse ETFs** aim to deliver performance that is the opposite of the tracked benchmark's performance. Inverse ETFs are commonly used for downside protection (hedging). For example, if you purchase the Inverse S&P 500 ETF, if the S&P 500 goes down 1%, the ETF should increase by 1%. An inverse ETF can protect your portfolio against a general market decline. In practice, however, as with leveraged ETFs, if your holding period is more than a day, the returns may differ materially from what you expect as a result of daily rebalancing. And as with leveraged ETFs, some investors may be disappointed with the results.

- **Active ETFs** are a hybrid of pure active management and pure passive management. These ETFs will have a benchmark but seek to do better rather than just match the benchmark return. Active ETFs provide the manager with some leeway to differ from the index by underweighting (taking a smaller position than the benchmark index) or overweighting (taking a larger position) in certain sectors or securities within the index. Fees for active ETFs can be higher. The popularity of active ETFs among investors is increasing, as evidenced by the 2016 partnership announcement between Dynamic Funds, a mutual fund company owned by Scotiabank, and BlackRock Canada, an ETF provider. This partnership will give Canadians interested in actively managed ETFs more investment choices.

  Be aware that when you purchase an active ETF, tracking error is a substantial issue. As Sandy McIntyre, Vice Chair of Sentry Investments, put it, "When you get into the world of active ETFs… you have no way of knowing if your price for the fund is in any way representative of the underlying net asset value of that fund. You are trusting the specialists/market makers to ensure that the spread is tight and that you are getting fair value on your trade."

- **Smart beta or intelligent ETFs** can be classified as a hybrid of active and passive management. Think of smart beta ETFs as normal ETFs with one substantial difference—these investments break the link with price and are not weighted by market capitalization (largest companies have the most weighting) but, rather, they use a different weighting methodology. One of the downsides to market-capitalization-weighted ETFs is that, due to the way they are structured, investors end up being overexposed to securities that are overvalued and being underexposed to securities that are undervalued. Common alternative weighting methods include, but are not limited to, equal weighting, whereby every stock has the same representation, and fundamental data such as valuation metrics (how cheap a given stock is or its dividend yield). If the weightings are based on fundamental data, stocks that rank better on the fundamental data would have a greater weight in the ETF. The smart beta approach does have drawbacks, including additional transaction costs. As such, smart beta products also tend to have higher fees than regular ETFs.

Here's a breakdown of some of the key differences between mutual funds and traditional passive ETFs whose goal is to mirror the return of a market benchmark.

Mutual funds	Exchange-traded funds
Diversified	Diversified, but may have many more securities than mutual funds, depending on composition of benchmark index
Active management (beat the market, or match the market with lower risk)	Passive management (mirror or track the market or an index)
Higher fee	Lower fee
Limited transparency (full holdings released once or twice per year)	Increased transparency (index constituents are known)
Minimum hold period 30–90 days (or else penalties can apply)	Trade on an exchange similar to a stock
Higher manager risk	Lower manager risk
Potential for higher turnover	Potential for lower turnover and better tax efficiency

Target Date Funds

Sometimes called a lifecycle fund or age-based fund, a target date fund (TDF) is best thought of as a mutual fund that provides an initial asset allocation and then, as you age and get closer to retirement (the "target date"), it progressively alters the asset allocation so that the asset mix becomes more conservative. For example, if you are 40 years old and plan to retire at age 65, the initial asset allocation would have a significant equity component. As you get closer to retirement, gradually the equity component will decline and the fixed-income investments will increase within the fund. The formula used to determine the rate at which asset allocation of the target date fund changes is often compared to how an aircraft comes in for landing, commonly referred to as the "glide path."

In summary, target date funds are designed to provide a simple investment solution. With a target date fund, it is advisable to "look under the hood" as, for a given target date, funds from different companies can have different allocations, so you really need to know what you are getting exposure to. The other aspect I worry about is that, given how expensive bonds are today, target date funds that are in de-risking mode could be buying bond assets that will fall in value in the future.

Platform-Traded Funds

Another type of investment product that is gaining popularity is called the platform-traded fund (PTF), which has been designed by Invesco Canada for use with fee-based accounts. PTFs allow advisors to effectively buy actively managed Invesco investment products for their clients just as they would purchase an ETF. Think about the PTF as an ETF that only trades once per day. Advisors who are registered as portfolio managers can also "bulk" trade these products, meaning that all their client accounts can be grouped in one block trade (and then the units purchased or sold are allocated appropriately), rather than the advisor having to put in separate buy or sell orders for each client account. The process is more efficient and less costly, allowing clients to have lower management fees, in some cases close to institutional investor rates. The PTF is an innovation and is not yet available on all dealer platforms. However, I expect to see the trend of innovative products such as the PTF gain more traction in the years ahead.

Individual Securities

As an investor, you have the option of purchasing individual stocks and bonds for your investment accounts. If you choose to go this route, be sure you do enough due diligence on prospective investments and focus on buying and holding securities in good-quality companies. I have found that individual investors may have two common misconceptions about purchasing individual securities, particularly stock. The first is reaching for yield—that is, blindly purchasing high-dividend stocks for their income stream; this is especially true in low-interest-rate environments. The challenge with this approach is that dividend yield is not always safe. Sometimes, dividends are unsustainable and are eventually reduced, which most often results in a significant reduction in the stock price and capital loss for investors.

The second common misconception is that price equals value. Many investors make the mistake of believing that a stock with a "low" price (such as $5 per share) is cheap and a stock with a "high" price (say, $100) is expensive. This is not necessarily the case. As mentioned earlier, the value of a stock can be determined only by comparing its selling price with the underlying earnings and cash flow generated by the company. Famed investor Warren Buffett is often quoted as saying, "Price is what you pay; value is what you get."

If you are participating in an initial public offering, be careful— these new securities can carry additional risk. In my experience, the average Canadian investor buying individual stocks would in most cases be better off holding a good-quality mutual fund or ETF. The reasons are threefold. First, investors often do not properly diversify their portfolios, making too-big bets on a few holdings. Second, the temptation of the latest stock tip is sometimes too hard to ignore. Third, it is easy to get caught in the trap of trading excessively and trying to time the market. A good advisor can help you avoid these mistakes and select appropriate investment products for your needs, while also keeping you on track to meet your broader financial goals and objectives.

Other Products

There are many other kinds of products available to investors, but unfortunately it is not possible to cover everything in this book, as much as I would love to. So I'll do the next best thing and draw your attention to other investment products, including closed-end funds, corporate-class funds, principal protected notes, and flow-through shares. If you are looking at using any product other than a regular mutual fund, ETF, or individual security, it is even more important to understand how the product works, the risk involved, the cost, and what assets you are buying. Start by doing an Internet search and then carefully research the risks of the product—or consult with an experienced financial advisor.

> **TAKE NOTE:** If you don't understand how a particular investment works, don't buy it!

Asset Allocation: How Much Do I Put in Each Bucket?

Now that you are familiar with the main asset classes, or buckets, the next step of "investing in buckets" is deciding what percentage of your investments to put in which bucket—this is called asset allocation. Different assets can be combined in an unlimited number of ways to form a portfolio. One of the main benefits of putting your money in more than one bucket is that different asset classes and styles of investing perform differently at different times. From year to year, there can often be a good deal of rotation as asset classes and investment styles go in and out of favour. This is nicely shown by the Callan Periodic Table of Investment Returns for 2015, on the facing page.

The Callan Periodic Table of Investment Returns for 2015

2010	2011	2012	2013	2014	2015
Russell 2000 29.09%	Barclays Agg 7.84%	MSCI Emerging Markets 18.63%	Russell 2000 Growth 43.30%	S&P 500 Growth 14.89%	S&P 500 Growth 5.52%
Barclays Corp High Yield 26.85%	Barclays Corp High Yield 4.98%	Russell 2000 Value 18.05%	Russell 2000 38.82%	S&P 500 13.69%	S&P 500 1.38%
Russell 2000 Value 24.50%	S&P 500 Growth 4.65%	S&P 500 Value 17.68%	Russell 2000 Value 34.52%	S&P 500 Value 12.36%	Barclays Agg 0.55%
MSCI Emerging Markets 19.20%	S&P 500 2.11%	MSCI EAFE 17.32%	S&P 500 Growth 32.75%	Barclays Agg 5.97%	MSCI EAFE -0.81%
Barclays Corp High Yield 15.12%	S&P 500 Value -0.48%	Russell 2000 16.35%	S&P 500 32.39%	Russell 2000 Growth 5.60%	Russell 2000 Growth -1.38%
S&P 500 Value 15.10%	Russell 2000 Growth -2.91%	Barclays Agg 16.00%	S&P 500 Value 31.99%	Russell 2000 4.89%	S&P 500 Value -3.13%
S&P 500 15.06%	Russell 2000 -4.18%	Barclays Corp High Yield 15.81%	MSCI EAFE 22.78%	Russell 2000 Value 4.22%	Russell 2000 -4.41%
S&P 500 Growth 15.05%	Russell 2000 Value -5.50%	S&P 500 Growth 14.61%	Barclays Corp High Yield 7.44%	Barclays Corp High Yield 2.45%	Barclays Corp High Yield -4.47%
MSCI EAFE 7.75%	MSCI EAFE -12.14%	Russell 2000 Growth 14.59%	Barclays Agg -2.02%	MSCI Emerging Markets -1.82%	Russell 2000 Value -7.47%
Barclays Agg 6.54%	MSCI Emerging Markets -18.17%	Barclays Agg 4.21%	MSCI Emerging Markets -2.27%	MSCI EAFE -4.90%	MSCI Emerging Markets -14.60%

Source: www.americancentury.com/content/dam/americancentury/direct/rd/pdf/educational_articles/Periodic_Table.pdf

In a diversified portfolio, when some investments are not performing well, others will pick up the slack for your portfolio. Every asset class marches to its own drum and has a different return-and-risk profile. In the industry, there is a concept called "correlation" that measures the extent to which prices of assets move together. Two assets can be positively correlated (meaning that prices tend to move in the same direction to some extent) or negatively correlated (meaning that prices tend to move in the opposite direction). Be aware that correlations can change. The world is more and more interconnected today, and so different asset classes can sometimes all move in the same direction. There's a saying in the industry, "When the %@$! hits the fan, correlations go to 1!" which means most asset classes move up or down together. Nonetheless, it is important to have assets in your portfolio that usually have different correlations, to reduce overall risk. Tony Davidow, Asset Allocation Strategist at the Schwab Center for Financial Research, has summarized this point nicely: "Having too many highly correlated assets is the equivalent of owning multiple homes in the same neighborhood. If local real estate conditions sour, all of their prices are going to suffer."

Understand that the way you allocate your assets should reflect your risk tolerance as well as your goals, objectives, and time horizon. If you do not know what your risk tolerance is, most advisors have risk tolerance questionnaires that can assist you; many are also available on the Internet. For most investors, the most important question is what percentage of your assets to put in cash, bonds, stocks, and other (alternative) investments. Your objective should be to have a portfolio that provides the highest level of return with the least risk—that is the sweet spot you should aim for.

Having the right asset allocation is one of the most important parts of the investment process, but there is no one-size-fits-all approach. A financial advisor will help you design a portfolio that is expected to provide the best return for the level of risk appropriate for you given your financial situation, individual risk tolerance, time horizon, and personal goals and objectives. But it is also critical that you know yourself. In thinking about risk, for example, know that though equities provide higher returns over time, they can be highly variable in the short term. If you will lose sleep over your portfolio temporarily moving up or down 10%–15% or more, a portfolio consisting entirely of equities may not be right for you.

Time horizon describes how long you have before you need to start drawing on your investments. If you are 40 years old and saving for retirement, you will likely have about 25 years before you need the money; you should therefore be able to tolerate market fluctuations more easily. But if you are retiring in five years, you may not want to take as much risk. Finally, your goals and objectives also factor in to the correct asset allocation for your portfolio. For example, if you earn a higher income and plan to live a modest lifestyle during retirement, you may be able to take less risk in your portfolio with lower equity exposure because you may not need a very high investment return to achieve your goals. Why take risk you don't have to? But if you are earning a modest income and want to at least maintain (or even somewhat enhance) your lifestyle in retirement, you may need to either modify your lifestyle goals, save more, or take more risk with existing investments by having higher equity exposure.

In the industry, there has historically been a rule of thumb about asset allocation. It suggests that, as a ballpark estimate, your portfolio should have equity exposure of 100% minus your age, with the remainder in bonds (fixed income). So if you're 40, your portfolio should be made up of 60% equities and 40% bonds. Recently, some have argued that this rule of thumb is outdated given that interest rates and returns available from fixed-income markets are so low, and people are living much longer. There have been suggestions that the new rule of thumb for equity asset allocation should be more like 110% minus your age, or even 120% minus your age. These guidelines should be used only as starting points for thinking about your asset allocation. Your risk tolerance and personal goals and objectives are far more important for determining the right asset allocation.

If you work with an advisor, he or she will be able to take you through a questionnaire to help determine the most appropriate

asset allocation for you. If you choose to manage your own invest-
ments, several good tools are available online (e.g., The Vanguard
Group's Investor Questionnaire or Charles Schwab Corporation's
Investor Profile Questionnaire).

....

➤ **TAKE NOTE:** There is no one-size-fits-all approach to asset allocation.
Make sure your asset allocation truly reflects your financial goals and risk
tolerance.

....

Basic Investment Principles

Can You Do Better Than Typical Investors?

We know that over time, markets rise in value as the economy grows
and the companies within the economy increase their earnings. If
investors were well diversified and stayed invested, we would expect
their portfolios to perform satisfactorily over the long term. But they
don't. Richard Bernstein of Richard Bernstein Advisors in New York
City recently did a study that compared the performance of the
"average investor" in the United States with the performance of a
wide variety of asset classes over a 20-year period. Factors including
total mutual fund sales, redemptions, and switches, along with the
returns of various asset classes, were used to determine the returns
of the average investor. The results of the study revealed that the
average investor performed worse than all but three of more than
40 asset classes. In addition, the average investor performed only
slightly better than inflation. While this study does not examine
the returns experienced by Canadian investors, given that human
behavioural tendencies typically do not change from country to
country, I would expect that the experience of the Canadian investor is similar.

Asset Class Returns vs. the "Average Investor"

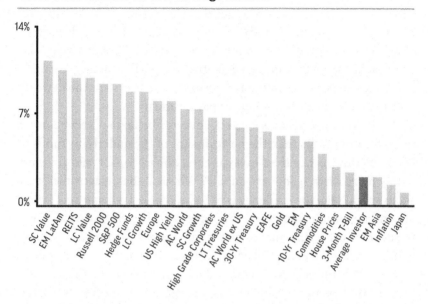

20 years annualized (12/31/1993–12/31/2013). *Richard Bernstein Advisors LLC.,*
Bloomberg, MSCI, *Standard & Poor's, Russell,* HFRI, *BofA Merrill Lynch, Dalbar,*
FHFA, FRB, FTSE.

In examining the reasons for the average investor's underperformance, Bernstein talks about investors making poorly timed asset allocation decisions; that is, investors consistently bought assets that were overvalued and sold assets that were unvalued—they did not buy low and sell high, as they should have, but instead did the opposite. Another organization, DALBAR, based in Boston, completes an annual study that measures the way investor behaviour related to buying, selling, and switching out of mutual funds affects returns. DALBAR's studies have repeatedly shown that the return average investors achieve is less than that of the mutual funds in which they invest. This is because investors are often irrational and buy and sell at exactly the wrong time, leading to underperformance. Based on DALBAR's 2014 study, the 20-year annualized return of the S&P 500 was 9.9%, but the average investor in equity mutual funds earned a 20-year annualized return of only 5.2%. So if you had invested $100,000 in the S&P 500 and earned an annual return of 9.9% for

20 years, your investment would be worth $660,620. For the typical investor who earned an average annualized return of 5.2%, after 20 years the investments would be worth $275,620. This is a difference of $385,000—a staggering amount. While some have criticized the DALBAR study methodology, suggesting the performance gap can be overstated depending on the timing of dollars invested, the key concept is that investor behaviour impacts returns.

As the DALBAR studies suggest, investor behaviour can be more important to results than the performance of the underlying funds is. For everything other than investments, don't people typically want to buy more when things are on sale? When clothes, electronics, and shoes are on sale, the tendency is to buy more. But when investments are on sale, people don't have this same tendency. In my experience, the average investor wants to invest when prices are up because they believe the asset's price will go up further. But when prices go down, fear prevents them from buying and in many cases leads them to sell because they're afraid they'll lose more money. This directly relates to investor psychology.

Behavioural Finance

Based on my personal investing experience and from working with my clients, I am absolutely convinced that one of the most important factors that will determine your investment success is your behaviour: your personal rate of return over time will be directly influenced by how well you control your emotions. All of us are human and subject to biases of various types. Behavioural finance is an emerging field that studies how and why people make irrational decisions when it comes to their finances.

One of the most common biases humans experience is overconfidence. As an example, a high percentage of drivers often rate themselves as above average even though testing shows otherwise. Overconfident investors overtrade too frequently and are prone to experience disappointing results. Investors will also succumb to confirmation basis—they will look for evidence that agrees with their view and ignore opposing points of view.

As an investor, to be successful you really need to not only understand how emotions can impact results, but you must also learn to control your own emotions, which is easier said than done. Below is one of the best graphical depictions I have come across that shows the myriad of emotions investors have to deal with.

Investor Emotion, Bias, and Decision-Making

Source: Dynamic Funds

Managing Your Emotions

When it comes to money, the two primary emotions that come into play are fear and greed. When a security begins to decline in value, fear of being wrong and losing money sets in and the typical investor is afraid to buy (even if the security is on sale) or is prone to sell to avoid further loss. Conversely, when a security increases in value, it feels great to be making money and greed kicks in, leading some investors to buy more even though the security may be fundamentally expensive. Giving in to emotions can cause investors to do exactly the wrong thing at exactly the wrong time. Famed investor Howard Marks has said "the discipline which is most important in investing is not accounting or economics, but psychology." The cycle of investing emotions is shown in the diagram on the next page.

The Cycle of Investing Emotions

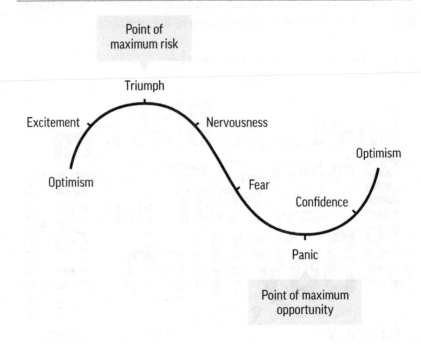

Point of
maximum risk

Triumph

Excitement   Nervousness

Optimism

Optimism   Fear

Confidence

Panic

Point of maximum
opportunity

For the average investor, emotions can be a significant hindrance to success. When the stock markets are roaring up and the news is rosy, you may be lulled into thinking the trend will continue and therefore buy when prices are high. Likewise, when the front page is dominated by the latest doom-and-gloom story, you might feel fearful and tired of watching the value of your retirement savings go down and be tempted to throw in the towel and sell when prices are low.

Barry Ritholtz, who runs a popular financial blog called The Big Picture, wrote a wonderful article in the *Washington Post* titled "Brexit happens. Know your investment plan, and stick to it." This article was in response to market reactions following the outcome of the 2016 Brexit vote, when the UK voted to leave the European Union. For a few days after the results, global stock markets sank, but then rebounded sharply thereafter. In his article, Ritholtz presents a list of important points that investors should remember when there is turmoil in the market, emphasizing that "markets surge and sell off. This is the ordinary course of events." He also talks about the difficulty of forecasting as the "world is filled with random outcomes, and the future is inherently unknown and unknowable." In investing, I agree entirely when Ritholtz says, "boring, steady portfolios can withstand about anything you throw at them" and "emotional reactions are bad for your portfolios." Remember, when it comes to investing, boring is good. The article emphasizes the importance of not only having a plan, but also having the discipline to stick with it. Let's examine how minimizing emotional reactions and sticking to a plan are critical to long-term financial success.

During the financial crisis of 2007-08, global stock markets declined significantly. Watching your investments decline is exceedingly difficult, and for investors at that time, future returns varied widely depending on how individuals handled their fear. I can best illustrate this with real client stories.

In January 2008 (before the Great Recession began), James and Kathy had identical portfolios of $1 million invested in a combination of high-quality equity mutual funds and individual securities. Both James and Kathy were retired and receiving pension income supplemented by dividends from their portfolios. Even though the market was declining, their investments were still generating the income they needed to live on.

James monitored the value of his investments daily and became concerned when the market began to drop in the fall of 2008. When the market continued to decline in 2009, he spent more and more of his day watching various business channels on television to hear what the experts were saying. There was no optimism that the market would come back. When his portfolio was down 20%, James called his financial advisor to discuss the situation. His advisor reassured him that his portfolio consisted of high-quality assets and that, even though the portfolio's market value had declined, there had been no change to the income it was generating. The advisor told James she was confident the markets would eventually come back and she strongly suggested that he ignore the doom-and-gloom media reports and focus on the long term. James agreed.

Nonetheless, he couldn't help monitoring the value of his portfolio daily. Several weeks later, the portfolio was down over 30%. James couldn't take it anymore. He called his advisor and asked her to sell all of his investments. The advisor had another discussion with James about emotions, and how selling now might be the wrong decision. But James insisted, and his investments were sold on March 10, 2009—the day the market bottomed. After he sold his investments, his portfolio consisted of $680,000 in cash. James was not comfortable reinvesting for quite some time. On June 1, 2011, he finally called his advisor, who reinvested the cash into a similar portfolio. On December 31, 2014, James's portfolio was worth $850,000.

In 2009, Kathy was aware that the value of her investments had dropped by about 20%. She was not overly concerned, however, because her portfolio continued to provide her with the income she needed to live on. She was confident her advisor was looking after her best interests and she remembered that her advisor had recommended that she ignore the noise and focus on the long term. She'd had a brief conversation with her advisor about the portfolio and agreed with the advisor's recommendation to stay invested. Several weeks later, the market bottomed and Kathy's investments started to regain value. By the end of 2014, Kathy's portfolio was worth $1.3 million. By better controlling her emotions and staying invested, Kathy had over $400,000 more in her portfolio than James, and the ongoing income she received from her investments never changed.

When you look at your portfolio and feel sick to your stomach due to the paper losses you see, that is usually the time to buy quality stocks. When the media is euphoric and you see magazine covers predicting never-ending investment gains or you hear taxi drivers talking about the latest stock idea, it is probably a good time to take some risk off the table and reduce your exposure. For those of you who are *Seinfeld* fans, you may remember an episode where George did the exact opposite of what he normally would do, and he ended up with far better outcomes. In investing, the same concept often applies and is called being "contrarian."

....

➤ **TAKE NOTE:** Being able to control your emotions is an important factor
in long-term investment success. You need to stick with your long-term
plan and avoid reacting to headlines.

....

Successful investing is hard, but it doesn't require genius. In fact,
Warren Buffett once quipped, "Success in investing doesn't correlate
with IQ." As much as anything else, successful investing requires
something rare: the ability to identify and overcome one's own psy-
chological weaknesses. Jonathan Clements once wrote in the *Wall
Street Journal*, "If you want to see the greatest threat to your financial future, go home and take a look in the mirror." Controlling your
emotions and avoiding self-destructive behaviour can be so much
easier with an advisor.

One of the key roles of an advisor is to act as a behavioural coach
and help clients manage their emotions and prevent them from making the wrong decision at the wrong time. The human brain is not
wired to deal effectively with the emotional side of investing. That's
why it is so important to have an advisor who can keep you calm and
focused on your long-term investment plan when the markets are
dropping and you want to sell, or when the markets are rising too far,
too fast and you are tempted to buy more than you should.

That said, over the years I have witnessed many investors do
astoundingly well just by keeping it simple, being well-diversified,
and investing regularly. If you don't want to hire a financial advisor,
I strongly believe that if you are disciplined and manage your emotions effectively, you will greatly enhance your probability of success.

Some investors understand the importance of having a long-term
investment strategy with annual rebalancing of asset classes but still
want to feel the adrenaline rush (or despair) of trading stocks. Some
want to follow the markets to try to generate profits. The reality is
that while this is certainly possible, it is difficult unless you dedicate
several hours every week to studying the financial markets and individual companies. Your returns will be directly correlated to the time
you are able to put toward selecting investments and to your ability
to control your emotions.

If you find yourself in this camp, my advice would be to invest your serious long-term money through a financial advisor who can keep you focused on obtaining good long-term results. Then put aside some risk capital (money you can afford to lose without negatively affecting your lifestyle) and open a discount brokerage account. This section covers some tips that will be key to your success.

....

➤ **TAKE NOTE:** Many investors achieve poor investment results because they react emotionally and buy high and sell low. A competent advisor will keep you focused on your long-term investment plan in good economic times and bad.

....

Invest—Do Not Speculate

For investors, distinguishing between speculating and investing can be difficult, but it doesn't have to be. In my experience, all forms of speculation have two features: attempting to predict and profit from short-term (days or weeks) movement in a stock or other investment, and taking on too much risk by purchasing an investment with a high-potential reward but also a high-potential risk.

Humans by nature are risk-seekers and many have difficulty resisting the opportunity to make a quick profit in the market. Maybe you got a stock tip from a friend or an idea from an expert on a business-themed TV program that sounds like a sure thing. So you go for it. If you're lucky, maybe it will work once, twice, or even several times, but in the long run, the greatest probability is that you will lose your hard-earned money. Those who blindly follow experts on TV should know that, at times, what an expert says on TV can be diametrically opposed to what they are doing personally. Keep that in mind. A senior executive from a well-known Canadian institutional investment manager once told me, "Whenever I'm on TV, I usually recommend a company that I'm selling." My message is, simply, take what you hear on TV with a grain of salt.

The best course of action to maximize the probability of being a successful investor in the long term is as follows:

- **Keep it simple.** Have a long-term asset allocation plan and stick to it, rebalancing your portfolio at least annually. This will force you to sell some of the investments that have increased in value and buy some of the investments that have decreased in value (rebalancing forces you to buy low and sell high). Do not buy stocks based on tips from acquaintances—do your own research.

- **Invest regularly and be patient.** Make regular contributions to your investments (this is also known as "dollar-cost averaging," which means you are averaging your cost over time because you're buying a certain dollar amount each month). Excessive trading usually detracts from performance and reduces tax efficiency.

- **Invest in quality.** Avoid concept stocks that only have a hope of revenue and earnings in the future. Instead, focus on buying the stock of companies that are well-established, have revenue and earnings streams, have reasonable debt levels, pay and grow dividends to shareholders, and can grow their business in most economic environments. I call this the GDQ™ approach to investing—if this sounds familiar, you are probably thinking about GDP, which relates to economic growth.

GDQ™ Investment Approach

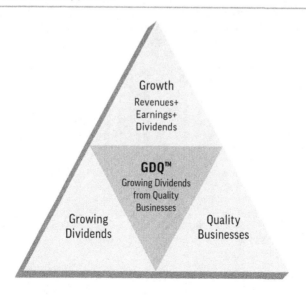

I would like to emphasize that dividends are a key component of investment returns, especially when reinvested on a regular basis. Reinvesting dividends is a form of dollar-cost averaging, allowing you to invest regularly at the prevailing market prices. Brian Belski, Chief Investment Strategist of BMO Capital Markets, made the following key conclusions in a 2016 research note titled *Elect Dividend Growth*:

- Dividend Growth Provides Superior Longer-Term Results,
- Dividend Growth Is Not Necessarily Just a "Defensive" Strategy, and
- Higher Interest Rates Are Not an Impediment for Dividend Growth.

In addition, Belski also examined yearly total returns of the S&P 500 going back to 1990, using different monthly end points rather than just a January and December year-end (this is referred to as a rolling monthly one-year return). His analysis showed that dividend growth investment strategies have tended to outperform in weak environments and still participate in up markets, although not as strongly. In other words, dividend growth protects on the downside, while also participating on the upside. This is illustrated in the graph below. (Note: dividend growth is not the same as just owning high-dividend-paying stocks—the growth is important!)

Dividend Growth Performance

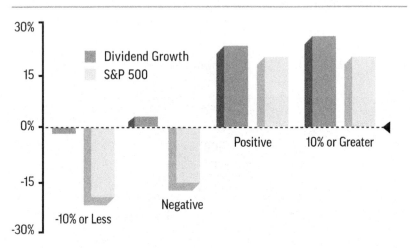

Rolling monthly 1-year S&P 500 total return. *Source: BMO Capital Markets*

If you insist on trading actively, or even speculating, before doing anything, educate yourself thoroughly by reading books such as Alexander Elder's *Trading for a Living*. When you get into active trading, do not expect to get rich fast—there are no shortcuts. Instead, focus on controlling your risk and be willing to accept that you will probably lose money before you make money.

In general, when you are buying a stock, keep in mind the following:

- **Make sure the valuation of the stock is reasonable.** Owning a stock gives you a right to a portion of the future earnings stream of the company. Your return will be largely based on the price you pay. Have some idea what type of a multiple of the company's earnings or cash flow you are paying, and how fast the company is growing its earnings or cash flow.

- **Check the stock's average daily volume.** The higher the average number of shares traded every day, the better. Higher volume means it will be easier for you to buy the shares (and eventually sell them).

- **Put in the right kind of order.** There are two main types of orders—limit orders and market orders. For the vast majority of stocks, you should put in a limit order, which requires you to specify the maximum price you are willing to pay. If you are buying shares in a very large, stable, well-known company, it is acceptable to put in a "market" order, which is the current price the shares are trading at in the market.

- **Avoid using stop-losses.** Some people try to protect profits or limit losses by putting in a sell order if the stock drops to a specific price. For example, assume you purchased 100 shares of ABC Inc. at $5. You are only prepared to lose 20%, so you put in a sell order that gets triggered if the shares fall to $4. Because markets and stock prices fluctuate, and sometimes in an exaggerated way if macroeconomic events occur, having a stop-loss order could result in your stock dropping in price and being sold (once the stop-loss is triggered) because of a short-term fluctuation—the stock could then quickly rebound back above the price at which you sold it.

- **Avoid the noise.** One of the best things you can do is tune out short-term price fluctuations. Prices move up and down for various reasons not related to the fundamental strength of your investment. For example, large institutional investors rebalancing their portfolios can cause a stock to drop temporarily. If you have done your research and have conviction in your investment, stick with it. Give it time to work out. I have learned this the hard way myself.

....

➤ **TAKE NOTE:** If you don't have the time to devote to doing your own investing, it is best to leave it to a professional.

....

➤ **TAKE NOTE:** If you want to speculate, set aside some risk capital you can afford to lose and leave your serious money in good-quality, long-term investments.

....

Avoid Timing the Market

The natural tendency for humans to take risks in the hopes of obtaining quick rewards explains why the temptation to time the market is so high. Why be patient, market timers think, and hope to achieve good long-term results when you could simply buy low and sell high every time? It sounds great in theory, but the problem is that almost nobody can time or beat the market consistently. If the best professionals cannot time the market consistently, do not make the mistake of expecting that you or your advisor can time the market. Peter Lynch, a legendary investor and author, once commented about temporary drops in the market, which are often referred to as corrections. Said Lynch, "Far more money has been lost by investors preparing for corrections or trying to anticipate corrections than has been lost in the corrections themselves."

You may be wondering whether you should be invested in the stock market at all, if you shouldn't bother trying to buy low and sell high. If you have a longer horizon, the answer, unequivocally, is yes, you should be invested in the market. Over time, as the economy grows, markets go up. In between, however, there is volatility—that is a fact of life. As David Rosenberg, chief economist and strategist at Gluskin Sheff + Associates in Toronto, says, "What really counts is time in the market, not timing the market." Markets go up and down for a wide variety of reasons. Sometimes the change is related to the economy, but many times it is for some other reason, such as a geopolitical event (e.g., Russia invading Ukraine), that may have nothing to do with the fundamentals of the economy. What causes the market to drop in these cases is uncertainty. As a rule, investors do not like uncertainty and so they may act impulsively, selling first and asking questions later. Don't let yourself fall into this trap. Stick to your long-term plan.

The challenge with trying to time the market and go to cash is that you have to be right not only once, but twice. Even if you do get lucky and successfully time the market by selling at the short-term top, would you be able to time the bottom and buy back in? It's unlikely. And chances are that as prices drop, fear may prevent you from buying because prices may drop even more. You will end up missing some of the best "up" days in the market, which will significantly affect your returns.

American finance firm J.P. Morgan Asset Management did a study that showed the dramatic difference in returns when an investor missed some of the best days in the market. The study examined the s&p 500 returns between 1993 and 2013. As the chart on the next page shows, missing the 10 best days of the market resulted in a 5.49% annualized return and missing the best 30 days resulted in an annualized return of 0.91%. If an investor missed even more of the market's best days, the results only got worse. But compare those results with the annualized return of 9.22% achieved by just staying invested in the s&p 500 over the entire 20-year period. The difference is astounding.

Missing the Best Days of the Market Is Costly

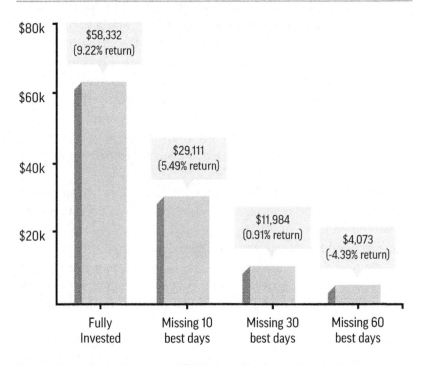

The performance of $10,000 fully invested in the S&P 500, Dec. 31, 1993–Dec. 31, 2013, compared with missing some of the market's best days. *Source: Adapted from J.P. Morgan Asset Management*

Timing the market consistently is exceedingly difficult, and the probability of an investor getting out at the top and having the courage to get back in after a big price decline is miniscule. Instead, invest regularly, diversify, and *stay* invested.

Save Early, Save Often, and Live within Your Means

The best way to dramatically increase the probability of meeting your financial and retirement goals is simply to live within or even below your means. Unfortunately, this is often difficult. Society today is focused on instant gratification. Every dollar you earn can be put toward consuming today, saving for future consumption, or paying off debt. Over the years, I have met many couples who, although in their 60s, still have mortgages and have little or no savings because they lived beyond their means their entire lives. If you are in this situation, you will likely need to keep working, drastically reduce your retirement-lifestyle expectations, or possibly rely on your family for help. Many retired couples I have talked to want to help their kids financially, but they want to see the benefits of their generosity rather than have the children receive an inheritance later. If you feel this way, just be careful to make sure the "helping" does not get out of hand, to the point where your own retirement is jeopardized.

Living within your means has different definitions for different people, but for me, this concept has two components. The first is buying what you can afford, or less than you can afford, and saving the excess. If you and your spouse can afford a $500,000 home but spend $450,000, you have money to save or you can pay down your mortgage sooner, which will save thousands of dollars in interest. The second component of living within your means is being financially prudent and avoiding excess debt. Do not fall into the trap of having to keep up with the Joneses or always having to have the latest car, best vacation, or top of the line electronics. Yes, you should enjoy life, but you can do that and be fiscally prudent at the same time. Every dollar you don't spend today is another dollar you can invest, grow, and then spend during retirement. David Chilton's books *The Wealthy Barber* and *The Wealthy Barber Returns* are timeless classics that discuss these principles and much more.

If you get stuck in the expensive-lifestyle trap, financial stress is likely to result. Not only that, but you will also have less financial flexibility to deal with the roadblocks life may throw at you. For example, what happens if you suddenly lose your job and can't find work for six months or more? If you live within or below your means, you will have a financial buffer. That buffer can help you through tough times or increase your savings to enable you to retire earlier and live the life you want.

Do you know what your lifestyle truly costs and what your means are? If not, you are not alone. In my experience, most people don't know. That is why budgeting is so important. If you do not already budget, start today! Many good online tools are available that will track your spending easily. Mint.com is a particularly good one. Your aim should be to take a good, hard look at what you spend every month and then think about whether any of those expenses are unnecessary. Reflect on whether any unnecessary expenses add value, meaning, or happiness to your life. If not, cut them!

The Power of Compounding

Albert Einstein is believed to have said that compound interest is the most powerful force in the universe. Simply put, compounding is interest (or dividends) earning interest (or dividends). The benefits of saving early and often, and living within your means, are magnified by compounding. But the negative effects of not taking these actions are multiplied by compounding too, as the case studies below illustrate:

CASE STUDY 1: GOOD COMPOUNDING

Daniella is 22 and recently graduated from university with an engineering degree. She started a full-time job and was able to invest $1,000 per month in a mutual fund focused on buying companies that pay and grow dividends over time. The investment provides a dividend of 3%, which is reinvested automatically. Assuming the total return of the mutual fund is 7% per year (net of investment costs), and Daniella continues to invest $1,000 per month, her account will be valued as follows in the future:

- 5 years: $71,592
- 10 years: $173,084
- 20 years: $520,927

CASE STUDY 2: BAD COMPOUNDING

Henri, 25, is working as a heavy-duty mechanic. He earns a decent income but is an impulsive spender, often buying more than he can really afford. His credit card debt is $10,000 and he can afford only minimum monthly payments. Henri does not follow his financial advisor's recommendation to stop overspending and continues to add $500 per month to his credit card balance while only making the minimum payments each month. The interest rate on the card is 18% per year and the minimum payment is 2% (currently $200 per month). This is what Henri's credit card debt will look like in the future:

- Monthly minimum payment:
  In 5 years: $789
  In 10 years: $1,389
  In 20 years: $2,589

- Total balance:
  In 5 years: $39,750
  In 10 years: $69,600
  In 20 years: $129,300

To paraphrase Albert Einstein: He who understands interest, earns it; he who does not understand interest, pays it.

In summary, keep these key points about compounding in mind:

- Compounding can work for everyone.
- Compounding can be your friend or enemy. If you are a saver, it is your friend; if you are in debt, it is your enemy.
- Use time to your advantage. The longer money compounds, the more it grows. It is wise to start saving and investing as soon as you can.
- Make regular monthly contributions. If you do not need the money your investment accounts earn, have it reinvested automatically. Have a plan to pay down your debt!

....

➤ **TAKE NOTE:** The best way to achieve financial success and the retirement you want is to live within your means. Doing so will also provide a financial buffer to deal with life's unexpected challenges.

....

Protect against Inflation

If compound interest is the most powerful force in the universe, then inflation is one of the most destructive. It is critical for investors to understand not only inflation, but also the negative impact it may have on your retirement lifestyle. Inflation is simply the annual rate at which the price for goods and services (the cost of living) rises.

In the past, inflation has varied substantially from just above 0% to upward of 12% in the early 1980s. In general, since the 1990s, inflation has been relatively modest, often between 2% and 3%, but this period of lower inflation will likely not last indefinitely. A 2% inflation rate means that in 20 years, $1 will purchase as much as 67¢ does today.

Most investors focus on the overall return of their portfolio before inflation—this is known as the "nominal" rate of return. Nominal returns are important, but what is more important is your return after factoring in inflation—the "real" rate of a return. If your investment portfolio returned 4% (nominal rate) and inflation was 5%, your real rate of return is –1%, which means you are further behind in terms of purchasing power. According to the Bank of Canada's online inflation calculator, a basket of goods and services that cost $100 in the year 2000 would cost $134.48 in 2016. As an investor, your goal should be to maintain or ideally increase your purchasing power by keeping ahead of inflation. If you retire and have planned such that all of your income will come from fixed-income investments, you may face a lower quality of life over time as your dollars no longer stretch as far.

How can you protect yourself against inflation? To answer this question, let's review what we know about the major asset classes.

- **Bonds.** If you purchased a $1,000 10-year bond with an annual interest rate of 5%, and inflation averages 3%, in 10 years when you get your $1,000 principal back, it will only be able to buy $745 in goods and services (after adjusting for inflation), which is much less than the $1,000 of goods and services it bought when you purchased the bond originally. In addition, the interest payment will be lower year by year in inflation-adjusted terms—for example, each year the $50 in interest you receive from that bond will buy fewer and fewer loaves of bread. Certain types of bonds offer better inflation protection, including floating-rate bonds, real return bonds, and inflation-linked bonds, but these products are more complex, so talk to your advisor to make sure you understand what you are getting into. But, generally, bonds do not offer much inflation protection.

- **Stocks.** Historically, stocks have provided better returns after inflation than bonds over the long term. One of the reasons is that companies, especially those in stable businesses, can raise prices in inflationary environments. For example, businesses such as cable and telephone companies have the power to raise prices. In addition, companies that pay dividends can increase those dividends, providing investors with a growing (rather than a fixed) income stream. Keep in mind that, over the short term, stocks are volatile and as an asset class can react negatively to significant increases in interest rates.

- **Alternative assets.** Real assets (sometimes referred to as "hard" assets—things you can touch and feel, such as real estate, oil, gold, and timber) have historically provided investors with some inflation protection, so these assets do have a role in a portfolio.

   As a general rule, it is important to have some inflation protection while saving for retirement and even during retirement. Equities and alternative assets can fulfill this role. The amount of exposure you should have to these asset classes depends on many variables, including your risk tolerance.

➤ **TAKE NOTE:** Inflation is the investor's enemy. Make sure you have inflation protection in your portfolio.

Invest Tax Efficiently

Another important consideration when it comes to your investments is taxation. Different accounts and different investments are taxed differently. When you invest, you can have two different types of accounts, non-registered and registered. A non-registered account is sometimes referred to as a cash, or open, account. Registered accounts have unique tax consequences and government regulations regarding their use—for example, they may have limits on or rules for contributions and withdrawals. Registered accounts include the following:

- Registered Retirement Savings Plan (RRSP)
- Registered Retirement Income Fund (RRIF)

- Tax-Free Savings Account (TFSA)
- Registered Education Savings Plan (RESP)
- Locked-In Retirement Account (LIRA)
- Life Income Fund (LIF)

As an investor, your goal should be to maximize your after-tax returns. There are three types of investment income you can earn: interest, dividends, and capital gains. For the purposes of this discussion, we will examine Canadian public market investments. Foreign and private investments are taxed based on similar principles, but you should consult your tax advisor for more information on these. In the public markets, each of type of investment income is taxed in a specific manner, as indicated in the chart below:

Type of income	Applicable investment	Tax efficiency
Interest income	Bank accounts, money-market funds, GICs, bonds, mortgages	Low
Dividends	Equities (individual, fund, or ETF)	Medium
Capital gains	Equities, Bonds (individual, fund, or ETF)	High

Interest income is earned on fixed-income investments. Any investment that carries an interest rate is considered to be paying you interest income. Investments such as cash in bank accounts, GICs, and bonds all pay interest income, which is taxed at your normal marginal tax rate. Effectively, this is the same tax rate that applies to every additional dollar of employment income you earn.

Dividend income is earned on equities or stocks (common and preferred shares). For example, assume you just purchased one hundred shares of Bank of Montreal at $50 per share for a total investment of $5,000. At the time of purchase, the income stream (dividend yield) from the shares was 4%. Each year, you could expect to receive $5,000 × 4%, or $200, in dividends. Because these dividends come from a publicly traded Canadian corporation, they are considered to be "eligible" dividends and receive preferential tax treatment, making dividends more tax-efficient than interest income.

Capital gains income is earned when an investment is sold for more than the original purchase price. The reverse is called a capital loss. In the public markets, capital gains income applies to any investment (stocks, bonds, mutual funds, etc.) that was sold for a profit. Tax rules could change in the future, but in 2016, capital gains were the most tax-efficient relating to interest income and dividends.

Now let's turn our attention to ways of minimizing these taxes. As an investor, there are several different tax levers you can control. The first is the type of income you receive. As long as you have a reasonably long time horizon and can withstand the up and down movements of the market, try to minimize the amount of interest income you earn. This applies especially to excess cash in bank accounts that you have no plans to use in the short term. It is always a good idea to keep a cash reserve of three to six months of expenses, and then invest the rest according to your long-term asset allocation plan, which should include some exposure to dividends and capital gains income, which receive preferential tax treatment.

The second lever in tax-efficient investing is deferring capital gains. Over the long run, buying shares in outstanding businesses and reinvesting dividends to take advantage of the power of compounding is a great way of generating wealth. By doing this, not only will you defer capital gains taxes and have more of your money working for you, but you could also save on transaction costs. Dividend reinvestment plans, also known as DRIPs, are a great way of doing this.

The third lever is controlling from where you take your income. One of the most important roles of your advisor, as you get into retirement, is to help you solve the retirement-income puzzle. Before retiring, you probably had one or two different regular paycheques. When you retire, you may have four or five different sources from which you can draw money, such a cash account, TFSA account, RRSP or RRIF account, LIRA or LIF account, rental property, and so on. Each of these sources of income is a piece of the retirement puzzle. A good advisor can help to put the puzzle together and figure out how best to draw your income (how much and from which account) to make it the most tax-effective so that you can pay the least tax possible and maintain government benefits.

A wonderful book discussing this topic is Daryl Diamond's *Your Retirement Income Blueprint: A Six-Step Plan to Design and Build a Secure Retirement*. Diamond talks about the stark differences between accumulation of assets in your working years and decumulation of assets in retirement. He emphasizes the unique nature of every retirement scenario, claiming that "planning retirement income is a very different art and science than planning the accumulation of assets, and there are few advisors who are proficient in it."

> **TAKE NOTE:** If you purchase mutual fund investments or other investment products near the end of the year, you may wind up paying taxes on income and capital gains generated by the investment during the year, even though you held it for only a short period. Be aware of this.

> **TAKE NOTE:** Tax-efficient retirement income planning is an art and a science.

Managing Investment Risk

The late American economist Benjamin Graham (known as the "father of value investing") once said, "The essence of portfolio management is the management of risks, not the management of returns." When it comes to investing, I am a strong believer in understanding the risks of your investments and taking steps to mitigate risk where possible. Earlier in the book, I referred to the analogy of tennis and making "unforced errors" when investing. In my experience, most investors make far too many unforced errors, many of which result in significant investment losses that were avoidable. Over the years I have found there are several common unforced errors that individual investors often make, and in this section I will identify the actions you can take to avoid them.

Beware of the "G" Word

The "G" word is "guarantee." I cannot count the number of stories I've heard from investors about investments that were supposedly guaranteed but are now worthless. When you invest, you are taking a risk in the hopes of earning an adequate return. One of the basic principles in investing is that to get a return, you need to take risk. There are very few investments where your principal is guaranteed, the most common being GICs and cash. And in the world of investment products, returns on guaranteed investments depend on interest rates, which in the 2010s are very low—low risk, low reward.

If you hear about an opportunity that is "guaranteed," compare the predicted return of that investment with current GIC rates of the same maturity. GIC rates should give you some idea of what type of return would be appropriate for a guaranteed investment. Say you are offered a five-year investment opportunity to lend money to a real estate project (secured by the property) with a guaranteed annual return of 10%. Find out what the current annual interest rate is for five-year GICs from any major bank (it might be 3%) and compare the two investments. On one hand, you could invest in a guaranteed five-year bank GIC providing a 3% return; on the other hand, you could lend money to a real estate project for five years with a guaranteed annual interest rate of 10%. If both investments are truly guaranteed and have a similar risk profile, the returns offered should be approximately the same. But, in this case, the returns of the two investments are not even close. Your conclusion could be that there is likely more risk in the real estate investment opportunity, meaning it may not be guaranteed. That doesn't mean it's necessarily a bad investment—it might turn out to be great. You just need to understand what you are investing in and the true risk involved.

....

➤ **TAKE NOTE:** Few investments are truly guaranteed. If an investment is described as guaranteed, investigate further and ask questions. One smell test is to see if it offers a potential return greater than that of a GIC of the same term. If it does, be careful.

....

Avoid Permanent Capital Loss and Fraud

If it sounds too good to be true, it probably is. You've heard it before, no doubt more than once. When it comes to investing, it is a simple, easy-to-follow principle. But what *is* too good to be true? Over the long term, public stock markets have historically returned 8%–9% annually. There is a lot of lumpiness to those returns, however; some years are better and some are worse. Whenever you evaluate a potential investment, it's a good idea to compare its risk-and-return profile with the public stock markets.

Every now and then we read stories in the paper about how some investors have been victims of fraud. How does that happen? Simply put, the investor gets caught up in the emotion of making a "no-brainer" investment with great returns and doesn't see the red flags. In other words, the investor sees the potential return but not the risk. Remember that with potential return always comes potential risk.

How can you avoid becoming a victim of investment fraud? The U.S. Securities and Exchange Commission has a webpage dedicated to providing information to help investors to protect themselves from fraud, and the Ontario Securities Commission has also developed a list of questions to alert investors to situations where the probability of fraud is high. I have summarized their suggestions for avoiding fraud below, along with some of my own. Watch for these red flags:

- **The investment is presented as having high return potential with minimal risk.** Risk and return always go hand in hand. It doesn't matter what it is; if there is high return potential and little or no risk, something is likely wrong. If you hear the word "guaranteed," be very cautious.

- **The investment's return history graph shows very little fluctuation, instead showing a consistent increase in value over time.** If the graph goes up in a straight line at a 45° angle, like this: /, be cautious—the value of very few, if any, investments go up in a straight line. There should generally be some zigging and zagging. Market conditions change continually and all investment values fluctuate. A consistent positive return despite varying market conditions was a hallmark of Bernie Madoff's Ponzi scheme.

- **The investment strategy is too complex to understand, or it's described as a "hot tip."** Always understand at least the basics of the investments you own. Also be aware that those offering tips may have ulterior motives.

- **You can't verify the investment with a credible third-party source.** If an opportunity sounds too good to be true, talk to a registered financial advisor, an accountant, a lawyer, or a regulatory body to get a second opinion.

- **The investment is offered only to a few exclusive investors, and there is only a short time to decide.** Pressure tactics are never a good sign. Don't sign anything you haven't read and had time to think about.

- **Little information is provided.** Always ask for details about the investment. Never make an investment that doesn't have proper written documentation.

- **The investment is sold by a person who is not licensed with the appropriate regulatory bodies.** Do your due diligence on the person selling the investment.

- **Interest payments are late.** Interest payments should always be received on time, every time. If they're not, you should be concerned.

Here's an example of how an investment can go wrong. Ivan, a sophisticated, wealthy businessman owning a chain of auto repair shops, invested in shares of a private company that provided short-term loans to other businesses (a practice known as "bridge financing"). Ivan was initially attracted to the investment by its 18% returns, and he started by investing $100,000. He met with the principals of the private company several times and was assured that the investments were doing well. For the first several years, Ivan received his interest payments on time. Over time, as he gained further confidence in the investment, he invested more and suggested to family members that they throw in too. Together, Ivan and his family invested a total of $6 million, which represented over 50% of their collective net worth.

A year after the additional investment was made, interest payments began to be late. At first they were a month late, and then more.

Ivan followed up on this but was satisfied with the explanations he received. He was even told he could withdraw his money if he wanted to, which reassured him that everything was OK. What was really happening was that, as new money from investors stopped flowing in, no money was available to make the interest payments to existing investors. Eventually, it was discovered that the owners of the company were running a Ponzi scheme. In total, investors lost over $50 million in this fraud. The owners disappeared and none of the money was recovered.

How could Ivan have avoided participating in this investment fraud? When told that as an investor he could expect a return of 18%, he should have realized the investment was too good to be true. Also, Ivan forgot about the principle of diversification and invested far too much of his net worth in this investment.

➤ **TAKE NOTE:** Protect yourself from fraud by understanding your investments, asking the right questions, and looking out for red flags.

Diversify

When it comes to investing, diversification is critical. You can view the concept of diversification in many ways. For example, you can see it from the perspective of different asset classes (stocks, bonds, real estate, etc.), the market value of the companies you invested in (small, mid-size, or large blue-chip companies), geography (Canada, US, Europe, Asia, etc.), and the industry or sector of the economy you are investing in (banking, healthcare, oil and gas, metals and mining, etc.). The concept of diversification can mean different things to different people, but in the end it can be summarized simply as not putting all your eggs in one basket.

An astute reader might point out that some of the best investors in the world did not diversify but rather made their wealth by investing in just a few select companies. This is absolutely true! But investors who choose not to diversify generally approach investing from a business-owner perspective—they know the businesses in which they invest inside out and are comfortable holding these companies for a long period regardless of any movement (up or down) in the share price. In my experience, this is not true for average investors, who have a much stronger tendency to look at the market prices of their investments too frequently and are more susceptible to the emotions of greed and fear, which most often lead to bad business and investment decisions.

The first step to diversifying is to have a written long-term investment strategy—your investment policy statement (IPS). The IPS should summarize your financial situation, your risk tolerance, and your long-term asset-allocation strategy (target percentages of stocks, bonds, and cash in your portfolio). You should revisit your IPS annually with your advisor and rebalance your portfolio back to the target asset allocation. This will force you to sell high and buy low. Even do-it-yourself investors should have an IPS and look at it annually.

The second step is to make sure that within each of your asset classes, you are adequately diversified, holding no more than 10% of your portfolio in any one investment, and your exposure to any one sector of the economy (such as energy or financials) should not be more than about 25% of your portfolio.

For example, in the stock component of your portfolio, investments should be diversified based on geography and sector in the economy, with most of the investments being in higher-quality, larger companies. Diversification is where an advisor can add a lot of value, in addition to helping you to create an IPS. It is particularly important to ensure that all your investments are not in any one country or one sector of the economy. For example, what if you had all your stock investments (60% of your portfolio) in Canadian energy stocks? When energy prices declined sharply between 2014 and 2016, the average energy stock was down 50% or more, so this would equate to a 30% loss of your entire portfolio (60% × 50% = 30%). Remember, you will win by not losing (avoiding big mistakes).

Diversification is so important because sometimes things that seem impossible can occur. You may have heard certain events such as the 2007-08 financial crisis or the 2014-15 drop in oil prices described as "black swans." The term became popular in 2007 when Nassim Nicholas Taleb published a book called *The Black Swan: The*

Impact of the Highly Improbable. From an investing perspective, the basic premise is that sometimes unexpected events that nobody believed could happen, do happen, and these outlier events have an extreme impact on markets. In my experience, black swan events can occur with more regularity than most people think! For example, it was highly improbable that the price of crude oil would decline from over US$100 per barrel in 2014 to less than US$30 per barrel at one point in 2016. Very few, if any, forecasters thought this was even a remote possibility. If your investments are too concentrated in a single country, sector, or asset class that is devastated by a black swan event, your savings could be significantly damaged.

Many Canadian investors suffer from "home-country bias," which is a global phenomenon that prevents investors from diversifying geographically. Because of this, many Canadians have most or all of their stock investments in Canadian companies. But did you know that the value of all the stocks publicly traded in Canada represents only 3.6% of the value of world stocks? A study published in 2015 by Vanguard Investments called *Home Bias and the Canadian Investor* showed that, despite Canada representing less than 4% of world stock value, Canadian investors on average have 59% of their stock holdings in Canadian companies. The implications of overweighting Canadian investments are particularly important because of the heavy resource focus of the Canadian economy. The Canadian stock market is weighted heavily in three industries: financials (banks and insurance companies), oil and gas, and metals and mining. Some very important sectors such as healthcare and technology are grossly underrepresented in Canada as a result of the resource-based nature of our economy. Sometimes being overweighted to Canada will work for you and sometimes it will work against you, but in the long run, having at least a reasonable amount of global exposure is important. I highly recommend being globally diversified.

With global investments, you also have to consider currency risk and foreign withholding taxes on dividends. In the long run, currency movements will work themselves out, but in the short term they can cause significant swings to portfolio values. Some investors manage or "hedge" currency risk and others do not. Interestingly, in times of uncertainty, having exposure to US investments in your portfolio can help because there can be a flight to safety, resulting in a rise in the US dollar. Two options for managing currency risk, if you so desire, are finding a mutual fund manager who can hedge currency risk if they see fit or using a hedged version of an ETF. Talk to your advisor for further information.

> **TAKE NOTE:** Make sure your portfolio is well-diversified by asset class, sector, and geography. Keep in mind the currency risk of foreign investments.

Your Employer's Stock

I'd like to say a word about holding stock in the company you work for. Many companies offer retirement programs that allow employees to purchase stock at a discount to the price it trades at on the stock market, and sometimes companies even match the employee's purchase to a maximum level. For example, an employee may put a certain percentage of their salary toward buying company shares and the company will match that amount. If the stock pays dividends, these can be reinvested into additional shares. This is a great way of building long-term wealth.

However, I strongly recommend that your overall exposure to the stock of your employer not exceed 10% of your total investment portfolio. For company executives this percentage can be higher, but the concept is the same. This is part of diversification. If the company you work for has business challenges and its stock declines substantially, in a worst-case scenario not only can you lose your job and salary, but your retirement savings could be jeopardized as well. Investors often hold more of their company stock than they should because they work at the company and know it well. That's all well and good, but remember the black swans—sometimes things happen that nobody expects. In 2014-15, for example, when the stock prices of many energy companies collapsed by 50% or more, job losses followed. Imagine the situation for oil and gas company employees in their mid-50s who just lost their jobs and had their retirement savings drop substantially as well—not a good scenario.

No matter how well you know the company you work for, avoid having excessive concentrated ownership in the stock of that company. That way you will never be risking both your livelihood and retirement savings on one company.

....

➤ **TAKE NOTE:** Review and diversify your company stock holdings annually. Have a maximum ownership of 10% of your portfolio in your company stock.

....

Rebalance Your Portfolio Annually

One of the most powerful forces in investing is called "reversion to the mean." Simply put, this means that asset classes performing poorly because they are out of favour will eventually perform better and regain investors' confidence. The reverse is also true. The easiest way to understand this phenomenon is to remember that when you are buying an investment, you are purchasing a right to the future underlying cash flows or profits the investment generates. So you want to make sure you are paying a reasonable price for the future cash flows you will receive—you want to ensure you're getting good value. When it comes to investments, portfolio managers of mutual funds and other institutional funds are the ones who move the market. These managers pay attention to value. When assets that have been performing well get too expensive, they sell, which eventually causes those assets to perform less well (more shares are sold than bought, and the price falls). When the assets that have not been performing well get too cheap, fund managers buy and that eventually causes those assets to start going up in price (buying is exceeding selling).

As an investor, you can use reversion to the mean to your advantage by owning a diversified portfolio of different assets and rebalancing your portfolio annually. Rebalancing is critical, but it simply means that you make adjustments so that your portfolio is in line with your long-term asset allocation objectives. For example, assume your asset allocation target is 70% equities and 30% fixed income. You look at your portfolio at year-end and it's at 75% equities and 25% fixed income. This probably happened because, during the year, the equities you owned did better than the fixed-income portion of your portfolio. To rebalance your portfolio, you sell 5% of your equities and use that money to buy fixed income so that, going into next year, your asset allocation is where it should be. You will have sold some of your better-performing assets (equities) at higher prices to buy some of the weaker-performing assets (fixed income) at lower prices. Doing this takes advantage of the power of mean reversion.

The concept of mean reversion applies not only to asset classes, but also to different categories within the market (such as large-cap stocks versus small-cap stocks, growth stocks versus value stocks, or domestic stocks versus international stocks).

Be Careful about Borrowing to Invest

Investors often ask me, "Should I borrow money to invest?" Borrowing to invest is known as using leverage or margin. Interest paid on the money borrowed to invest is also tax-deductible. When markets are going up, leverage can be a great idea. When markets decline, however, watching investments you bought with borrowed money decline in value can be a gut-wrenching and emotional experience. Let's look at an example of different investment returns when borrowing $100,000 at an interest rate of 4.5%.

	Happy scenario	Not-so-happy scenario
Amount borrowed	$100,000	$100,000
Portfolio return	15%	−15%
Account value	$115,000	$85,000
Interest charged	($4,500)	($4,500)
Net account value	$110,500	$80,500
Result	Investor has gained $10,500	Investor has lost $19,500

NOTE: the above does not include any tax benefit from the deductibility of interest on borrowed money.

As you can see, leverage is a double-edged sword. If your investments do well, it can work very nicely—but if they don't, it's not so great. Borrowing to invest can be appropriate for investors with higher incomes and little other debt. Even then, however, borrowing must be done prudently. Only borrow what you can afford to lose. You do not want to be in a situation where you are forced to sell investments in a down market because the investments have been made with borrowed money.

So, where should you borrow money from if you do want to borrow to invest? You can use a margin account at a full-service or discount brokerage, where you borrow the money from the brokerage. However, you will likely pay a lower interest rate if you borrow the money using a home equity line of credit at your bank. As mentioned, don't forget to keep track of the interest you pay on the borrowed money because it's tax-deductible.

> **TAKE NOTE:** Borrowing to invest is a higher-risk strategy. If you do borrow to invest, borrow only what you can afford to lose.

Defence Wins: How to Be an Investing Champion

In sports, champions have great defensive skills; teams that win the Stanley Cup, for example, typically play a solid defensive game and have a great goalie. A solid offence is wonderful too, but it's usually unsustainable over time. You can become an investing champion if you keep the importance of defence in mind. Increase your odds of winning by keeping the following key principles in mind:

1. **Have an appropriate long-term asset-allocation plan and rebalance your portfolio annually.** It should include a mix of the major asset classes in your portfolio. Review your plan annually with your advisor and adjust as necessary. Rebalancing your portfolio ensures the weights of the asset classes in your portfolio remain at the right level; this also forces you to buy low and sell high.

2. **Diversify, diversify, diversify.** As some of your investments perform well, others will not. Diversify by asset class, geography, and economic sector.

3. **Ignore short-term market movements.** Invest for the long term. Short-term market movements are largely due to investors' emotional reactions. As a result, nobody can accurately predict them. Long-term market movements are a result of the profitability of the companies in which you invest.

4. **Ignore hot stock tips from friends and family.** It is human nature to join the crowd, but doing so is acting on the emotion of greed, and people tend to talk only about their investment successes, not their losses. There are no shortcuts to investment success.

5. **Start early with dollar cost averaging.** Take advantage of the power of compounding. The earlier you start investing, the better your long-run results will be. A regular monthly investment, even if it's small, will enable you to take advantage of market fluctuations. Reinvest your gains to further compound your growth.

6. **Control your emotions.** Remember that it is normal for markets to move up and down. Have an appropriate long-term plan and stick to it. When markets go up, do not be greedy. If markets drop, do not let panic override your long-term plan.

7. **Keep it simple.** Have a straightforward plan, own quality investments for the long term, and invest regularly. The more complex your investments, the less likely you are to really understand them and the greater the potential that something could go wrong. Resist making investments in areas that are outside your risk comfort zone and investment plan.

8. **Avoid borrowing money to invest.** If the investment doesn't work out, your losses will be magnified.

9. **Minimize mistakes (especially big ones!) and unforced errors.** Investors can do harm to themselves in some many ways. Be vigilant! I suggest reading Larry Swedroe's *Investment Mistakes Even Smart Investors Make and How to Avoid Them.*

10. **Find a great advisor.** The vast majority of investors would bene-fit from the help of an experienced, qualified advisor. Having an advisor you trust, who is looking out for you and who can guide you in making investment decisions and sticking with your plan, can add immense value to your long-term results.

Action Call

1. Think about your long-term goals and develop your invest-ment policy statement or plan.

2. Understand your asset allocation and costs of investing.

3. Control your emotions and avoid falling into common investing pitfalls.

4. Stick to your plan.

3

YOUR FINANCES BEYOND INVESTING: INSURANCE AND ESTATE PLANNING

Insurance 101

INSURANCE IS ESSENTIALLY a contractual arrangement by which a company (the insurer) provides a guarantee of compensation for specified losses, damage, illness, or death in exchange for a specified payment (the premium). When you think about your financial goals and objectives, don't forget about the risks that can get in the way of success. If they are not addressed appropriately they can have a significant financial impact down the road. Identifying when and where these risks should be insured is critical; after all, the future is uncertain. Unfortunately, when most people think about their finances, they do not pay enough attention to risk management.

While the probability of something catastrophic happening to you may be low, it is not zero. If you became seriously ill or severely disabled, what would the impact be on you and your family? If you died suddenly, would your family have sufficient financial resources to ensure that their lifestyle would not be drastically affected? Being adequately insured can mean the difference between leaving your family in a strong financial position and leaving them to cope with outstanding debt and an insufficient income. Insurance is meant to provide you and your family with financial assistance when you need it most. This section of the book focuses on the role of life, disability, and critical illness insurance as part of your overall financial health.

Insurance is founded on two key concepts:

- **Pooling of risk.** Because many people purchase insurance, insurance companies are able to "pool risk" and offer coverage at lower prices than would otherwise be possible. To illustrate how this works, let's consider the risk of a house fire. Say your home insurance costs $75 per month and while you are away on vacation, your home burns down in a fire that started at your neighbour's house. As long as your home insurance is in force, the insurance company may, depending on your specific policy, pay for a new home to be built, replace your possessions, and cover temporary living expenses. The cost to the insurance company could easily top $500,000, which means that even if you have been paying home insurance premiums for 30 years, the insurance company will suffer a substantial loss in paying your claim (relative to what you have paid in premiums over the years). The reason the insurance company can afford to do this is due to the pooling or diversification of their risk. Because thousands of people purchase home insurance but relatively few make claims, it also allows insurance companies to offer reasonable prices. They know that while they will suffer losses on a few policies, their business will most likely be profitable overall. The same concept of pooling of risk also applies to other types of insurance such as life, disability, and critical illness.

- **Transfer of risk.** When you purchase an insurance policy, you transfer risk from yourself (the insured, or the policyholder) to the insurance company. If your house burns down, the insurance company carries the financial risk and will pay for the damages, not you. If you don't have insurance, the financial risk remains with you.

Insurance companies are also very careful in managing their own risk. One of the key tools used by insurance companies for this purpose is called "reinsurance." In simple terms, reinsurance is insurance for insurance companies. In this manner, an insurance company can transfer a portion of its risk to a different company (called the reinsurer) to reduce the possibility of having to pay out a large claim. The reinsurance company taking on the risk will do so in exchange for a portion of the premium.

Key Terminology

An insurance policy can be considered to be a contract, to which there are typically three parties—the policy owner, the life insured, and the beneficiary. You've probably heard these terms before, but let's make sure the meanings are clear. For the purposes of explaining the key terminology, I will use life insurance as an example; however, the concepts are similar for other kinds of insurance.

- **Policy owner:** With life insurance, the policy owner is the individual with whom the insurance carrier forms a contract. The policy owner has the right to name a beneficiary to receive the benefit specified under the terms of the insurance contract. The policy owner is also commonly referred to as the policyholder or the insured. In most cases, the policy owner is the one who pays the premiums.

- **Life insured:** The person on whose life the policy is based. When talking about life insurance, "the insured" should not be confused with "the life insured." The policy owner is the insured because he or she is the individual who can direct the receipt of the insurance benefit, whereas the life insured is the person on whose life the policy is based.

  Be aware that life insurance policies can cover a single life or multiple lives; for example, the life insured could be a single individual or a couple. Policies that cover multiple lives could be set up as joint first-to-die or joint last-to-die. In the case of a joint first-to-die policy the claim would be paid on the first death, while on a joint last-to-die policy the claim would only be paid on the second death. Because the insurance company will not have to make a claim until a point further in the future, joint last-to-die policies can have lower premiums than individual life insurance policies.

- **Beneficiary:** The beneficiary of an insurance policy is the person who will receive the benefit from the insurance policy (i.e., payment from the insurance company once a claim is filed and processed). In the case of life insurance, the beneficiary is the one named in policy to receive the proceeds of the death claim. The policy owner has the opportunity to name a desired beneficiary in the insurance application or contract, and this designation can be either irrevocable or revocable.

An irrevocable beneficiary designation is one where, while the beneficiary who is initially selected remains alive, the policy owner may not alter or revoke the designation without prior consent of that beneficiary. The policy owner could, however, change an irrevocable beneficiary with the original beneficiary's consent. In essence, the irrevocable beneficiary controls the proceeds of the insurance policy, which at the same time limits the policy owner's control over the policy. Most irrevocable beneficiary designations result from legal proceedings, such as a divorce decree. If an irrevocable beneficiary dies before the insured, the policyholder generally has the right to name a new beneficiary.

A revocable beneficiary designation allows the policy owner to retain control of the policy and the ability to alter the beneficiary designation without obtaining prior consent from the person who was initially selected as beneficiary. A revocable beneficiary has no legal right to the insurance policy or to the proceeds until after the death of the life insured(s).

When it comes to life insurance, there are also primary and contingent beneficiaries. The primary beneficiary (also known as the direct beneficiary) is the one who receives the proceeds of the life insurance policy when the insured person dies, unless the primary beneficiary dies before the insured. If this happens, the contingent beneficiary receives the proceeds if named. Note: naming a contingent beneficiary is optional.

Minor children should generally not be named as beneficiaries because they lack the legal capacity to receive the insurance proceeds. A will can direct insurance proceeds to the guardian of a minor beneficiary *but* the beneficiary is legally able to obtain the full proceeds upon reaching the age of majority. A policy owner should put thought into how proceeds should be managed and distributed to children (not just minors). Your will could specify a trustee who can receive the life insurance proceeds on behalf of the children or the life insurance could be paid into a trust for the children as set out in your will.

Note that if you name your estate as the beneficiary of your life insurance policy, the insurance proceeds will be subject to probate (the legal process by which a will is validated or invalidated in court) and its associated costs, delays, estate taxes, and claims of creditors. Having the estate as a beneficiary would, however, provide the estate with immediate liquidity to settle debts and other obligations. On the other hand, having a direct beneficiary for proceeds from a life insurance policy will bypass probate.

Keep in mind that, for other types of insurance such as disability and critical illness, when a claim is made the person who is the insured will be alive and will usually be receiving payments from the insurance company, as a beneficiary.

- **Premium.** The premium is the amount of money the insurer charges (annually or monthly) for a certain amount of insurance coverage. The premium can change over time.

- **Underwriting.** This is the risk-management process the insurance company goes through to review your application and determine whether to issue insurance to you.

This following discussion will concentrate on three types of insurance that I particularly focus on as an advisor—life, disability, and critical illness. For each of these types, you need to understand how much coverage is appropriate for your situation and then decide whether you will purchase coverage or take your chances and "self-insure." Note: there are several other types of insurance, such as long-term care, health and dental, travel, and group benefits. While also important, these areas are not the focus of this chapter.

Life Insurance

Do I Need It?
Life insurance can be a "need" or a "want" depending on your situation. Many people need life insurance to pay final expenses and debts (such as a mortgage or line of credit) and provide an ongoing stream of income to ensure a comfortable standard of living for their family. If you are a business owner, you may *need* life insurance so that your business partners have money to buy your share of the business upon your death. Other people, especially high-net-worth individuals, may not strictly need life insurance because if they passed away, their

families would have enough money to live comfortably and in the lifestyle they wish. Similarly, people without financial dependents may not truly need life insurance. However, such individuals may *want* life insurance for reasons such as to provide a gift to a loved one, cover tax liabilities at death, provide a larger estate to survivors, or leave a charitable legacy.

Life insurance has applications beyond protecting your family. It can also be used to accumulate tax-sheltered investment assets. By moving investment assets from a tax-exposed investment vehicle, such as a non-registered investment account, into a tax-exempt life insurance policy, the funds can accumulate on a tax-deferred basis in the life insurance policy. Of course, you need to be sure that the benefits of this type of a strategy outweigh the costs for your particular situation. Proceeds from life insurance policies, including accumulated investment assets, are distributed to beneficiaries or the estate tax-free. As mentioned, probate is also bypassed as long as a direct beneficiary is named.

There are two main types of life insurance—temporary (or term) and permanent—and each will be discussed separately below. From a life-cycle perspective, goals and objectives can change as people age, and insurance requirements may need to change to reflect this. For example, a couple in their 30s with a mortgage and young family would likely be focused on obtaining life insurance that is the most cost-effective coverage, and that is temporary insurance. As the couple ages, eliminates debt, saves for retirement, and has more discretionary cash flow, their goals and objectives may become more focused on maximizing the estate for their children and therefore they may consider obtaining permanent life insurance, which is generally more costly than temporary insurance.

What is most important is that you have adequate life insurance to cover the needs of your family. I often come across younger people who are inadequately insured, thereby putting their families in a potentially vulnerable position. Some of these people purchase modest amounts of more costly permanent life insurance that would not truly cover their family's needs in the event of death (permanent insurance is more costly, so they bought only what they could afford). In many cases, these individuals would have been better off spending the same amount but having a much higher level of temporary coverage or term insurance. In this way, if something catastrophic occurred, their family's needs would be fully covered.

If you are unsure about whether you need life insurance, ask yourself the following question: Do I have any financial responsibility toward others (such as a spouse or any children)? If you answer yes, you likely need life insurance. An advisor who is life insurance-licensed (also referred to as a "life insurance agent") can help you confirm this and also help you decide how much life insurance you need and what type is best for you. It is best to purchase life insurance when you are younger and healthy, because it's cheaper then. Recently, the Canadian Life and Health Insurance Association launched www.notimelikenow.ca that is geared toward educating younger adults about life insurance.

A Note on Group Insurance

If you are employed, you may have some insurance coverage (life and disability) through your employer, generally referred to as group insurance. In my experience, many people make the mistake of dismissing the need for personal insurance because they have group coverage. But keep a couple of things about group coverage in mind: First, you do not own or control your coverage—your employer does. Second, often you are insured only while you are a member of the group (i.e., while you're employed by the company). If your employment status changes, you may have an opportunity to keep the coverage, but the terms may make it cost-prohibitive. In the worst case, you could lose your coverage. While you may feel your employment situation is very stable and unlikely to change, anything can happen. So even if you have some coverage through your employer, you may want additional coverage that will remain in place if your job changes.

How Much Do I Need?

Determining the amount of life insurance you need can be challenging on your own. Most banks and insurance companies in Canada have web-based insurance-needs calculators; however, I caution you to use these tools only as a starting point. The right amount of life insurance is more than just the answer to a mathematical question—a lot of subjective components should be considered as well, especially your goals and objectives. You can use online tools to get a basic idea of what coverage you might need, but be sure to meet with a licensed insurance advisor to fine-tune the amount of insurance required.

In general, there are two approaches for calculating your life insurance needs:

- **Capitalization of income (or human life value) approach**—As cold as it sounds, the capitalization of income approach involves calculating the lifetime economic value of your lost income if you were to pass away. The calculation tells you how much money you would need today as a lump sum in order to replace the income you would have earned over the remaining course of your working life. In theory, the amount of the lump sum would be invested at the prevailing interest rate to provide your family with an alternate source of income.

  Here's the formula: annual income ÷ interest rate = insurance need. Annual income is your current annual income, and the interest rate is a reasonable current rate of return that can be earned on conservative investments. For a quick "back-of-an-envelope" calculation, an interest rate of 4%–5% is reasonable. So if you earn $100,000 per year and use an interest rate of 5% in the calculation, you would need $2 million of insurance to provide your family with $100,000 per year. Given the low level of interest rates today, one could argue that a lower interest rate should be used in the calculation. However, the 4%–5% is only a guideline and should be viewed as such.

- **Capital-needs approach**—The capital-needs approach is more detailed and tailored to the needs of you and your family. The calculation has two main components: the first is calculating immediate cash needs, and the second is calculating the value of the annual income that has to be replaced for the family.

  In determining immediate cash needs, final expenses need to be examined, including funeral costs, taxes, and any debt, such as a mortgage, that may be outstanding. This amount is then deducted from available assets, such as cash in bank accounts. If there is more cash available than is required to cover immediate cash needs, the excess is used to reduce total insurance requirements. If there is not enough cash, the cash deficit is added to total insurance needs. Assume you passed away and your final expenses consisted of $20,000 for funeral costs and $180,000 to pay off your mortgage, and you had $10,000 in the bank. There would be a cash need of $20,000 + $180,000 − $10,000, or $190,000.

The ongoing-requirements part of the calculation takes into account the needs of surviving family members for ongoing living expenses. The period for which the family requires income is called the dependency period. To calculate this, the difference between continuing income and continuing expenses is required. The value of this amount as an ongoing income stream is then calculated by dividing it by the appropriate interest rate. If you passed away and your spouse continues working, earning $50,000 per year, but your family has household expenses of $90,000 per year, there is a funding requirement of at least $40,000 per year. This would result in an insurance need of $800,000 using a 5% interest rate ($40,000 ÷ 5% = $800,000).

To arrive at the total insurance need, the amount required for immediate and ongoing requirements is calculated. The formula for the calculation is as follows: immediate cash needs + (continuing income less expenses ÷ interest rate). In our example, the total insurance need would be $190,000 + $800,000, or $990,000.

The above are simple examples that provide a basic idea of how insurance needs are calculated, ignoring any effects of income tax. I strongly recommend talking with an advisor who is insurance-licensed to determine whether you are adequately insured. Determining the insurance you need is not a simple undertaking. Having the right advice is critical.

Term or Temporary Life Insurance
The most cost-effective type of life insurance is called term or temporary insurance. This form of insurance is for a specific period of time, hence the name. Most commonly, term insurance is bought for a period of 10 years (Term 10 or T10) or 20 years (Term 20 or

T20), but the length of the term can vary. Term insurance is most effective in cases where higher amounts of coverage are required for a specific period of time for reasons such as mortgage and debt repayment, replacing income, or any other temporary need. For example, in the case of a young couple with children and a mortgage, term insurance would likely be appropriate—it would cover the mortgage and lost income if one spouse passed away. In general, term life insurance is often best for meeting short-to-medium-term needs at a reasonable cost.

Other notable features of term insurance are as follows:

- Premiums are guaranteed to be the same for the duration of the contract. That is, if you purchase a Term 10 policy, your premiums are guaranteed to be the same for 10 years. After this, if you renew your policy, your premium will change. Remember, premiums increase as you age, in stair-like fashion.

Term Insurance: The Premium Staircase

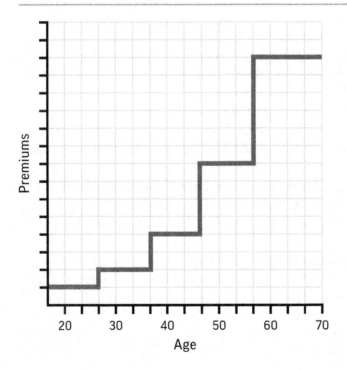

Age

- You can renew your policy at the end of the term without submitting additional medical evidence. However, the price will increase substantially because of the increase in your age. Because the insurance company has no idea about the state of your health and thus can't assess its risk in renewing your policy, the new premium can be three or four times the premium you paid for the initial policy. If you reach the end of your term (e.g., 10 years) and, after a review with your insurance agent, you still require life insurance coverage, you will want to compare the cost of renewing the existing policy against reapplying for a new policy. The latter will require you to submit a new application and medical information, but it may save you a lot money. If you are considering renewing, it usually makes sense to submit a new application with new medical information so you can get a better premium. Keep your current policy in place until the new policy is approved, though—that way, if your new application is not approved, you can still keep your old coverage, albeit at the higher cost.

- You can convert the term policy into a permanent policy.

- The insurance is in force as long as you pay your premiums on time.

....

➤ **TAKE NOTE:** If possible, pay your premiums annually rather than monthly—this will generally save you about 9% on the premium. If you are set up to pay premiums annually, make sure you do not miss the payment due date. While the insurance company will give you a 30-day grace period after your premium due date, if the premium remains unpaid after this time your policy will lapse—the insurance company will cancel your policy.

....

Permanent Life Insurance

Permanent life insurance is exactly what the name suggests—coverage for your entire life. While term insurance to age 100 (Term 100 or T100) is also considered to be a form of permanent insurance, this discussion will focus on the two main types of permanent life insurance—whole life and universal life. Whole life provides a guaranteed death benefit, and a guaranteed premium that remains fixed throughout the lifetime of the policy. Universal life, on the other hand, is a flexible permanent insurance plan that combines life insurance protection and a tax-deferred investment account. This combination can be an ideal financial-planning tool for those looking for comprehensive permanent coverage and a tax-effective savings account. Depending on your situation, permanent life insurance can be a great way to build and transfer long-term wealth for future generations. Keep in mind, though, that there is a limit to the dollars that can be accumulated inside of the life insurance policy (remember: if it sounds too good to be true, it probably is!).

A life insurance policy is exempt from annual taxation as long as the cash value or equity in the policy (more on this later) is below what is known as the Maximum Tax Actuarial Reserve (MTAR). Effective January 1, 2017, new income tax rules change the way the MTAR and other items pertaining to permanent life insurance policies are calculated. The result of this is that the maximum amount of money that can accumulate within the policy on a tax-exempt basis is lower. Policies issued prior to January 1, 2017, have "grandfathered" status, whereby the old rules still apply. That said, there are specific events that could result in policies issued before January 1, 2017, losing their "grandfathered" status. For example, any change to an existing permanent life insurance policy that requires medical evidence will cause that policy to lose its grandfathering status.

Let's now take a more detailed look at the two main types of permanent life insurance.

WHOLE LIFE INSURANCE

Whole life insurance is permanent life insurance that provides coverage for the rest of your life. A whole life policy has a fixed premium that will not change as you age. Premiums can be paid for the rest of your life or on a limited-pay basis, meaning premiums are paid over a specified number of years or until a certain age—for example, a 20-pay policy requires premiums to be paid annually for 20 years. If you pay premiums over a shorter period they will likely be higher because the insurance company is seeking to create enough cash value inside the policy during the premium payment years so that the policy can be self-funded once premiums are no longer being paid.

During the early years of a whole life policy, because the cost of insurance is lower due to the fact that you are younger and premiums are fixed, the amount of premium you pay above the cost of insurance is invested by the insurance company and creates a policy reserve or cash reserve, also known as the cash surrender value (CSV) or cash value (I use all three terms interchangeably in this book). The policy owner can access the cash value of the policy in several ways:

- **Fully surrendering the policy.** If you give up the insurance policy, you are entitled to the cash value within the policy. However, there may be tax consequences. Every whole life policy has an adjusted cost, which is based on a specific formula. Policyholders are required to include in taxable income any gains realized upon the disposition of all or a portion of their interest in a life insurance policy. The income inclusion, or "policy gain," is the amount by which the CSV exceeds the adjusted cost base (ACB), which is the policyholder's cost of the insurance policy for tax purposes. Be careful before surrendering your life insurance policy and be sure to discuss it in depth with your advisor.

- **Partially surrendering cash value.** Permanently removing any portion of the cash value from the policy will inherently reduce the amount of cash value that remains inside the policy. This will impact future growth of cash value and could also impact the benefit payable. Tax consequences, similar to that discussed above, also apply.

- **Obtaining policy loan from insurer.** The insurer provides a loan which is secured by the CSV. In this way, the policy continues to grow as it would otherwise. Commonly, there is a limit whereby a maximum of 90% of the CSV can be borrowed. Interest is charged on the amount borrowed, and the loan is repayable. At death, any loan amount that is unpaid (plus accrued interest) is deducted from the policy proceeds before being paid to the beneficiary. Taking a policy loan from the insurer is a simple, hassle-free way of accessing CSV. Rather than going to the traditional process at a bank, simply call the advisor who set up the policy for you to request the loan. There can be tax consequences to be aware of when taking out policy loans, so be sure to understand this as well.

- **Obtaining loan from third party.** To access the csv, the policy can be assigned to the third-party lending institution. The lender will then have security to back the loan or line of credit that is provided to you. Interest is payable on the loan and the policy continues to grow as it would normally. If the life insured passes away, the lender will be repaid any balance (plus accrued interest) owing, and the remaining funds will go to the beneficiary of the policy. While better financing terms could be obtained from a third party, there is also more administrative work required as the borrower has to go through the lender's loan approval process.

When people purchase permanent life insurance, usually the intent is to keep the insurance forever; however, circumstances can change. In an extreme case, if somebody was unable to continue to pay premiums, they would "default" on the policy, the policy would eventually lapse, and any cash value in the policy would be given up. One of the features of permanent life insurance is that there are choices if the policyholder wants to discontinue paying premiums. Considered as "lapse protection," a non-forfeiture option allows for premiums to stop being paid after a certain period of time, but the policyholder does not lose all the benefit of the policy. Non-forfeiture options include the following:

- **Automatic premium loans**—The insurance company issues a loan against the csv of the policy to pay unpaid premiums in order to keep the policy in force. The policyholder is charged interest on the amount borrowed from the cash value until the debt is repaid.

- **Reduced paid-up insurance**—The csv is used as a single premium to buy a reduced amount of permanent insurance.

- **Extended term insurance**—The cash value is used to pay for a certain amount of term life insurance. This way, the policyholder continues to have some coverage through term life insurance.

Before exercising any of the above options, discuss the concepts with your advisor to make sure you are meeting your goals and objectives in the most effective way possible.

Whole life insurance is available as a non-participating or a participating policy. A non-participating policy is simple—all the key factors (value of the death benefit, csv, and amount of the premium) are determined when the policy is issued and cannot be changed. Non-participating policies have lower premiums than participating policies.

Participating policies offer features similar to non-participating policies—lifetime protection, cash values, and guaranteed premiums. Plus, they also generate an annual dividend. When you purchase participating life insurance, your premiums go into an account called the participating account, together with funds from other participating policyholders. The insurance company then invests these funds. The funds are managed by professionals in a diversified manner that includes exposure to bonds, stocks, and alternative assets such as real estate. The investments will grow in a tax-sheltered environment over time. Each year, based on several factors, including the insurance company's actual expenses and claims experience as well as performance of the investments in the participating account, a dividend will be paid to policyholders of participating policies.

Note: these dividends are different in character, especially from a tax perspective, than dividends declared by public companies. Dividend rates can fluctuate from year to year, and there is no guarantee that the insurance company will pay a dividend in a given year. Most life insurance companies in Canada continue to pay dividends, even in today's low-interest-rate environment. In fact, many of Canada's life insurance companies have paid a dividend yearly for over one hundred years! The annual dividend can be taken in cash or used to accumulate additional cash values, buy additional life insurance, reduce future premiums, or purchase additional term insurance. Another important concept to be aware of is premium offset, which allows the policyholder to stop making additional cash premium payments. Premium offset allows the policyholder to pay premiums using the policy's dividends. Remember that policy dividends are not guaranteed and that projections about when your premium offset date will take effect will be very sensitive to dividends received. Even once the policy qualifies for premium offset, changes to dividends received can impact whether the policy continues to qualify.

For those readers who are history buffs, you will find it is interesting to note that originally insurance companies were typically owned by their policyholders. These insurance companies were known as mutual insurance companies. During this period, any profits earned by a mutual insurance company were rebated to policyholders in the form of dividend distributions or reduced future premiums. Starting in the 1980s, several mutual insurance companies converted into publicly traded companies through a process known as demutualization. For example, now Manulife and Sun Life are owned by investors who have purchased company stock. Any profits generated by a stock insurance company can be distributed to the investors without necessarily benefiting the policyholders. Today, the dividends you receive as a participating policyholder is a portion of the insurance company's profits that is paid as if you were an investor or stockholder. Each year, based on a review of the performance of the participating account and other factors, the insurance company will determine the amount of profit or policy dividends available to be distributed to participating policyholders. Note that, in recent years, largely due to the low-interest-rate environment we are in, dividends have tended to be in decline. When interest rates increase, dividends may also rise.

....

➤ **TAKE NOTE:** If you want permanent life insurance but don't want to manage investments, whole life insurance is a good choice. Premiums for participating policies are generally higher than premiums for non-participating policies.

....

Universal Life Insurance

Universal life insurance is the other type of permanent policy. While there are many similarities with whole life policies (such as cash values, non-forfeiture options, and having tax-exempt status dictated by the Maximum Tax Actuarial Reserve), there are also some important differences. In essence, universal life insurance combines insurance and a tax-deferred investment component in a manner that offers more flexibility, but also more responsibility to the policyholder.

When you purchase a universal life policy, your deposits are first made into an investment account; then, each month, insurance charges and fees are deducted, while the balance earns interest based on the performance of the investments you have selected in your policy. A unique feature of universal life policies is that all costs relating to the policy are "unbundled" or shown separately. What that means to the policyholder is that you can see the cost of insurance, administration expenses, or other fees being deducted from the investments every month, which then grow on a tax-preferred basis. With whole life policies, you see one premium that includes all cost components.

Another key difference between universal life and whole life policies is that, for universal life, the policy owner is responsible for selecting investments and managing the investment account. Your advisor can assist you, but ultimately you are responsible. This places a greater responsibility on the policyholder to implement regular monitoring of the policy's investment component. In general, each insurance company will have several different investment choices. For example, at the time of writing this book, one well-known insurance company in Canada has investment choices available that include floating rate investments and guaranteed interest investments, portfolio managed accounts, mutual fund-managed accounts, and indexed accounts. When it comes to universal life policies, having sufficient knowledge in the area of investments is important.

I mentioned that one of the features of universal life is flexibility. As a policyholder, in addition to selecting the investments, you can do the following:

- **Choose** the cost of insurance using one of two methods:

1. Level cost of insurance—the cost will stay the same over the entire life of the policy.

2. Yearly renewable term (YRT) or annual renewable term (ART)—the cost of insurance is similar to that of a term insurance policy in that it increases as you age. In this case, the cost of insurance is good for a single year, and increases each year thereafter. In the early years of the policy, YRT costs less than the level cost of insurance,

leaving more money available to go into the investment part of the policy. In the long term, however, the cost of insurance for YRT will be higher and the policy will be more expensive to sustain.

It is important to understand that if the investments within the policy perform poorly and do not keep up the cost of insurance, there can be a shortfall. In such a case, the policyholder can be put in a position where they have to choose between paying the additional premium, reducing the death benefit, or allowing the policy to lapse entirely. Policies that are based on YRT are particularly vulnerable to this possibility. The difference between level cost of insurance and YRT is shown graphically below.

Cost of Insurance (COI): YRT vs Level

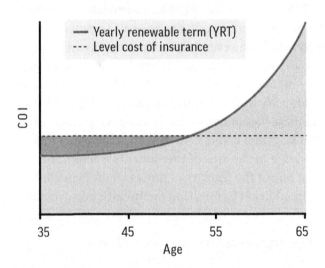

- **Select** the type of death benefit, the most common of which are the "level death benefit" and the "increasing benefit" (also known as "death benefit plus policy fund value").

  As its name suggests, in the level-death-benefit option, the death benefit remains constant throughout the life of the policy. Over time, as the investment account grows, the insured amount drops while the investments contribute an increasing proportion of the total death benefit. For example, let's consider the example of a universal life policy with a level death benefit of $1,000,000 and an investment account valued at $200,000. At payout, the insurance company would pay the $1,000,000 death benefit; however, this is really composed of $800,000 from the insurance company plus the $200,000 from the investment account. While the death benefit remains constant, the insured amount actually decreases as the investment account grows. Unsurprisingly, with the level-death-benefit option, the cost of insurance is typically lower. In cases where the investment account is higher in value than the level death benefit, the death benefit will be for the higher amount. In the example above, if the investment account was valued at $1,200,000, the beneficiary would receive that amount, not the level death benefit of $1,000,000.

In a universal life policy with an increasing death benefit, the insured amount remains the same and the death benefit will increase as the investment account grows. In the example above, if the death benefit of the policy was $1,000,000 and the investment account value was $200,000, then the total death benefit would be $1,200,000. Other types of death-benefit options include death benefit plus return of premium and death benefit plus cost-of-living adjustment. Remember, the more bells and whistles on your policy, the higher the premiums are likely to be.

- **Increase or decrease** the face amount of the policy with satisfactory evidence of insurability.

- **Increase or decrease** the amount (as long as there is enough to cover the cost of insurance) or duration of the premium.

In summary, universal life is permanent insurance that is flexible and also unbundles the costs of insurance, investments, and administrative expenses. Managing the investments is the policyholder's responsibility. Universal life policies are best suited for people who want to actively manage the investment component and who want flexibility in their premium deposits and investments. If you have a universal life policy, be sure to monitor the investments within the policy on an annual basis.

Disability Insurance

A very important but often overlooked type of insurance covers your income if you become disabled and are unable to work. According to the 2012 *Canadian Survey on Disability* released by Statistics Canada, an estimated 3.8 million adult Canadians reported being limited in their daily activities by a disability. This represents 13.7% of the adult population. So the probability of becoming disabled during your working years cannot be dismissed. If you do become disabled and do not have sufficient insurance, you may be forced to withdraw money from RRSPs or other sources to cover expenses. Doing so has two consequences: 1) taxes are withheld when you withdraw money from RRSPs, and 2) your long-term retirement savings are diminished.

To illustrate this point, I will share an experience of one of my clients, Teresa. Now 60 years old, Teresa was working full-time for many years before suffering a back injury in her 40s that rendered her unable to work. She had modest disability insurance coverage through her employer, but unfortunately it was not enough. To make ends meet, Teresa used up most of her retirement savings as well as a portion of her home equity. Today, Teresa wishes she would have had the foresight to enhance her disability coverage before her back injury.

Disability benefits are structured to replace a portion of your pre-disability income, usually between 60% and 85%. Depending on the plan and how the premium is paid, benefits can be tax-free or taxable. If multiple sources of disability benefits are in force, then these benefits are coordinated so that the claimant does not receive more than his or her normal pre-disability income. Disability insurance is very important because your lifestyle and your financial goals and objectives depend heavily on your ability to earn income. Imagine if you were suddenly disabled and your paycheque stopped—how would you manage?

Disability insurance policies can be complex, and the list of things to consider can be long—this is where having an advisor can be very helpful. When considering a disability policy, it is critical to understand

- exactly what definition of disability is being used,

- how long you have to wait to receive benefits (this period of time is known as the elimination or waiting period and could be 90 days or longer) and the length of your benefit period (the amount of time you are eligible to collect benefits while on a disability insurance claim),

- whether you are entitled to any partial or residual disability benefits, and

- whether your benefits will be subject to cost-of-living increases to keep up with inflation.

It is also important to know whether your benefits will be taxable or not. If you have a personal policy and pay premiums with after-tax dollars, your benefit is tax-free. If you are in a group plan, however, and the employer pays the premium for you, your benefits may be taxable (unless the employer premium payments were a taxable benefit to you). Some employers may provide you with an option to pay with after-tax dollars—if that is the case and you choose this option, then your benefits would also be received on a tax-free basis.

It is important to note that you must have income to replace when you apply for disability insurance—you don't qualify if you have no income. Also be aware that an insurance company may not cover disabilities that result from self-inflicted injuries, acts of war, transplant surgery, normal pregnancy/childbirth, or pre-existing medical conditions. The specific exclusions will vary by insurance company. In cases of obvious and permanent loss (such as loss of vision, hearing, or limbs), the insurance company may make a determination of presumptive disability, which means it assumes you will never recover from the disability, and will pay you benefits until the end of the benefit period.

When purchasing a disability insurance policy, it is very important to understand what definition of "disability" is being used. The most common definitions of disability are **own occupation, regular occupation**, and **any occupation**. Let's address these one at a time:

- **Own occupation**—To meet this definition of disability, the person who is insured must be under the care of a physician licensed in Canada and, as a result of illness or injury, be unable to perform the duties of his or her usual occupation. The insurance company will continue to provide you with a benefit as long as you cannot do your own specific work, even if you are able to perform other work. For example, if you are a dentist who, after your disability, can teach but not practise dentistry, you will continue to receive your disability benefits. The own occupation definition provides the strongest form of protection and is also the most expensive. This definition is only available to certain professions, such as medical doctors and dentists.

- **Regular occupation**—Sometimes referred to as "own occupation, not working," the regular occupation definition of disability requires the insured to be under the care of a physician licensed in Canada, be unable to perform the duties of his or her normal occupation as a result of illness or injury, and not be working in any other occupation. Under a regular occupation definition of disability, the dentist who is unable to practice dentistry but is teaching at a university would not receive disability benefits.

- **Any occupation**—The person who is insured would meet the any occupation definition of disability if he or she is under the care of a physician licensed in Canada and, as a result of illness or injury, is unable to perform the duties of any occupation for which he or she is reasonably qualified. This is the weakest form of protection, because once you are able to do any type of work at all, the insurance company considers you to be employable and your coverage will stop.

Some disability policies also pay benefits if you are not totally disabled and can work. Think of any condition which *reduces* your ability to work without eliminating it completely. These benefits may be included in your policy or may have to be purchased as an add-on, or rider, to the base policy. There are two types of coverage in this area—residual disability and partial disability.

Residual disability considers the amount of income you have lost as a direct result of your disability. In order for residual benefits to be applicable, the insured must be working, be under the care of a doctor licensed to practise in Canada, and have a loss of income of between 20% and 80%. Residual disability benefits are based on a comparison of how much money you were making before you became disabled and how much you are making now as a result of an injury or illness. If you were earning $5,000 per month before and are earning $2,500 after the disability, you are losing 50% of your income and will receive 50% of your total monthly disability benefit.

Partial disability coverage is similar to residual disability coverage. The benefit is based on how many hours (time) or important duties you could work before you were disabled compared with how many hours (time) or important duties you can work after. For example, if you were working 60 hours a week and are now working 30 hours, you are unable to work 50% of the time and eligible to receive 50% of your total monthly disability benefit.

Critical Illness Insurance

Critical illness insurance provides a single lump-sum payment if you are diagnosed with one of several serious medical conditions. The conditions covered can vary among insurance companies, but most commonly include heart attack, stroke, and cancer. Health risks are unpredictable and critical illness insurance is meant to ease the financial burden during a time of illness. You can use the proceeds from a critical illness policy for anything you wish, including health-care expenses, childcare costs, reducing debt, or simply allowing you to take more time with your family and focus on getting well. Having additional financial resources during times of critical illness can mean you don't have to use retirement or other savings earlier than planned.

What are the odds that you will develop a critical illness during your lifetime? It varies by condition, but according to the *Canadian Cancer Statistics* publication for 2015, 40% of all Canadians will develop cancer in their lifetimes. So the risk of developing a serious illness is not negligible.

As a consumer you have to weigh the risk versus the cost of insurance. You can choose to self-insure, meaning you take on the financial responsibility if you become seriously ill. One situation in which critical illness insurance can definitely make sense is if you are a stay-at-home parent of small children and cannot get disability insurance because you do not have earned income. Think about how your family's situation would change if you, as the stay-at-home parent, were critically ill. Aside from the emotional strain the illness would put on your family, it would also be very expensive to hire somebody to provide childcare.

Let's look at some other important considerations for critical illness insurance:

- To claim, you must be diagnosed with one of the conditions stated in your policy. Be sure to understand what these are.

- To receive the benefit, you must survive a certain waiting period (known as the elimination period), which can be 30-90 days, depending on the illness and the terms of the policy.

- Pre-existing medical conditions may exclude you from getting coverage (for example, if you had a heart attack before you applied for critical illness insurance, you may be ineligible and declined for coverage). Be sure to understand any exclusions that apply to your policy.

- Policies can usually be purchased until age 65 and can be structured as a limited pay policy, where you pay the premium for a certain number of years, or as a level premium policy, where you pay premiums regularly until the policy expires.

How Insurance Premiums Are Determined

Insurance premiums are based primarily on three factors—probability of mortality (life insurance) and morbidity (critical illness and disability insurance), interest (return on investments), and administrative expenses or operational costs.

Mortality and Morbidity Cost

To determine the appropriate price for insurance products, insurance companies employ actuaries to develop projections of death, critical illness, and disability. The role of the actuary is to use statistics to figure out the probability that any given person will die or suffer an illness or disability based on their characteristics. The insurance company needs to know what the probability of claims and size of the claims that will be payable are likely to be. This information is then used to determine the premium the insurance company collects from policyholders. The premium dollars collected by the insurance company are used to pay operational expenses and/or are invested and eventually used to pay out insurance claims.

What consumers need to know is that the most important determinants of premiums have to do with *you*—your age, gender, health (including family history of medical conditions), and lifestyle. For the insurance company, everything is about risk. The riskier the insurance company considers you to be, the higher your premiums will be. Based on your health, if you are considered an average risk for the insurance company, you are classified as a "standard" risk. If you are in better health than the average for your group, the insurance company would consider you to be a "preferred" risk and your premium would be slightly lower. Finally, if you have a personal or family history of certain medical conditions, your premiums could be "rated," meaning you would pay a higher premium than somebody who is considered a standard risk. Ratings are expressed in percentage terms and could be 125%-200% or more of standard-risk rates. A rating of 150% simply means you would pay one-and-a-half times the standard premium. Everything else being equal, insurance policies for younger people are cheaper than those for older people. Premiums for non-smokers are lower than those for smokers.

Interest Rates
Insurance companies conservatively invest the premiums you pay, using various types of investments including bonds, real estate, and some stocks. The money is invested so that the insurance company has enough money to pay out claims, while also generating profits for shareholders of the insurance company. The insurance company also focuses on what is called asset-liability matching, whereby premiums are invested in such a way that future cash flows are available to meet anticipated liabilities. This minimizes the risk of the insurance company being unable to pay a liability on time.

Generally, the portfolio of any insurance company has significant exposure to bonds due to the lower-risk profile of this asset class.

The returns on these investments help the insurance companies pay claims when a death, critical illness, or disability occurs. Insurance companies have armies of actuaries and statisticians working for them, to calculate mortality and rates of disability and critical illnesses, with a goal of projecting what the liabilities of the insurance company might look like in the future. The insurance company aims to match their assets with the longer-term forecasted liabilities.

Insurance companies need to invest money that is received as premiums, until they pay claims. The return on these investments is critical. In general, interest rates impact how much insurance companies earn on their investments, which then in turn may impact the premiums they charge. If interest rates are very low, insurance companies can earn less on these investments, which may force them to charge higher premiums to make up the difference. Insurance companies have certainly been challenged by the low-interest-rate environment that has persisted in the aftermath of the 2007-08 financial crisis.

It is important to keep in mind, however, that the significance of interest rates also varies by insurance product—not all products are impacted by changes in interest rates to the same extent. Longer-term policies, such as permanent life insurance, are more sensitive to interest rates because the premiums are set at the beginning of the policy. For shorter-duration policies, changes in interest rates are less important.

Administrative Expenses or Operational Costs

This area refers to the cost of operating the insurance company and selling its products. These include marketing costs (advisor or agent compensation, costs of operating sales offices, and advertising expenses) and non-marketing costs (the cost of constructing and maintaining company buildings, salaries of executive officers and staff). Operating expenses vary among insurance companies.

The Insurance Application Process

The insurance application process can be broken down into the following steps:

1. Meet with your advisor to determine your insurance needs, including both the right products to meet your goals and objectives and the amount of coverage. Your advisor will provide you with a policy illustration that clearly explains how the particular insurance product works, along with any applicable guarantees. The advisor will also provide you with a quote or the anticipated cost for the policy you are applying for. This quote is approximate because, depending on your situation, the insurance company may charge a higher premium, especially if you are rated. If you are in good health, you may qualify as a "preferred risk," which can lower your premium.

2. Complete and submit the insurance application form. To complete the form, your advisor will collect personal information and ask you detailed questions about various things, such as your employment status, existing insurance coverage, medical history (such as height, weight, prior conditions, last time you saw a physician, medications you take, medical conditions running in your family), and lifestyle (such as smoking, drug and alcohol use, and the types of recreational activities you participate in). You will be required to provide the insurance company with consent to obtain your medical records if they need this information to make a decision. Depending on the type of policy and amount of coverage, there may be medical tests (such as blood work) required, and a nurse may visit you for this purpose, as well as to obtain a more detailed medical history. I would like to point out that major insurance companies such as Sun Life are trying to modernize the insurance application process to have less onerous medical testing requirements and, in some cases, "instant approval," where possible.

   On the insurance application form, you also have to select the beneficiary(ies) of the policy.

   Your advisor will also have to submit what is known as the advisor's report. This is a summary, from the advisor's perspective, of the purpose of the insurance policy being applied for and any other comments that may help the insurance company make a decision on your application. The more information your advisor can provide to the insurance company (particularly, why you are a good risk), the better. The objective of the advisor's report is to give your advisor the opportunity to paint a picture of you for the insurance company, so that you are not just another number.

If your eligibility for insurance is questionable for reasons such as medical conditions or lifestyle issues, your advisor may consider submitting what is called a "trial" application. Trial applications are preliminary applications that can be submitted to determine eligibility before proceeding with arranging for medical evidence. If eligibility is likely, based on feedback from the insurance company, then the medical evidence can be completed and the formal application submitted.

The insurance company will "underwrite" your application and make a decision. During this process, the company will obtain your medical reports as needed. Depending on the policy you have applied for, the insurance company may request additional medical testing and information from your physician. This is called the attending physician's statement. Additionally, the insurer may obtain information from the MIB Group (formerly Medical Information Bureau), which is a membership corporation owned by over four hundred insurance companies in Canada and the United States. Through a proprietary database, the MIB allows its members to see what underwriters from other insurance companies know about an insurance applicant (from prior insurance applications). If you have applied for insurance before, your information may be in this database and the insurance company could review it. The insurance company may request further information at this stage.

3. Once the decision is made, you will have a certain period of time to accept the policy. If you accept it, you and your advisor will meet and your advisor will verify that nothing material has changed with respect to your health status. Then you will sign the final paperwork and receive a copy of the policy contract (this step is known as "delivering the policy"). Once the policy is accepted and you have paid the premium, the policy is considered to be

"in force." Be sure the premiums are paid on time. Most policies have a 30-day grace period if your premium is late. If you exceed the grace period without paying the premium, your policy will be considered lapsed, meaning you no longer have the insurance coverage. There are reinstatement procedures, but success in having your policy reinstated is not guaranteed. The insurance company may request additional medical information if reinstatement is being requested. A good rule of thumb is that if you are applying for a policy to replace an existing policy, do not cancel your existing policy until the new one is delivered.

When you apply for life insurance, you can obtain temporary coverage, through a temporary insurance agreement (TIA), while your application is going through the approval and underwriting process. To qualify for the temporary coverage, you must pay one month's premium at the time of application and be able to answer "no" to several specific medical questions. Temporary life insurance commences once the life insurance application has been signed and payment has been received. If you die before your insurance application is approved, the TIA will pay the lesser of the amount of coverage you applied for or a maximum amount, usually $500,000 to $1 million. If there is any material misrepresentation on the application, then the insurance company will not be liable to make payment on a claim. Once your policy is approved, the TIA is cancelled. Note, you can only apply for temporary life insurance at the time your policy application is submitted.

Riders

When you hear the word "rider," it's often in relation to the list of things a well-known musician or band requests to have in their dressing room backstage before a show, but the term applies to the insurance world also. Used in this sense, a rider is an additional feature or "extra" that can be added to the base insurance policy you are purchasing. Essentially, riders are optional features that provide additional flexibility or benefit to either the beneficiary or policy owner. Riders are issued with the policy and add an extra cost to the premium. Because riders can be costly, be sure to purchase only what you need, and not more. In the case of whole life and universal insurance policies, riders do not change cash surrender non-forfeiture values. Commonly available life insurance policy riders include the following:

- **Waiver of premium.** If you become totally disabled and cannot work, you no longer have to pay your premium. With a waiver of premium rider, the insurance company will pay the monthly insurance premium while you are totally disabled.

- **Guaranteed insurability.** In the future, you can purchase additional life insurance without going through a subsequent medical exam or additional testing.

- **Critical illness.** In the future, if you are diagnosed with one of the critical illnesses specified in the policy, you will receive a lump-sum payment from the insurance company.

- **Disability income.** If you become totally disabled, the insurance company will provide a monthly income stream, subject to the limitations outlined in the policy.

- **Return of premium.** For a term insurance policy or other living-benefit policies (such as critical illness, disability, and long-term care insurance), if you live past the end of the term you will get all or a portion of your premium back. With this rider, a key consideration is how the extra cost of the premium compares to investing that extra money over time.

The following riders commonly apply to disability insurance:

- **Cost-of-living adjustment (COLA).** Inflation means that, over time, prices increase and your purchasing power decreases. The purpose of the COLA rider is to maintain your purchasing power. This rider will increase the benefit you receive either by a fixed percentage or based on changes in the consumer price index, which measures inflation. COLA riders can have caps on benefit increases. If you are young, a COLA rider is critical in case you become disabled at an early age.

- **Future purchase option.** Also known as a future income option, this rider allows you to increase your monthly benefit as your income rises over time without evidence of insurability being required. You will, however, have to prove that your income has increased, and your total insurance premium will likely increase since your total coverage is also increasing. Usually, the option to increase future income must be exercised by a certain age (usually 50). This is an important rider, particularly for young professionals who anticipate large income increases in the future.

Contestability

In the insurance industry, there is a concept called "contestability," which refers to the legal right of the insurance company to challenge the validity of your insurance contract. Incontestability means the insurer cannot challenge the contract. The insurance company can challenge a contract for a period of two years from the date of issue, which is referred to as the contestable period.

For example, with a contestable contract the insurance company can challenge the payment of the death benefit if the insurer finds there to be material misrepresentation on the insurance application after the fact. If evidence of outright fraud is found, the insurance contract can be terminated regardless of when the policy was put in place. Because of contestability, it is essential that you do not make any misrepresentations on your insurance application. Also, keep in mind that when you replace a policy with a new one, the contestability clock starts again, meaning your new policy is now contestable for two years.

Insurance-Based Investment Products

Note: to sell the insurance products described below, your advisor must be life insurance-licensed.

Segregated Funds

Segregated funds are a type of investment available from life insurance companies. These funds are not securities products but rather insurance products also known as individual variable insurance contracts (IVICS). The easiest way to understand segregated funds is to think of them as mutual funds with an extra layer of insurance, known in the industry as an insurance "wrapper." Here are some key features of segregated funds:

- An IVIC provides two guarantees: the maturity guarantee and the death benefit guarantee. Combined, the two guarantees are referred to as the principal guarantee.

- IVICS have a 10- to 15-year minimum holding period for the guaranteed maturity benefit. The maturity guarantee provides for the return of at least 75% of deposits on maturity of the contract 10 years after the investor signs it. For 100% maturity guarantee, the holding period must be 15 years or longer. When the contract matures, the investor receives the greater of the maturity guarantee or the market value of the contract.

- During the contract period, the death benefit guarantee provides for payment to a beneficiary of at least 75% of deposits if the owner of the contract dies (some segregated funds provide a 100% guarantee). The beneficiary receives the greater of the guaranteed death benefit or the market value of the contract on its maturity.

- You can purchase segregated funds in different types of guarantee combinations. For example, the 75/75 product provides a 75% guarantee at contract maturity and 75% if you die before the maturity date. The 75/100 product provides a 75% guarantee at contract maturity and 100% if you die before the maturity date. The 100/100 product provides a 100% guarantee at contract maturity and 100% if you die before the maturity date.

- The guarantees limit losses. As the owner of the contract, you know the minimum amount you or your beneficiaries can expect to receive.

- Some segregated funds allow their value to be locked in during contract period. This is called the reset feature. If the fund has increased in value since you purchased it, resetting allows you to lock in that value so that gains cannot be eroded by a future market downturn. As the fund continues to grow in value, additional resets can be used to lock in the fund value at ever higher levels. Death and maturity guarantee benefits will be based on the reset amount and so will be higher than when the contract was purchased. Reset terms can be different depending on the company that issues the product, and there can be a maximum number of resets allowed over a given period of time. Some resets are set to happen automatically at certain times, but others require the advisor to request the reset. Keep in mind that when the reset feature is exercised, the maturity date is likely to be extended to 10 or 15 years (whatever the original term was) from the reset date.

You might want to consider owning segregated funds because they

- provide growth potential through exposure to investment markets with the ability to lock in gains;

- offer security of capital with a long-term guarantee of at least 75% of gross contributions, which minimizes exposure to market downturns;

- protect the value of your investment for beneficiaries through the death benefit guarantee;

- are not subject to probate or other estate-settling fees (as long as proceeds are not paid through the estate), leaving more money for your family;

- provide privacy in the event you pass away because the beneficiaries are paid directly rather than through the estate and probate process (probate files are public court records anyone can obtain); and

- can protect your registered and non-registered assets from creditors in the case of bankruptcy or being named in a lawsuit. It is critical to understand, however, that if you purchase segregated funds with the knowledge that you are going to be bankrupt, the legal system can void your transaction in the future, which will leave your assets exposed to creditors.

Segregated funds have many features that can be beneficial depending on your specific goals and objectives; features such as the guarantee levels will depend on your specific contract. Segregated funds have the same kind of fees as mutual funds, including sales (load) charges and MERs, but the fees for segregated funds are slightly higher because there is a cost for the guarantees (this is similar in concept to the cost of insurance) and other features. As a consumer, you have to decide whether the additional features provided outweigh the additional costs. Think about this in the context of your financial goals and objectives. Keep in mind that different insurance companies may also have a maximum age at which segregated funds can be purchased or certain guarantee options are available.

Your financial advisor should be familiar with segregated funds and be able to recommend whether they meet your objectives. The following provides an overview of the four situations where segregated funds can make sense:

- **Guarantee of principal is important.** Chenguang is 50 years old and has $100,000 cash in her bank account, where it is earning very little interest. She does not see herself ever needing this money and would like it to grow to enhance her estate. She understands that over the long term the stock market provides the greatest opportunity for growth, but she once had a bad experience in the stock market and still has some negative emotions about it. Segregated funds could make sense for Chenguang because she wants higher returns in order to leave a larger estate and she realizes she needs exposure to the stock market to achieve this. She is able to make a long-term investment and is more comfortable doing this because of the guarantee of principal. Chenguang comes to the conclusion that paying the additional fees associated with segregated funds is better than having her money sit in her bank account, earning very little interest.

- **Death benefit and probate advantages are needed.** Anais is 70 years old and is married to Harry; both she and Harry have children from previous marriages. Anais inherited $500,000 from her mother and would like to pass this money directly to her own children. Currently, the money is in a bank account, earning little interest. Anais wants the funds to grow, but does not want to lose any of the principal. Segregated funds are appropriate for Anais because if she passes away when the markets are going down, her children will receive the value of at least the original investment (assuming she chooses the 100% guarantee). The funds will pass directly to the children she has named as beneficiaries without going through probate.

- **Principal guarantee and death benefit resets are desired.** Jacob invests $100,000 in a segregated fund and wants the ability to lock in investment gains in the future; three years later, his investment has grown to $130,000. After an automatic reset, $130,000 becomes the new guaranteed amount—the amount he will receive on maturity or that his beneficiaries will receive on his death.

- **Creditor protection is needed.** Miriam is a business owner with a net worth of $20 million. Although her business is performing well and she has never been named in any lawsuits, Miriam would like to protect a portion of her assets from creditors. By investing in segregated funds and naming her spouse or child as the beneficiary, Miriam can protect her personal assets from creditors if the business fails or she is named in a lawsuit. To further illustrate this point, a former advisor provided me with a case study that is startling. Donald, 73 years old, sold his business for $4 million—these funds were intended to be used as retirement capital. Shortly after selling his business, Donald was involved in a severe car accident where he was at fault and subsequently sued. The settlement was for $5 million, and Donald's auto insurance covered a maximum of $2 million. As a result, the remaining part of the settlement ate up most of Donald's retirement nest egg, severely impacting his retirement in a negative way. In this case, if Donald had invested the proceeds of the sale of his business (or at least a portion of it) into segregated funds, creditors would not have had access to this money.

➤ **TAKE NOTE:** Understand which investment products your advisor is licensed to sell. Advisors who are only insurance-licensed have access only to segregated funds. Likewise, advisors who are only securities-licensed, will not be able to provide access to segregated funds. When considering segregated funds, make sure you need their specific—and more expensive—features before buying.

Guaranteed Withdrawal Benefits

Another product that is built on the foundation of segregated funds is called the Guaranteed Minimum Withdrawal Benefit (GMWB) or the Guaranteed Lifetime Withdrawal Benefit (GLWB). In essence, when you purchase these products, you are exchanging a lump sum of capital for a series of payments that may last for a certain number of years or for your lifetime. These products also offer possibility of increasing payouts if stock and bond markets perform well. But there's a trade-off: you get upside potential if markets do well, but the minimum guaranteed income can be less than you get from a conventional fixed annuity. For the purposes of this discussion, we will use the GMWB to illustrate the basic concepts. See your advisor for more detailed information.

When you purchase a GMWB, you also select particular investments for market exposure. The basic idea is that when you purchase the product, you receive a guaranteed income floor, which may be in the range of 4%-5% of your investment—let's call this the base rate. In addition, if the performance of the investments you select proves better than the base rate, you may be eligible for bonus income. Your total payment is composed of payments consisting of the minimum income (established initially) plus any applicable bonus income. If you purchase a GMWB product before you are ready to retire and can wait several years before drawing a payment, you will receive a bonus (usually in the range of 5% for each year you delay payments). Note: this is not a cash deposit, but rather it increases the amount that is guaranteed for future income withdrawals. Bonuses are only on the original investment and not compounded.

GMWB products provide the potential for resets to occur periodically, thus giving investors the opportunity to participate in the upside of the markets. Sometimes these products are referred to as variable annuities. But the resets are not guaranteed. If the markets do well, then you have a chance to increase the amount of income you will receive in the future.

The first GMWB product was brought to market by Manulife in 2006. Due to the financial crisis of 2007-08 and the resulting severe market decline, the GMWB guarantees paid off for product owners.

Insurance companies had liabilities and had to set aside capital to cover them. Since that period of time, the features of these products have been pared back.

GMWB products may or may not be right for you. If you have a defined-benefit pension plan already, or you have more money then you will ever need, this product may not be for you. However, GMWBs can fill a gap for people without defined-benefit pension plans, and can provide a reliable income stream to meet basic non-discretionary expenses during retirement. This will safeguard you against longevity risk, or the possibility of running out of money during retirement. For some people, the peace of mind alone makes these products worth considering. If you are in this situation, you need to weigh the peace of mind against the higher product fees and the fact that your cash flows may not be protected against inflation. Consider also the impact on your estate— withdrawals can proportionately reduce death benefit guarantees. The alternative is to have a fixed annuity provide a basic income stream and protect against market fluctuations, and then own a good quality portfolio of companies that pay and grow dividends. This option would likely have a lower total fee, but it comes with some market risk. As always, do your due diligence and make sure you read the fine print. As with all products, if you don't understand it, don't buy it.

Annuities

Annuities are another investment product issued through insurance companies. With an annuity, you sign a contract with an insurance company and pay a lump-sum annuity premium. The insurance company will invest your money and pay you back a guaranteed, fixed income stream for the remainder of your life or for a certain period, depending on how you structure the annuity. Annuities provide you with peace of mind—you will receive a guaranteed amount of money for the life or term of your annuity.

The amount of income you receive is called the "benefit." The benefit is composed of three different components, as described below. Over time, while the overall payment received will remain the same, the proportion coming from each of the three different components will change.

- **Return of capital**. A portion of every payment you receive consists of a return of the capital you initially contributed.

- **Interest**. The insurance company invests the premium dollars you provide, and a portion of each payment you receive consists of interest or income earned from the investments. Note, in general, that the benefits received are sensitive to interest rates. When interest rates are low, benefit payments are usually smaller simply because the insurance company earns lower returns on your premium dollars. When interest rates are higher, the insurance company earns more on the investment earnings and can pay annuity holders more. Benefit levels are established and set at contract signing.

- **Mortality credit**. There is a portion of the payment you receive that is linked directly to the age of the annuitant—this is referred to as mortality credit and is discussed in more detail later in the chapter.

The key principles to understand about annuities are twofold. First, when you purchase an annuity you are in effect exchanging a large sum of money for a guaranteed income stream for a certain period of time. At the end of your life, depending on the specific contract terms of your annuity and when you pass away, there may or may not be any capital left for your estate. This is very important to understand. Second, as just explained, the benefit payments are sensitive to interest rates. In every annuity contract, the four main parties are

- the contract owner, who pays the premium;
- the person who receives the annuity benefit (the annuitant);
- the person who receives a benefit if the annuitant dies (the beneficiary); and
- the insurance company.

Types of Life Annuities
Though the key principle is the same, several different types of annuities are available:

- **Straight life annuities** provide the maximum payments because there are no beneficiaries in this contract (the concept is that when you die—even if you die early—payments stop).

- **Cash refund annuities** provide your beneficiaries with a lump-sum payment at the time of death if the total principal (or premium) you paid has not already been returned or paid back.

- **Guaranteed annuities** provide guaranteed benefit payments for a certain period of time. For example, if you have a 10-year guarantee and die in Year 3, your beneficiary will receive benefit payments for the next seven years. The duration of the guarantee can vary and depends on your contract.

- **Joint last-to-die annuities**, commonly used by couples, cover the lives of both spouses. When one spouse dies, the surviving spouse will continue to receive benefit payments (the amount may or may not be the same, depending on how the annuity was structured). When the second spouse passes away, there are no payments to beneficiaries.

- **Term-certain annuities**, also known as fixed-term annuities, provide a guaranteed benefit for a specified period. The length of the term, be it five years or 20, is the choice of the contract owner. Term-certain annuities can also be provided to a certain age. In principle, term-certain annuities are similar to term life insurance policies in that there is an expiry date. If you pass away within the term of the annuity, your beneficiaries can receive the benefit payments. The key risk with these annuities is the danger that you may outlive the benefit payments.

There are different subtypes of annuities that vary depending on the answers to three questions—when do the payments start, how long do benefits last, and is the annuity purchased with registered or non-registered money?

When Do the Payments Start?
Annuity payments can start immediately or they can be deferred. When you purchase an immediate annuity, the payments start within

your first "annuity period." For example, if you have an annuity that will provide yearly income, your first payment will come within a year of when you purchased the annuity; if you have an annuity that will provide monthly income, your first payment will start within a month of purchase. An immediate annuity is typically purchased with a single premium because benefit payments begin so quickly.

You can instead elect to start taking the income at some point in the future—this is called a deferred annuity. A deferred annuity begins to pay benefits to the annuitant a year or more after the annuity was purchased. Because the benefits are deferred, the annuity can be funded either through a single lump-sum payment or with a series of payments over time.

How Long Do the Benefits Last?

Annuities can provide benefits for the rest of your life (life annuity) or for a certain period of time (term-certain annuity). Life annuities work on the same principle as permanent insurance in that they provide lifelong protection. Benefit payments can be guaranteed for a certain number of years and if the annuitant dies before receiving the guaranteed number of payments, benefits will be paid to the contract beneficiaries either as a lump sum or in instalments, depending on the specifics of the annuity contract.

Insurance companies can offer annuities because insurers can pool risk—in the case of life annuities, the risk to the insurance company is that you will live longer than anticipated, meaning it has to pay out an income stream to you for longer than expected. But because of the large volume of annuities an insurance company will place, it will be able to mitigate its overall risk. Some people will live longer than expected, but some people will live for a shorter period—this way, the insurance company can manage its overall risk. As mentioned earlier, mortality credit refers to the portion of each annuity payment that is linked directly to the age of the annuitant. The mortality credit plays a larger role in the payments as you age. The key concept is that when some annuitants pass away earlier than expected, the premiums they paid are now available to the overall pool and can be part of the pool of money to provide for the remaining annuitants.

Annuity Taxation

As a rule of thumb, an annuity will retain the same form of taxation as the source of the funds used to purchase it. For example, if you use your RRSP or RRIF to buy the annuity, you are using registered money and the annuity income is fully taxable as regular income in the year it is received. When the annuity income is fully taxed as regular income, it is referred to as a "non-prescribed annuity." If, on the other hand, the annuity is purchased with non-registered money, it may be characterized as a "prescribed annuity."

The distinction is important because of the tax consequences. Remember that when you buy an annuity, part of the cash flow you receive will be interest (because the insurance company has invested the money you provided) and the remainder will be your principal (or return of your capital). When you purchase an annuity with non-registered funds, tax is payable on the interest but the principal returned to you is tax-free (it is your own money and was taxed when you earned it). Prescribed annuities provide tax advantages such as tax deferral through levelling taxable income over the duration of the contract. To qualify as a prescribed annuity, it must meet several conditions based on the *Income Tax Act*.

Non-prescribed annuity taxable income is higher in the early years and decreases over time as principal is reduced. Non-prescribed annuities (interest is taxed as it is earned) are less tax-efficient because in the earlier years, payments comprise a greater amount of taxable interest than principal. This proportion shifts over time so that, in later years, you receive more non-taxable principal and less interest. In summary, in the earlier years taxable income is higher (higher tax and less cash flow after tax) and in the later years taxable income will decline (less tax and higher cash flow after tax).

Note that, as of January 1, 2017, the federal government implemented new rules regarding the taxation of prescribed annuities which increase the taxable portion of payments. As a result, prescribed annuities will be less tax-effective than before. However, prescribed annuities are still a valuable tool to mitigate the risk of living too long. If you have any questions about how taxation works with annuities, see your tax specialist.

Who Are Annuities Appropriate For?

Generally, Canadians nearing retirement age should consider annuities as part of their overall income strategy because annuities provide a guaranteed source of income to cover essential living expenses and to supplement income from government pensions or benefits such as the Canada Pension Plan and Old Age Security pension program. An annuity has less (or little) appeal for somebody who is very wealthy and not at all concerned about meeting fixed living expenses.

A term annuity can also be useful as an "income bridge." For example, you may be retiring at age 60 but will not receive payments from your defined-benefit pension plan until age 65. A five-year annuity could bridge the gap. Having a guaranteed source of income helps to create an "income floor" so you do not have to worry about covering basic expenses. If you employ this type of strategy, you may feel more comfortable about having the remainder of your investment portfolio exposed to traditional equity and fixed-income investments for the long run. While it is most common for people approaching retirement to begin looking at annuities, these products can be appropriate for people of other age groups looking for an income for a certain period of time.

How Is the Benefit Level Determined?

An annuity's level of benefits is based on several factors, including the sex and age of the annuitant, the level of prevailing interest rates, timing (whether the annuity is immediate or deferred), the duration of the annuity (defined-term or lifelong), and any special terms, such as guarantee periods. The most important concepts to understand about annuity benefits are as follows:

- The older you are when you purchase an annuity, the higher the annuity payment will likely be—from the insurance company's perspective, if you are statistically more likely to die sooner, the insurer can pay you more and still be profitable. If you are ill with a serious medical condition, such as cancer, and you purchase an annuity, your annuity could be "rated," whereby the insurance company provides a higher payment because you are likely to live for a shorter period of time given the illness. In general, annuities tend to make the most sense when people are in their 60s or early 70s. However, depending on your goals, objectives, and financial circumstances, an annuity can also make sense at a younger age.

- Higher interest rates provide the insurance company with better returns on the investment of the money you pay as the annuity premium, meaning the insurer is in a better position to provide higher benefits. When interest rates are low, annuity benefits will likely be low and/or premiums will likely be higher. It is also important to keep in mind that shorter-term annuities are more sensitive to interest rates, while longer-term annuities are less sensitive to interest rates because insurance companies have the ability to better match their assets and liabilities in the longer term.

- The more bells and whistles you have in the annuity contract, the greater the likelihood that the benefit payments will be reduced or the premium will be higher. For example, if your annuity contract has a guaranteed benefit period as well as a benefit indexed to inflation, the benefit payment may be lower or you will have to pay more for the annuity. There is always give and take between you and the insurance company. The greater the protection, the greater the cost or the lower the benefit. One way or another you will pay for these features.

In general, annuities are a great way to exchange capital for a specific level of income for either a defined period or your lifetime. Keep in mind that once you exchange the capital for income, there will be less capital eventually available to your heirs as part of your estate. On the flip side, however, you may end up living longer than expected and you will continue to receive annuity payments even though all of your capital has really been returned to you by the insurance company. Essentially, when you purchase an annuity you are making a trade-off between certainty of cash flow or income and having less in your estate at death. This can be mitigated to some extent by ensuring that the annuity that is purchased has guaranteed payments for a set number of years. This way, theoretically, if you die the day after you purchase an annuity, your estate will receive some value. Because annuities can be complex, it is critical to have an advisor help you to make sure you are meeting your specific needs. Read the fine print and ask lots of questions.

How Are Advisors Paid for Insurance Products?

Generally speaking, when you purchase an insurance policy, your advisor is paid an upfront commission that varies based on the type of policy sold. As a rule of thumb, the commission to your advisor will be approximately equal to one year's worth of premiums for your policy. This is for determining your need for a life insurance product and advising you. For example, if you purchase a $1-million term life policy with a premium of $2,500 per year, the gross commission to your advisor will be about $2,500. This amount will then flow through the dealer's grid and the advisor will receive a net amount. In addition, your advisor may receive a small ongoing residual payment, similar to the way advisors who sell traditional mutual funds receive an ongoing income stream for a certain period of time. The residual income is meant to pay for ongoing service and advice to the client—so make sure you take advantage of this.

For segregated funds, advisors can receive compensation through initial or deferred sales charges, as well as an ongoing trailer fee for service (this is similar in principle to advisor compensation received from mutual funds). For annuities, advisor compensation is typically a percentage of the amount of the annuity. Annuities have a modest front-end deposit-based commission and that's it. It is usually 3% of the first 100,000 and then 1%-2% on the balance.

With insurance products, a substantial part of advisor compensation can come from commissions at the initial sale. Because of this commission payment structure, there is a potential conflict of interest. The best way to mitigate this possible conflict is to select the right advisor.

Conclusions about Insurance

In summary, insurance is an often overlooked yet critical part of protecting your financial capacity and allowing you to leave a legacy to your family and/or charitable organizations. Insurance requirements should always be examined in the context of your overall financial plan, and the solutions need to be custom-built for your plan. Over time, your insurance needs will change. In your earlier years, the focus of insurance should be on making sure your family can pay off debts and replace income if you were to pass away or suffer a critical illness or disability. As you age and move toward retirement, the focus will likely change to using insurance as an estate-planning tool to maximize the estate for your children or to leave a permanent legacy to humanity, or a combination of the two. Insurance products can also be very useful for retirement income planning purposes.

I strongly suggest thinking about insurance as another asset class and a diversifier for your overall financial portfolio. It may also help to think about your financial portfolio as a pie with several slices that include real estate (your home or rental properties), a traditional investment portfolio consisting of stocks and bonds, and insurance products. I recommend reviewing your insurance annually, to make sure you are adequately insured and that the insurance you have in place is working as you need it to.

I often hear comments such as "insurance is never a good investment" or "insurance is not worth it." Nothing could be further from the truth. Yes, you may pay premiums and never make a claim. But being adequately insured is absolutely critical because in life you never know what will happen. In addition, insurance can be a very powerful tool for business owners and for general estate-planning purposes. Be sure to discuss your specific goals and objectives with a qualified advisor.

Estate Planning 101

Estate planning is something few people want to think about, let alone talk about. That's understandable. Death is not a pleasant subject. But the reality is that life is short and time is limited; one day you will die. Yet, according to a 2012 study by LawPRO, over 50% of

Canadians have not signed a will! This is inexcusable. Because death is inevitable, estate planning is critical.

What is estate planning? Different people have different definitions. To me, it boils down to answering the following questions: "What would happen if I were to suddenly die or become incapacitated?", "How do I want my assets distributed?", and "How can I control the amount of tax payable to the government on my death?" You must understand what your goals are, what is important to you, and what you are trying to accomplish through your estate plan.

For the sake of your loved ones, it is imperative that you have three important documents: a will, power of attorney, and personal (medical) directive.

Your Will

Commonly, a person's will is the only written words they leave behind. Thomas Deans wrote a wonderful book titled *Willing Wisdom: 7 Questions to Ask Before You Die*. This book presents a thought-provoking discussion about how to pass wisdom to the next generation and engage families in collaborative conversations about wills. I highly recommend it.

The basic purpose of a will is to ensure that, when you die, your assets will be distributed the way you want them to be. In Canada, if you die without a will, the government considers you to have died "intestate." This means the legislation set out in the province in which you resided will decide how your assets are divided.

A common assumption is that if you die without a will, your assets simply pass to your spouse. But this assumption is only partially correct. In most provinces, what really happens is that only assets held jointly between spouses with right of survivorship pass to the surviving spouse automatically. This would include joint bank and investment accounts, along with TFSAs that have the joint right of survivorship designation. If you die intestate, your legal spouse and any children may share the rest of your estate. The calculation of each share varies depending on provincial rules. Spouses may receive a certain amount of the estate first, usually ranging from the first $40,000 to the first $200,000, with the remainder being divided between your spouse and children. Realize that if you die without a will, your estate may not be divided the way you wanted it to be and your wishes may not be respected, even if your family knows what they were. Furthermore, you could leave your heirs open to potential challenges and a legacy of litigation and family disputes. For people with non-traditional families, there could also be other complications, such as common-law spouses being left out of the estate owing to a lack of recognition of spousal status.

Selecting an Executor

One of your most important estate-planning decisions is naming an executor (sometimes referred to as a personal representative) to ensure that your wishes are carried out as stated in your will. Most people appoint their spouse or common-law partner as their first choice. You should also name at least one other person as an alternate executor in case your first choice is unwilling or unable to act as executor.

While being an executor historically has been an honour to be bestowed on a family member or friend, it is important to understand that being an executor can be a very demanding and time-consuming role. To get things done quickly and without added costs, and to meet all legal and financial responsibilities, your executor has to be knowledgeable in many disciplines and interact with many different parties, as shown below. If not, specialists may have to be hired, with their fees charged to your estate. The duties of an executor can be quite extensive. Some of the tasks are as follows:

- Reviewing the will and applying for grant of probate
- Creating inventory of all asset and liabilities
- Arranging valuations of real estate, securities, personal property, and automobiles
- Settling debt obligations, including closing credit card accounts
- Closing bank and brokerage accounts
- Selling property and other assets, as required
- Dividing and distributing assets
- Completing previous year and terminal tax returns

Executors Wear Many Hats

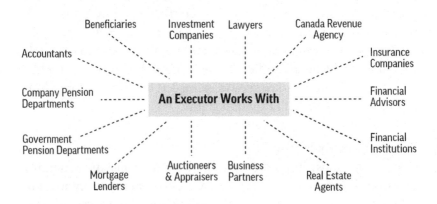

An executor works with many parties. *Source: Fiduciary Trust*

When selecting an executor, you also have to think about the emotional pressure on this individual. He or she may be held personally liable if mistakes are made, and the executor has to stay completely impartial during what can be a very stressful time.

It is important to keep in mind that having an executor who lives outside of the province where you reside, or outside of Canada, can cause complications to the estate. In the case of an out-of-province or out-of-country executor, because the government may have less control, a court can insist that a bond is in place to ensure that assets are not taken out of the province or country and disbursed improperly. The bond requirement could be waived if all beneficiaries agree to this, but there is no guarantee that all beneficiaries would agree. Everything else being equal, it is better to have an executor who lives in your province of residence. If there is nobody in your province of residence whom you trust to make sure your final wishes are taken care of, think about appointing a local trust company as a co-executor.

Most wills include a provision that grants the executor the power to hire professional advisors to help carry out their duties. One of the common errors individual executors make is trying to fulfill the role on their own, struggling and eventually realizing months later that help is needed once initial work has already been attempted (at which point, if the situation is "messy," a trust company may decline to take the file). Knowing all the complexities and responsibilities of being an executor, some people appoint a trust company as their executor. Choosing to have a trust company act as co-executor with a spouse, other family member, or friend (as mentioned above) is another option that is becoming increasingly popular. In this situation, the trust company takes responsibility for all the day-to-day administration and management activities related to settling the estate. Your beneficiaries will have the advantages of professional administration, and the trust company will be able to work with someone who was close to you, which is important especially when it comes to dealing with personal effects and wishes. Trust companies can be independent or owned by a large financial institution such as a bank.

To administer an estate, trust companies will charge a one-time fee that varies with the size of the estate. Such fees differ among companies but can be up to 3%–5% of the estate's value, and a minimum fee could apply. Note: generally the trust company is compensated similar to the amount that a "lay" executor can take, which is also 3%–5% of the value of the estate. Also be aware that trust companies may have a minimum size of estate that is required for them to work with you.

Additionally, trust companies can serve the role of trustee of a trust created by your will. In this case, most trust companies will want to manage a portion or all of the investment assets with the trust. The investment manager may be an investment management company that is related to the trust company (such as a subsidiary). Trust companies will charge an ongoing annual fee that is based on the size of the investment portfolio. Fee schedules can vary between companies.

Other Considerations for Your Will

In addition to selecting an executor, there are a few other things to keep in mind when creating a will.

- **Division of your estate.** Consider how you want to distribute your estate. Doing so in percentages may be better than specific dollar amounts because the value of your estate can change over time. To assist you in this process, prepare an updated list of all your assets (including investments, real estate, and any other valuables) and any liabilities (mortgages and other debt) for your executor. Most advisors will be able to help you with this.

- **Asset protection.** Individuals who have a higher net worth will want to think about protecting their wealth and passing down as much as possible to the next generation. Another consideration is protecting assets in the event of marital breakdown among your children. Be aware that in provinces other than Quebec, any inheritance your children receive is not considered matrimonial property—unless it is comingled with the assets of your child's spouse (for example, if the inheritance was used to pay down a mortgage), in which case the inheritance becomes matrimonial property. Even if the inheritance is kept separate, any growth of those assets is classified as matrimonial property. In general, asset protection objectives can be achieved through the use of more complex structures known as "trusts." When considering trusts, seeking appropriate legal advice is critical.

- **Guardianship of minor children.** If you have children under age 18, in case your spouse or common-law partner does not survive you, you will need to appoint a guardian to care for your children until they turn the age of majority.

- **Specific bequests.** Prepare a letter instructing your executor to give away certain items as you instruct.

- **Burial instructions.** You can include burial and funeral preferences in your will or put them in a letter of instruction for your executor.

- **Tax efficiency.** Consider ways to minimize any tax owing at your death through the use of charitable giving or additional insurance (see the estate tax section below).

- **Legal review.** Obtain advice from a wills and estate lawyer when preparing your will—this is absolutely critical. The creation of a will is important and must be done correctly. Attempting to do it yourself using an off-the-shelf will kit could cause unnecessary legal complications for your executor and heirs.

Review your will annually or at least biannually, particularly to make sure that it is aligned with your estate plan. Over time, personal, financial, and tax circumstances can change and your will needs to reflect those changes. Think of the periodic review as similar in concept to checking your smoke detector—you have to check it annually to make sure it is working for you!

Power of Attorney

Life is unpredictable at best. How would you handle your financial affairs if you were hit by a bus and were incapacitated and unable to make financial decisions? The purpose of the power of attorney is to appoint a representative to make financial decisions for you if you are unable to do so.

While I highly advise getting proper legal advice to create a power of attorney, in most cases you will want to give your financial representative the authority to manage your financial affairs only if you become incapacitated—this is known as a "springing" power of attorney. Usually at least one medical professional has to confirm your inability to make financial decisions. Some lawyers will draft the power of attorney document such that two medical professionals have to make this confirmation. Without a power of attorney, your family may have to go to court to obtain permission to manage these areas of your life when you are no longer able to.

Personal Directive

Also known as a medical directive or power of attorney for healthcare, a personal directive allows you to appoint a representative to make medical decisions for you if you are unable to do so. Included in the personal directive should be items such as your preferences for end-of-life care. Your personal directive becomes effective when you no longer have the capacity to make medical decisions (this usually has to be confirmed by two medical professionals). If you do not have a personal directive, your healthcare preferences may be unknown and therefore not carried out. Your family could be put in the position of having to make difficult decisions, which can lead to strains in family relationships when opinions differ.

A key decision you have to make is who to appoint as your representative. It should be somebody you trust and in whom you have the highest confidence. It also obviously needs to be somebody willing to act in that capacity. Most people appoint their spouse as their first choice and name an alternate (such as a very close friend or family member) in case their spouse is not able or not willing to make the decisions.

Estate Tax

Note: the discussion that follows is current at the time of writing, but keep in mind that tax rates and government policy are subject to change.

As Benjamin Franklin famously said, in life there are only two certainties—death and taxes. There is no specific estate or inheritance tax in Canada; the death of an individual can still trigger a large tax bill for the estate. The Canada Revenue Agency (CRA) considers the entire estate to be sold at death unless it is inherited by a surviving spouse or common-law partner, in most cases. For couples, in practical terms what this means is that when the first spouse passes away, assets will be rolled over to the surviving spouse, and when the surviving spouse dies, the estate may owe tax. Be aware that Canadians (who are non-US citizens) can be subject to US estate tax if they have a substantial estate and die owning US assets, such as property and US-listed stocks and bonds. Luckily, there are tax credits available under the Canada-US Income Tax Treaty such that, as of 2015, if the estate value is less than $5.4 million, US estate tax will generally not apply. High-net-worth individuals should seek advice from a qualified tax specialist.

In Canada, tax consequences vary depending on the type of assets involved. Let's take a closer look at some of the potential tax implications at death and how the taxes can be minimized.

Non-registered Investments

When someone dies, the CRA assumes that all non-registered assets are disposed of immediately at fair market value. This is known as a "deemed disposition." Half of any gains are reported on the final tax return (the "terminal" return) of the deceased individual. Those gains are taxed at the person's marginal tax rate. Note that capital gains rates and tax rules may change in the future.

Here's an example: Assume you died with investments in non-registered accounts worth $500,000 that had an ACB of $100,000, resulting in a paper gain (the gain has not yet been realized by selling the investments) of $400,000. Half of that is taxable at your normal marginal tax rate. In 2016, for an Alberta resident in the top tax bracket, the tax bill would be $400,000 × 50% × 48%, or $96,000. This includes federal and provincial tax.

If non-registered assets are passed on to a surviving spouse, the tax on them will be deferred until the death of that spouse. The surviving spouse will inherit the assets and the ACB that comes along with them.

Registered Retirement Investments

As with non-registered assets in cash investment accounts, the CRA assumes that assets inside registered retirement plans such as RRSPs and RRIFs are disposed of at death. Because of the tax-advantaged status of these accounts, the entire fair market value is taxable at the deceased's applicable marginal tax rate.

Using the previous example, if you were to pass away with a portfolio of registered investments worth $500,000, the tax payable at death would be calculated as follows: $400,000 × 48%, or $192,000.

If registered assets are passed on to the surviving spouse's RRSP or RRIF through a beneficiary designation or through the will by making an election, the tax will be deferred until the death of the second spouse. As the spouse withdraws funds from the RRSP or RRIF, this income will be taxed at the appropriate marginal tax rate. When the surviving spouse passes away, any remaining investments in the RRSP or RRIF will be subject to the CRA's deemed disposition rules—that is, the entire fair market value of those accounts then remaining will be taxed at the applicable marginal tax rate for the second spouse. In the case where beneficiaries are named for registered accounts such as RRSPs or RRIFs, these assets are generally not probated. It can also be possible to leave RRSP assets to a financially dependent child or grandchild. If the child or grandchild is not of majority age, he or she could use the funds to purchase an annuity to age 18. This can potentially lower the total amount of tax paid as the income is spread over a number of years. If the child or grandchild is over 18, the proceeds will be included in his or her income (potentially at a lower average tax rate, depending on the situation).

Principal Residence

Principal residences are generally tax-exempt at death. The property will be dealt with according to the will. If the property goes to your heirs, any future growth in value or income received from the property will be taxed in their hands. Note that, beginning in the 2016 tax year, the CRA now requires that individuals report details about the sale of their principal residences, in order to claim the full principal residence exemption.

Reducing Taxes at Death

As part of completing your estate plan, your advisor should provide you with an estimate of what your estate tax could be. Remember that planning is very sensitive to assumptions, so this tax projection is only a ballpark estimate. But with the rough estimate in hand, you can consider whether you wish to take steps to reduce estate tax using charitable or planned giving, insurance coverage, or a combination of these. The key point here is that by using some of these tools, you can implement a self-directed tax plan at death. Instead of the government being a financial beneficiary of your death, you can direct the dollars that would have gone to the government in tax to registered charities of your choice. The government will benefit indirectly, as the charitable organizations will have increased resources, thus requiring less support from the government (in theory). This can be referred to as a "self-directed tax plan."

Remember that additional life insurance used for the purposes of reducing taxes owed by the estate will cost you money in insurance premiums while you are alive. This may or may not be affordable depending on your health and cash flow situation. Let's take a look at a specific example in which someone dies with a $2-million estate comprising real estate, non-registered investments, and registered investments, with a total tax liability of $500,000. We will examine several different scenarios.

SCENARIO 1: NO CHARITABLE DONATIONS

- Planned giving to registered charity: $0
- Insurance policy proceeds: $0
- $500,000 to the CRA
- $1.5 million to heirs
- Tax savings: $0

SCENARIO 2: CHARITABLE DONATIONS OF $500,000 IN YEAR OF DEATH

- Planned giving to registered charity: $500,000 to charities, resulting in tax credit to the estate of 50% of value of donation (tax credits vary slightly among provinces and may change in the future)
- Insurance policy proceeds: $0
- $250,000 to the CRA
- $1.25 million to heirs (initial estate of $2 million – $500,000 charitable donation – $250,000 to CRA)
- Tax savings: $250,000

SCENARIO 3: INSURANCE POLICY OF $1 MILLION AND CHARITABLE DONATIONS OF $1 MILLION IN YEAR OF DEATH

- Planned giving to registered charity: $1 million
- Insurance policy proceeds: $1 million
- $0 to CRA (charitable donation wipes out tax)
- $2 million to heirs (initial estate of $2 million + $1 million insurance payout – $1 million charitable donation)
- Tax savings: $500,000

(Note that Scenario 3 does not include cash outflow to pay for the insurance premiums and it assumes that donations save $0.50 of tax for each dollar donated. The actual tax benefit for donations will vary based on the province where you reside and your income level.)

Giving the proceeds of an insurance policy to a registered charity has a number of advantages. First, it provides an affordable way for an individual to leave a substantial gift to charity, maximizing the impact of their legacy. Second, when structured properly, the proceeds of the policy can pass directly to the charity on the donor's death, bypassing probate and estate administration fees. This also protects the donation from creditors, relatives, or others who might wish to contest an estate with a sizeable charitable bequest written directly into the will. Furthermore, a charitable tax receipt equal to 100% of the insurance proceeds will be issued to the donor, reducing the overall tax liability of the estate.

Whether or not you wish to reduce the tax owed by your estate is entirely a personal decision. I have found that some people wish to minimize the estate tax to maximize the value of their estate for the benefit of their children or charitable organizations, while other people are not so concerned with the tax and are comfortable with their estate paying whatever tax will be owed, and the balance going to their family or charitable organizations.

Using Donor Advised Funds (DAFs)

Another way to facilitate charitable giving is to establish a donor advised fund (DAF). The basic concept behind this approach is that you find an established registered charitable foundation, either through the dealer firm your advisor works with or another organization that can facilitate your DAF. For example, you can set up the Mr. and Mrs. Jack Caldwell Family Foundation account. Your DAF account is then used for charitable giving, either by having the funds go directly to charity (a one-time lump-sum donation) or by acting like an endowment, producing income that is donated to charity on a yearly basis. The "host" charity handles administration of the fund, making DAFs a lower-cost and simpler alternative to setting up and managing a private family foundation. By using a DAF rather than a private foundation, you eliminate having to go through what can be time-consuming and potentially costly administrative activities, like setting up a trust or a not-for-profit corporation, registering as a charity, annual CRA reporting, and tasks such as processing donations, providing tax receipts, bookkeeping, and processing and tracking grants. The DAF account can also facilitate anonymous giving. Interestingly, Facebook founder Mark Zuckerberg and his wife opted to utilize a donor advised fund.

DAF accounts are usually opened many years before death, but are then funded as part of the will and estate plan. This is another reason that integrated planning is so important. For example, your advisor may estimate your tax liability to be $500,000 at death. You can open the DAF and leave instructions to fund the account with $1 million when you pass away. The $1-million donation would give your estate a tax credit of $500,000, effectively wiping out the tax liability (assuming each $1 of charitable donation reduces tax owed by the estate by 50¢).

As part of the instructions in your DAF and estate documents, you can specify either that the $1 million will go to one or more registered charities of your choice in one lump sum or that it be invested, and the income from the investments will be given to the charities annually. This creates a permanent legacy for you. Some people appoint their children or grandchildren as fund advisors and request that they meet every year to decide where to donate the year's investment income. This is a wonderful way to not only leave a permanent legacy, but also have your family come together to support charitable endeavours.

While DAFs are most often funded at death, this does not have to be the case—it can make sense to fund it during your lifetime if, for example, you have a large capital gain from the sale of a business or from exercising stock options that have produced a substantial tax liability. Keep in mind, though, that the maximum DAF contribution that can be claimed for tax credit is 75% of your net income for the year. The exceptions are the year of death and the year prior to the year of death. In these two years, the estate can claim donations of up to 100% of the net income of the deceased.

Key points to keep in mind about DAF include the following:

- Your donation is considered to be irrevocable. The tax credit, however, can be used in the year the contribution is made or carried forward for several years.
- The charities named to receive the funds in the DAF can be changed as you wish.
- Publicly traded securities are exempt from capital gains tax if donated to a registered charity.

- When you donate an asset to a DAF, you remove that asset from your estate and the probate process.
- DAF accounts can be open and funded during your lifetime. This makes sense in certain circumstances, such as if you have a large capital gain and wish to make a donation to reduce your tax burden while also creating a legacy.

In summary, the main advantage of DAFs is that they give donors the ability to achieve the same objectives they could achieve through a private foundation, but at a much lower cost and with less administrative and other complexities.

Advanced Estate Planning

Rather than directly distributing assets to your heirs, you can also consider the use of trusts, which are a slightly more complex way of transferring assets. In essence, a trust serves as an intermediary between you and your heirs. Trusts can be created during your lifetime (known as an inter vivos trust or a living trust) or at death based on language in your will (known as a testamentary trust). One example where a trust may be useful is in second marriages with blended families. For example, if you were to pass away, a spousal trust may be an effective way to provide an ongoing income stream to your current spouse while also providing you with peace of mind that your biological children will eventually receive the capital in the trust on the death of your spouse. There are many, many applications of trusts and it is critical to get professional advice if you are considering utilizing a trust as part of your estate plan. Keep in mind that there are one-time start-up costs for trusts as well as some ongoing maintenance costs (e.g., tax filing). Estate planning can be as complex as you make it. I strongly advise trying to achieve your goals and objectives in the simplest way possible. Keep in mind these words from Richard Branson: "Complexity is your enemy. Any fool can make something complicated. It is hard to keep things simple."

Action Call

1. Seriously consider the situation you want to be in, or you want your family to be in, if you are disabled, suffer a serious illness, or suddenly pass away.

2. Review existing insurance coverage you have in place.

3. See an advisor to help assess whether existing coverage is adequate.

4. Make sure your will package is updated and in force and that the documents were drafted by a lawyer.

4

YOUR FINANCIAL
FUTURE IS
IN YOUR HANDS

YOU SHOULD NOW have a good idea of how the financial advice industry in Canada works, the different types of advisors that are available, and the areas in which advice is typically needed. You should also understand the key principles of investing, insurance, and estate planning. It should also be clear why an integrated approach to financial advice is so important.

Know Your Rights

As a consumer of financial services, it's up to you to ensure you're getting good value for what you're paying. As I've said throughout this book, in the media we often hear that the advisor fees Canadian investors pay are too high. While in some cases this is true, it often isn't; and if the advisor is delivering great value, fees could even be too low! Good financial advice is invaluable, and in my experience the vast majority of us need the advice that an advisor can provide to make sure our financial affairs are well taken care of.

It is also critical for you to understand the level of service and professionalism you can expect from an advisor and what your rights are as a consumer. The CFA Institute has developed a Statement of Investor Rights, which I believe is ideally what all consumers should look for in their advisor—I strongly believe that it should be used by all

Canadians as a guideline of what they should expect from a financial professional. The Statement of Investor Rights is summarized below:

1. Honest, competent, ethical, law-abiding conduct

2. Independent and objective advice that is based on diligence and prudent judgment

3. Consideration of the client's financial interests over those of the advisor and the advisor's firm

4. Fair treatment with respect to other clients

5. Disclosure of existing or potential conflicts of interest

6. Understanding of the client's circumstances to ensure that advice is suitable and appropriate based on the client's goals and objectives

7. Clear, accurate, complete, timely communications in plain language and a format that conveys information clearly

8. An explanation of all fees and costs charged

9. Confidentiality

10. Complete and appropriate record-keeping

You can find the full text of the Statement of Investor Rights on the CFA Institute's website.

Forms

Every Canadian should be an active participant in their own financial affairs. You can choose to delegate the work to an advisor, but it is critical that you understand, from a financial perspective, where you are, where you want to go, and how you will get there. Nobody will ever care as much about your money and financial future as you do. Remember, it is fine to delegate your financial affairs, but never abdicate! I strongly suggest that you (and your spouse if you have one) set aside one day annually or semi-annually to go through all your financial affairs and make sure you're on track. Call it Family Finance Day.

To help you do that, I've created the Financial Check-up Form™. It's just one of the forms and resources included on the following pages for those who are currently working with an advisor or those who are looking for one:

- Financial Advice Needs Assessment™
- Financial Advisor Interview Questionnaire™
- Financial Advisor Reference-Check Form™
- Financial Advisor Ranking System™
- Advisor Meeting Summary Form™
- Annual Advisor Review Form™
- Annual Net Advisor Value Summary™
- Annual Financial Check-up Form™
- Sample Investment Policy Statement

Some of these resources will also be useful if you're a do-it-yourself investor and manage your own finances. For those in that camp, the Financial Advice Needs Assessment, Financial Check-up Form, and Sample Investment Policy Statement are the resources that will be useful for you.

FORM 1

The Financial Advice Needs Assessment that follows will help you better understand the areas in which you may require financial advice. (*Adapted from Mackenzie Investments*)

Financial Advice Needs Assessment™

Name:

Age:

Anticipated retirement date:

Number of years until retirement:

Investment knowledge

Check the appropriate box:

- ☐ None (If you have no or limited investment knowledge, then you likely need an advisor.)
- ☐ Limited—I have had some exposure to investing, but I am not confident in doing it on my own. Dealing with my finances makes me nervous.
- ☐ Good—I have read several books on investing and I am comfortable investing on my own.
- ☐ Sophisticated—I am a very well-educated investor and am comfortable using complex strategies.

Risk tolerance

Check the appropriate box:

- ☐ Low—I avoid risk as much as I can.
- ☐ Average—I am willing to take average risk to achieve average returns.
- ☐ High—I am willing to take high risk for the possibility of high returns, acknowledging that I may lose capital.

Level of personal involvement desired

Check the appropriate box:

- [ ] I want to be informed but delegate day-to-day management of my financial affairs to someone I trust. (If so, use an advisor.)
- [ ] I want to make day-to-day decisions on how my finances are managed but consult with an advisor from time to time. (If so, you are likely a do-it-yourself investor and may wish to consider fee-only advice annually.)

Services required

The more services you require, the higher the likelihood you will need an advisor. Check all that apply:

- [ ] Budgeting
- [ ] Business planning
- [ ] Debt management
- [ ] Estate and legacy planning
- [ ] Goal setting
- [ ] Insurance review (life, disability, critical illness)
- [ ] Investment review, asset allocation, and investment selection
- [ ] Retirement and financial planning
- [ ] Tax planning

FORM 2

The Financial Advisor Interview Questionnaire™ that follows will assist you in selecting a financial advisor who is appropriate for your needs. When you're looking for an advisor, you should interview at least three individuals. (*Adapted from Mackenzie Investments and the National Association of Personal Financial Advisors*)

Financial Advisor Interview Questionnaire™

---

1. How long have you been in the financial industry?
(Tips: More experience is better—it means the advisor has managed through market cycles.)

_____

_____

_____

2. Tell me about your educational background and designations. Do you have experience working with US persons (if applicable)?

(Tips: CFP = Certified Financial Planner, CLU = Chartered Life Underwriter, CIM = Chartered Investment Manager, CFA = Chartered Financial Analyst. Designations indicate commitment to further education and excellence but should not be relied on in isolation.)

_____

_____

_____

_____

_____

3. Which platform do you operate under and which regulatory bodies are you licensed by (MFDA, IIROC, insurance only, investment counsel)? Have you ever been disciplined for regulatory reasons by a regulator? Do you manage assets on a discretionary or non-discretionary basis?

(Tips: Platform affects products available to you. Ideally, your advisor should be licensed to provide mutual funds, securities, and insurance to provide comprehensive service. If an advisor has been disciplined, be sure to investigate further.)

_____

_____

_____

_____

4. What is your investment philosophy? What was your biggest investment mistake and what did you learn from it? What is your opinion of macroeconomics and how do you apply this to your investment philosophy? What are your views about building portfolios that are adequately diversified? Do you provide clients with a customized investment policy statement? How do you invest your own money?

(Tips: Look for a clearly articulated investment philosophy. The advisor should be able to articulate how macroeconomic factors influence markets and investments. Chasing trends or hot investments is a danger sign. Ensuring the advisor adequately diversifies portfolios is critical.)

_____

_____

_____

_____

5. What services do you provide and what can I expect to receive on an ongoing basis? Do you provide comprehensive tax reporting, including gain/loss reports? Do you coordinate with my accountant and lawyer when required? Provide an example. Can you give me samples of the reports and plans your clients receive?

(Tips: Understand all the areas in which advice is provided (refer to The Advice Wheel). Comprehensive advisors provide annual cash flow projections and guidance on insurance and estate planning. A gain/loss report is valuable for taxable accounts.)

_____

_____

_____

_____

6. How many clients or families do you work with, and what are the total assets you manage? What is your average yearly client turnover? Would you provide me with contact information for two or three of your long-term clients or professional partners (such as accountants or lawyers) as references?

(Tips: It is difficult for an advisor to serve more than 100 families (as a rule of thumb, a single advisor can serve 100 families). Great advisors have low client turnover.)

_____

_____

_____

_____

_____

7. Explain how you are paid. Do you charge hourly or receive fees based on assets under management, commissions, or ongoing trailing commissions? Are there other charges I should be aware of? Are your fees transparent?

(Tips: Advisor should be upfront when discussing compensation and fees or trading, maintaining registered accounts, transferring in or out.)

_____

_____

_____

_____

_____

8. Explain how your interests are aligned with your clients' interests. Does your investment dealer have any relationship with a manufacturer of investment products? Explain to me how you are independent. Do you have any incentive to recommend certain products?

(Tips: Alignment of interest is critical. Be aware of whether the investment dealer has a relationship with a product manufacturer (such as a mutual fund company). Advisor independence is important.)

_____

_____

_____

_____

_____

9. Tell me about your team and their qualifications. Who would I be working with primarily? If not you, can I meet this person? When do you plan to retire, and what is your succession plan?

(Tips: It is important to get along with the people you will be working with. The advantage of a team is that if your primary advisor is away, another advisor could assist you. Teams may also provide broader perspective and expertise.)

_____

_____

_____

_____

FORM 3

Before hiring an advisor, it is critical that you speak to at least two, but preferably three, of the advisor's current clients to see what their experience has been. I designed the Financial Advisor Reference-Check Form™ to facilitate this process. I strongly recommend asking all the questions on the form and taking notes during the conversations. After speaking with all the references, you should have a good idea of the overall experience each advisor provides to their clients, as well as the individual strengths and weaknesses of each advisor. Note: you could also speak to any other professionals (such as accountants or lawyers) the advisor works with, and ask them to answer the questions on the following Financial Advisor Reference-Check Form based on the feedback they have received from clients about the advisor.

Financial Advisor Reference-Check Form™

Advisor:

Firm:

Reference #1 name:

Reference #2 name:

Reference #3 name:

1. How long have you been with this advisor?

Ref #1:

Ref #2:

Ref #3:

2. Do you feel the advisor understands your financial goals and objectives and your risk tolerance?

Ref #1:

Ref #2:

Ref #3:

3. Is the advisor proactive in arranging meetings to review your financial affairs?

Ref #1:

Ref #2:

Ref #3:

4. Does the advisor communicate with you regularly?

Ref #1:

Ref #2:

Ref #3:

5. Is advice provided in areas beyond investments, such as insurance, retirement planning, and estate planning?

Ref #1:

Ref #2:

Ref #3:

6. Has your investment portfolio performance been satisfactory?

Ref #1:

Ref #2:

Ref #3:

7. Does the advisor focus on providing advice rather than selling products?

Ref #1:

Ref #2:

Ref #3:

8. In what areas does the advisor do best?

Ref #1:

Ref #2:

Ref #3:

9. In what areas could the advisor improve?

Ref #1:

Ref #2:

Ref #3:

10. Would you refer your close friends and family to this advisor?

Ref #1:

Ref #2:

Ref #3:

FORM 4

After you've interviewed each prospective financial advisor and completed the reference checks, I recommend using the Financial Advisor Ranking System™ that follows to score each advisor. Once completed, it will give you a comparative analysis on the advisors you interviewed, which will be very useful in helping you select the one who may be most appropriate for you. Note: do not solely rely on the score to select your advisor; rather, choose your advisor using your overall comfort level with the person and your trust and confidence in them. The Financial Advisor Ranking System should be used as a framework to provoke thought and discussion. (*Adapted from Mackenzie Investments*)

Financial Advisor Ranking System™

Candidate 1

Name:

Firm:

Candidate 2

Name:

Firm:

Candidate 3

Name:

Firm:

Scoring: 0 = very weak, 5 = very strong

Advisor's experience and education

Score #1_____ #2_____ #3_____

Comments:
_____

_____

Strength of advisor's team

Score #1_____ #2_____ #3_____

Comments:
_____

_____

Advisor's breadth of services provided and ability to meet my needs

Score #1_____ #2_____ #3_____

Comments:
_____

_____

Advisor's ability to ask questions and listen

Score #1_____ #2_____ #3_____

Comments:
_____

_____

Advisor's understanding of my goals and objectives

Score #1_____ #2_____ #3_____

Comments:
_____

_____

Advisor's investment process, philosophy, and portfolio construction. Consider investment acumen. Will the advisor be a patient steward of my money?

Score #1_____ #2_____ #3_____

Comments:

Alignment of interest between advisor and his or her clients. Is my advisor independent?

Score #1_____ #2_____ #3_____

Comments:

Personality fit

Score #1_____ #2_____ #3_____

Comments:

Feedback from references

Score #1_____ #2_____ #3_____

Comments:

Overall confidence and trust in advisor and team to deliver the service and advice I need.

Total score #1_____ #2_____ #3_____

FORM 5

Advisor Meeting Summary Form™ (*Adapted from Mackenzie Investments*)

Advisor name: _____

Date of meeting: _____

Meeting type (phone call, in person, electronic): _____

Investment portfolio

Summary: _____

_____

_____

Advisor recommendation: _____

_____

_____

Action: _____

_____

Follow-up required: _____

_____

Insurance

Summary: _____

_____

_____

Advisor recommendation:

_____

_____

_____

Action:

_____

_____

Follow-up required:

_____

_____

Retirement planning

Summary:

_____

_____

_____

Advisor recommendation:

_____

_____

_____

Action:

_____

_____

Follow-up required:

_____

_____

Estate planning

Summary:

_____

_____

_____

Advisor recommendation:

_____

_____

_____

Action:

_____

_____

Follow-up required:

_____

_____

Other

Summary:

_____

_____

_____

Advisor recommendation:

_____

_____

_____

Action:

_____

_____

Follow-up required:

_____

FORM 6

While your advisor may have a branch manager or other authority they report to, remember that your advisor works for you too. And so, just as your boss or a human resources representative may give you an annual review to provide you with feedback on your work performance and suggestions for improvement, it is important that you review your advisor's performance every year, along with the relationship you have with him or her, to ensure that your needs are still being met. The Annual Advisor Review Form™ that follows will assist you with this process. (*Adapted from Mackenzie Investments*)

Annual Advisor Review Form™

Advisor name:

Date:

Personal qualities

☐ Yes   ☐ No   My advisor takes the time to understand my needs.

☐ Yes   ☐ No   My advisor asks questions.

☐ Yes   ☐ No   My advisor puts my interests first.

☐ Yes   ☐ No   My advisor is well qualified and is committed to continuing education.

Service provided

☐ Yes   ☐ No   I meet with my advisor at least once per year.

☐ Yes   ☐ No   My advisor is proactive in contacting me.

☐ Yes   ☐ No   My advisor looks at my overall financial picture (including insurance, financial planning, and estate planning), rather than only focusing on investments.

☐ Yes   ☐ No   My advisor explains concepts to me in a way that I can understand.

☐ Yes   ☐ No   My advisor is not focused on selling me financial products.

☐ Yes   ☐ No   My advisor's interests are aligned with mine.

Investments

☐ Yes ☐ No My advisor is knowledgeable about investments.

☐ Yes ☐ No My advisor can articulate a sound long-term investment strategy.

☐ Yes ☐ No My advisor invests at least some of their money in a portfolio similar to that of their clients.

☐ Yes ☐ No My investment portfolio is reasonably diversified around the globe.

☐ Yes ☐ No No individual position is worth more than 10% of my portfolio.

Costs

☐ Yes ☐ No My advisor is transparent with regard to costs for his or her services.

☐ Yes ☐ No My costs are reasonable.

FORM 7

Annual Net Advisor Value Summary™

Needs assessment: Is advice needed? (Complete Financial Advice Needs Assessment annually.)

☐ Yes   ☐ No

Comments:

\
\
\

Advisor service: Is the service satisfactory? (Overall service and advice, beyond just investment recommendations.)

☐ Yes   ☐ No

Comments:

\
\
\

Value proposition: Approximate total cost

Comments:

\
\
\

Summary comments:

\
\
\

FORM 8

I strongly suggest that every Canadian perform an annual financial check-up. I have designed the Annual Financial Check-up Form™ exactly for this purpose. Completing the form will give you a clear idea of whether your financial house is in order or not. If it is, congratulations—you are on your way to long-term financial success. If not, the Annual Financial Check-up Form that follows will show you which areas need work. You can then do that work yourself or seek professional advice.

Annual Financial Check-up Form™

Investment plan, process, and results

Scoring: 0 = very weak, 5 = very strong

I have a long-term asset allocation plan that I understand.

Score _____
Comments:

My investment portfolio is not too concentrated in any one holding (i.e., no more than 10%).

Score _____
Comments:

My portfolio is rebalanced annually.

Score _____
Comments:

I have an investment policy statement that I abide by.

Score _____

Comments:

_____

_____

Financial and retirement planning

I have a financial and retirement plan that is realistic and understandable.

Score _____

Comments:

_____

_____

If close to retirement, I understand where my retirement income is coming from such that it is tax-efficient.

Score _____

Comments:

_____

_____

I have a budget.

Score _____

Comments:

_____

_____

Will and estate planning

I have a will, power of attorney, and personal directive that have been reviewed in the past year.

Score _____

Comments:

_____

_____

My estate-planning goals are clear and I understand the tax rules that apply at death.

Score _____

Comments:

_____

_____

Insurance

My life insurance needs have been reviewed in the past 12 months and I am adequately insured. For permanent policies, the funding status of my policies and the investments within the policies have been reviewed.

Score _____

Comments:

_____

_____

My disability and critical illness insurance needs have been reviewed in the past 12 months and I am adequately insured.

Score _____

Comments:

_____

_____

Total score _____

(Note: If your score is less than 50, you have work to do!)

FORM 9

Having a clear, regularly updated investment policy statement is absolutely critical, whether you have a financial advisor or not. The IPS has often been compared to a GPS—if you don't have a clear path to your destination, your probability of getting lost goes up dramatically. An IPS provides a framework of guidelines for your investment portfolio. The closer you stick to the guidelines you establish in your IPS, the higher your probability of being a disciplined investor (and the higher your probability of long-term investment success).

The sample IPS that follows is a good starting point and will be sufficient for most investors with basic needs, including do-it-yourself investors. If you work with an advisor, he or she may have a different (and possibly more detailed) document. Be sure you understand what is in your IPS. I recommend sitting down as a family and reviewing the information annually—and don't make any investments outside of what is permitted in your IPS.

Sample Investment Policy Statement

Date last revised:

Summary of family goals and objectives (describe goals, e.g., saving for retirement, children's education, recreation property):

Risk tolerance

Understanding that markets go up and down, my/our risk tolerance for loss of capital is (check appropriate level):

☐ Low (can tolerate maximum negative returns of –5%)

☐ Medium (can tolerate maximum negative returns of –10%)

☐ High (can tolerate maximum negative returns of –20%)

Investment parameters

Time horizon (enter number of years
before withdrawal of capital is required) _____

Minimum cash balance (enter amount
required for major upcoming needs) _____

Other unique circumstances
_____

_____

Asset allocation

Assets to be allocated according to the following percentages:

_____ Cash and equivalents
_____ Fixed income (bonds)
_____ Equities (stocks)
_____ Other (private or alternative investments)

100% Total

Other guidelines/constraints

Investing using borrowed money will be permitted: ☐ Yes   ☐ No

Portfolio will be rebalanced annually to bring
asset allocation in line with long-term targets   ☐ Yes   ☐ No

Who will be responsible for investment
selection? (enter name) _____

Maximum percentage of a single investment
holding in the portfolio (enter percentage) _____

Taxation issues (such as US citizenship) _____

Any specific companies or sectors not
to invest in (e.g., tobacco stocks) _____

Signed: _____

Date: _____

Final Thoughts

W HEN I BECAME a financial advisor, I thought my job was all about getting the best investment returns I could for my clients. After all, in the media the term "investment advisor" is often used synonymously with financial advisor. As I began working with clients, however, I quickly realized that being a financial advisor is not just about producing the best investment returns possible. Being a financial advisor is about providing good, risk-adjusted investment results, yes; but it's also about taking care of all the other financial aspects of your clients' lives—The Advice Wheel.

And that is really where the inspiration for this book comes. It was born out of frustration because navigating the financial advice industry in Canada can be very confusing, but it doesn't need to be. For the first time in Canada (that I am aware), there is now a single resource that clearly and simply outlines how the financial advice industry in Canada is structured, providing basic principles about investments, insurance, and estate planning that every Canadian should read and understand.

I have put my heart and soul into this book, hoping that by sharing with Canadians the knowledge I have acquired over my career, it will make a difference. You work hard for your money, so you need to make sure your money is working for you most effectively. I sincerely believe that by having read this book, you are now armed with what you need to know to take control of your financial future. J.P. Morgan is often credited for saying, "You can ignore economics and finance; the scary part is that they will not ignore you." There is so much truth to that statement! In her 1998 report, *Investment Funds in Canada and Consumer Protection: Strategies for the Millennium*, Glorianne Stromberg concluded by arguing that the well-being of consumers and investors cannot rest alone on governments and regulators, and that investors "have to do their part. They have to help themselves. They cannot abdicate their responsibility to act prudently and with full knowledge of the facts." I sincerely hope this book will help you do your part.

Gaining more control over your financial future can be a daunting task, but taking the first step is the most important. My suggestion is to start by taking stock of your financial goals and objectives, and understanding what your risk tolerance really is. Invest regularly, be disciplined, and avoid making big mistakes. Make sure you have adequate insurance to deal with catastrophic events, and ensure that you have basic estate-planning documents, at minimum. Above all else, remember to keep it simple. As Albert Einstein said, "Everything should be made as simple as possible, but no simpler."

I wish you all the best in getting your money's worth.

Sincerely,

SHAMEZ KASSAM
Canada's Candid Advisor

Further Resources

AFTER READING THIS book, you should now be armed with knowledge in a wide range of areas. If you would like to learn more, the resources listed below can help. This list is by no means exhaustive, but these resources are a wonderful place to start.

General Information

Canadian MoneySaver Magazine
De Goey, John. *The Professional Advisor* IV (2016).
Financial Planning Standards Council (www.fpsc.ca)
Canadian Financial Literacy Database

Financial Literacy and Advocacy

CanadianFundWatch.com
Canadian Foundation for Advancement of Investor Rights
    (www.fair.canada.ca)
Canadian Foundation for Economic Education (www.cfee.org)
Financial Consumer Agency of Canada
Small Investor Protection Association (www.sipa.ca)

Investing

American Association of Individual Investors (www.aaii.com)
Canadian ETF Association (www.cetfa.ca)
Canadian ShareOwner (www.investments.shareowner.com)

Fisher, Philip A. *Common Stocks and Uncommon Profits and Other Writings* (Wiley, 1996).

Graham, Benjamin, Jason Zweig (Contributor), Warren Buffett (Contributor). *The Intelligent Investor.* (HarperBusiness, 2006).

Hagstrom, Robert G. *The Warren Buffett Way: Investment Strategies of the World's Greatest Investor*, 2nd ed. (Wiley, 2005).

InvestingIntroduction.ca

Investment Funds Institute of Canada (www.ific.ca)

Investment Industry Regulatory Organization of Canada (www.iiroc.ca)

Mutual Fund Dealers Association of Canada (www.mfda.ca)

National Association of Personal Financial Advisors (www.napfa.org)

O'Neil, William J. *How to Make Money in Stocks: A Winning System in Good Times or Bad* (McGraw-Hill Companies, 2002).

Ontario Securities Commission (www.osc.gov.on.ca)

Portfolio Management Association of Canada (www.portfoliomanagement.org)

www.stockcharts.com (technical analysis)

Insurance

Canadian Life and Health Insurance Association (www.clhia.ca)

NoTimeLikeNow.ca

Financial/Retirement Planning

Chilton, David. *The Wealthy Barber Returns* (Financial Awareness Corp., 2011).

Diamond, Daryl. *Your Retirement Income Blueprint: A Six-Step Plan to Design and Build a Secure Retirement* (Wiley, 2011).

Sellery, Bruce. *Moolala: Why Smart People Do Dumb Things with Their Money (and What You Can Do About It)* (McClelland & Stewart, 2011).

Wills and Estate Planning

Deans, Thomas William. *Willing Wisdom: 7 Questions to Ask Before You Die* (Detente Financial Press, 2013).

Douglas Gray and John Budd. *The Canadian Guide to Will and Estate Planning: Everything You Need to Know Today to Protect Your Wealth and Your Family Tomorrow*, 3rd ed. (McGraw-Hill Education, 2011).

Blogs, Podcasts, and Media

Barron's (www.barrons.com)

Barron's Next (www.barrons.com/next)

Consuelo Mack WEALTHTRACK: *The Right Track to Your Financial Health* (www.wealthtrack.com)

Financial Post (FP Investing)

GetSmarterAboutMoney.ca

Globe and Mail: "Globe Investor" and "Globe Investor Weekend" (Portfolio Strategy and Investor Clinic)

Investor's Business Daily (www.investors.com)

Jason Zweig: A Safe Haven for Intelligent Investors (www.jasonzweig.com)

Money Talks with Michael Campbell (www.cknw.com/money-talks)

Mostly Money, Mostly Canadian with Preet Banerjee (podcast)

The Investors Podcast: We Study Billionaires (www.theinvestorspodcast.com)

WhereDoesAllMyMoneyGo.com

YoungandThrifty.ca

References

BarclayHedge. Assets under management. (Available at www.barclayhedge.com/research/money_under_management.html.)

Barclays Wealth. *Understanding the Female Economy: The Role of Gender in Financial Decision Making and Succession Planning for the Next Generation* (2011).

Belski, Brian. *Elect Dividend Growth* (2016).

Bernstein, Richard. *Business Insider.* "Investors Always Do the Wrong Thing When They Hear the Sounds of Stock Market Chaos," August 12, 2014.

Bernstein, Richard. *Style Investing: Unique Insight into Equity Management* (Wiley, 1995).

BlackRock. *BlackRock Global Investor Pulse Survey* (2015).

BlackRock. Press Release. "BlackRock Global Investor Pulse Survey: Canadian Women Face 'Gender Gap' in Retirement Planning and Investing," March 5, 2015.

Blanchett, David and Paul Kaplan. *Alpha, Beta, and Now... Gamma.* (Morningstar, 2013).

Bradshaw, M. et al. *Analyst Target Price Optimism around the World* (2012).

Brown, Lawrence D. et al. *Inside the "Black Box" of Sell-Side Financial Analysts* (2013).

Canadian Cancer Society, Government of Canada. Canadian Cancer Statistics. *Special Topic: Predictions of the future burden of Cancer in Canada* (2015).

Canadian Securities Administrators. CSA *Staff Notice 33-318 Review of Practices Firms Use to Compensate and Provide Incentives to their Representatives* (2016).

CFA Institute. *Statement of Investor Rights.* (Available at www.cfainstitute.org/learning/future/getinvolved/Pages/statement_of_investor_rights.aspx.)

Chilton, David. *The Wealthy Barber Returns* (Financial Awareness Corp., 2011).

DALBAR. *Quantitative Analysis of Investor Behaviour* (2015).

Davidow, Anthony B. *Are You Really Diversified?* (Charles Schwab, 2014).

Davis Advisors. *The Wisdom of Great Investors: Insights from Some of History's Greatest Investment Minds.* (Available at davisadvisors.com/davissma/downloads/WGI.pdf.)

Dvorak, Tomas. "Do 401k planners take their own advice?" Paper presented at the American Economic Association Conference, 2013.

Ellis, Charles. *Winning the Loser's Game: Timeless Strategies for Successful Investing* (McGraw-Hill Education, 2013).

Fiduciary Trust Canada. *The Role of an Executor.* (Available at www.fiduciarytrust.ca/ca/ftcc/en/pdf/servicing/FTCC_TheRoleofanExecutor.pdf.)

Foerster, Stephen et al. *Retail Financial Advice: Does One Size Fit All?* NBER Working Paper No. 20712 (2014).

Graham, Benjamin. *The Intelligent Investor: The Definitive Book on Value Investing* (HarperCollins, 2006).

J.P. Morgan Asset Management. *Guide to Retirement* (2015).

Kinnel, Russel. *Fund Spy: Morningstar's Inside Secrets to Selecting Mutual Funds that Outperform* (2009).

Law Pro. "Survey: More than half of Canadians do not have a signed will." Press Release (2012). (Available at www.lawpro.ca/news/pdf/Wills-POAsurvey.pdf.)

Lortie, Pierre. *A Major Setback for Retirement Savings: Changing How Financial Advisors are Compensated Could Hurt Less than Wealth Investors Most* (University of Calgary School of Public Policy, 2016).

Marowits, Ross. "Financial advisers aren't just for the rich and nearly retired." *Globe and Mail*, October 12, 2012.

Martijn, Cremers et al. *Indexing and Active Fund Management: International Evidence* (2015).

McIntyre, Sandy. *Passive vs. Active Management (Part II).* (Sentry Investments, 2016).

McKinsey & Company. *Mapping Global Capital Markets* (2011).

McKinsey & Company. *Thriving in the New Abnormal: North American Asset Management* (2016).

Ontario Securities Commission. *Investment Fraud Checklist.* (Available at www.osc.gov.on.ca/en/Investors_res_investment-fraud-checklist.htm.)

Ontario Securities Commission. *Statement of Priorities for fiscal 2015-2016* (2015).

Pakula, David C. et al. *Global Equities: Balancing Home Bias and Diversification: A Canadian Investor's Perspective* (2014).

PricewaterhouseCoopers and Advocis. *Sound Advice: Insights into Canada's Financial Advice Industry* (2014).

Ritholtz, Barry. "Brexit happens. Know your investment plan, and stick to it," *Washington Post.* June 24, 2016.

Sellery, Bruce. *Moolala: Why Smart People Do Dumb Things with Their Money (and What You Can Do About It)* (McClelland & Stewart, 2011).

Shillington, Richard. *An Analysis of the Economic Circumstances of Canadian Seniors* (Broadbent Institute, 2016).

Statistics Canada. *Canadian Survey on Disability* (2012).

Taleb, Nassim Nicholas. *The Black Swan: The Impact of the Highly Improbable* (Random House, 2007).

U.S. Securities and Exchange Commission. *How to Avoid Fraud.* (Available at www.sec.gov/investor/pubs/avoidfraud.htm.)

Vanguard Group. *Putting a Value on Your Value: Quantifying Vanguard Advisor's Alpha* (June 2015).

Wanger, Ralph. *A Zebra in Lion Country: The Dean of Small Cap Stocks Explains How to Invest in Small, Rapidly Growing Companies Whose Stocks Represent Good Values* (Simon & Schuster, 1997).

Yale University. *The Yale Endowment* (2009).

Acknowledgements

A S I HAVE discovered, writing a book is an immense undertaking and involves much more work and effort than is initially expected. For me, having this book go from the concept phase to becoming a manuscript and then, finally, ready for physical production, was very much a team effort. I humbly and sincerely offer my thanks to the following:

My wife, Zahrah, for being so patient and accommodating my early-morning and late-night writing and editing schedule over the course of two years. I love you!

My family, for your continued support. I would particularly like to thank my parents, who came to Canada in the early 1970s with little but the clothes on their backs. Thank you for working multiple jobs to provide what our family needed. I don't know how you did it!

My sister, Zahra. I wish time and less distance permitted us to get together more often!

The staff and professors at both the University of Alberta and Columbia Business School, for providing me with such a tremendous educational experience.

Donna Dawson, for your instrumental work in taking my original manuscript and editing and organizing it in such a wonderful manner.

Peter Cocking, Jesse Finkelstein, Zoe Grams, Lindsay Humphreys, Gabrielle Narsted, and the rest of the team at Page Two Strategies, for bringing my book alive and assisting me in navigating the publishing process.

Deborah Kully, Marilyn Langevin, Julia Boberg, Holly Lomheim, Kate Farr, the late Dr. Einer Boberg, and all the current, former, and future staff of the Institute for Stuttering Treatment and Research, for giving a voice to people who stutter. The impact of your work on my life has been profound and cannot be explained in words. Dr. Boberg, I miss you.

My friend Zaylin Lalji, for your valuable feedback on multiple versions of the manuscript and for believing early on in my vision of how a book like this could help millions of Canadians achieve a more secure financial future.

Brandi Dickson, Franc Godri, Scott MacMillan, Irene Pfeiffer, and Shelley Waite, for reviewing the manuscript and providing valuable comments.

Felix Lin and Clark Schow, for providing your wisdom, insight, and support of my work.

George Hartman, I have learned so much from you over the years. Thank you for your valuable feedback and suggestions.

Goshka Folda, thank you for the wonderful research you do providing timely insights and analysis of the wealth management industry in Canada.

David Chilton, Patricia Lovett-Reid, and Bruce Sellery, thank you for your feedback and words of encouragement.

My friends Patricia Morgan and Martin Parnell, thank you for your guidance and for providing me with so many valuable ideas and connections along the way.

My friends Adil Lalani, Ken Phillips, Mary Hassanali, Nazir Kassamali, Paul Corona, and Zahir Dharsee, thank you for our long friendship and for your wise advice over the years.

Thank you to my friends who are wholesalers in the financial industry. Your insights have been very valuable.

Thank you to the great investors I have met over the years and from whom I have learned so much.

ACKNOWLEDGEMENTS 279

My clients, I have learned so much from you and I love working with you. Thank you for your trust.

The management of Raymond James Ltd. and Raymond James Financial: I truly appreciate the firm's values of client first, integrity, conservatism, advisor independence, and contributing to the community. I would particularly like to thank Peter Kahnert, Moira Rosser, Christopher Cooksey, Lindsay Swan, and Rachel Petford for your assistance and support not only on this project, but over the years.

To my business partners, colleagues, and all the wonderful advisors I have had the pleasure of meeting during my career, thank you for the great work you do to help Canadians achieve their financial goals and objectives.

To the authors of the countless investing books I have read over the years, thank you for sharing your knowledge and wisdom.

And finally, to you, the reader, thank you for taking the time to read this book. I wish you great success in your quest to secure your financial future and create new possibilities for your family and your community.

About the Author

SHAMEZ KASSAM, MBA, CFA, is a 2004 graduate of Columbia University's Graduate School of Business in New York City, where he majored in finance and economics. He holds the Chartered Financial Analyst (CFA) designation from the CFA Institute. Before entering the world of finance, Shamez completed an undergraduate degree from the Faculty of Rehabilitation Medicine at the University of Alberta and worked as an occupational therapist for five years. He spent the first several years of his finance career working with institutional investors, including BNP Paribas and Alberta Investment Management Corporation, and he began working with individual Canadian investors in 2010. Shamez firmly believes in the value of financial advice and that all investors can be successful by following key principles, managing their emotions, and avoiding big mistakes. He is passionate about improving the financial literacy of Canadians, particularly the need to improve financial education in the Canadian school system. A person who stutters, Shamez serves on the boards of the Institute for Stuttering Treatment and Research and Accessible Housing Calgary. Shamez is a financial advisor at Raymond James and is licensed to provide portfolio management services and investment advice both in Canada and the United States. He lives in Calgary with his wife and four-year-old son.